The Complete Chinese Cookbook

Kenneth Lo is one of the Western world's leading experts on Chinese cookery. He was born in Foochow, China, and studied physics in Peking before moving to England in 1936 and studying English Literature at Cambridge University. During the war he was Welfare and Labour Relations Officer at the Chinese Consulate in Liverpool and between 1946 and 1949 was Vice Consul for China in Manchester. For many years he was a director of Cathay Arts Ltd, a leading fine arts publishers, before becoming in 1966 a writer and consultant on Chinese food. He is the author of many books and feature articles on Chinese cookery, including *Peking Cooking, Chinese Vegetarian Cooking, Chinese Food, Cheap Chow, Quick and Easy Chinese Cooking, Step by Step Chinese Cooking* and *The Love of Chinese Cooking*. Mr Lo is Chairman of the Chinese Gourmet Club in London and has made numerous TV and radio appearances over the years.

The Complete Chinese Cookbook

KENNETH LO

This edition published 1996 by Diamond Books
77-85 Fulham Palace Road
Hammersmith
London W6 8JB

First published 1974 as *The Chinese Cookery Encyclopedia*
First issued in this abridged form 1978 by Fontana Books

Copyright © Kenneth Lo 1974, 1978

Printed in Great Britain

CONDITIONS OF SALE
This book is sold subject to the condition
that it shall not, by way of trade or otherwise,
be lent, re-sold, hired out or otherwise
circulated without the publisher's prior consent
in any form of binding or cover other than that
in which it is published and without a similar
condition including this condition being
imposed on the subsequent purchaser.

Contents

Introduction	7
Soup	55
Rice	71
Noodles	82
Vegetable and Vegetarian Dishes	95
Pork	106
Beef	139
Lamb and Mutton	151
Chicken	159
Duck, Pigeon, Turkey and Frogs	192
Fish	210
Seafood and Crustaceans	223
Eggs	247
Sweets and Snacks	256
Glossary	272
Index	277

Note on metrication

Metric equivalents and oven temperatures have been included in all the recipes throughout this book. Conversions based on 1 oz = 25 g, 1 pint = 500 ml and 1 inch = 2½ cm are in accordance with Standard British Practice. With larger amounts, quantities have been rounded up or down and have been appropriately balanced.

Introduction: The Importance of Chinese Cooking

One of the most exciting things about writing about Chinese food and cooking lies in the knowledge that one is writing about a subject which is undoubtedly one of China's unique contributions to the sum total of the world's civilization. If it is not her most important contribution, it is certainly one of the most living, extensive, and satisfying. And as such, its influence on the world at large must be considerable and quite immeasurable.

Few things in life are as positive as food, or are taken as intimately and completely by the individual. One can listen to music, but the sound may enter in one ear and go out through the other; one may listen to a lecture or conversation, and day-dream about many other things; one may attend to matters of business, and one's heart or interest may be altogether elsewhere. One can be bored and entirely indifferent.

In the matter of food and eating one can hardly remain completely indifferent to what one is doing for long. How can one remain entirely indifferent to something which is going to enter one's body and become part of oneself? How can one remain indifferent to something which will determine one's physical strength and ultimately one's spiritual and moral fibre and well-being?

Besides, in one's attitude towards food one can be driven by such a basic urge as gnawing hunger, and motivated by such a fundamental desire as physical appeal. For in food and eating, we are coming very near to that plane of life which is at the very root of human existence on earth, at which nobody is a bystander.

It is in this larger context and against this general basic human background that I should like to consider the subject of Chinese food and cooking. The significance of its conception and techniques has become a part and parcel of the Chinese way of life through the ages, and, it seems, will very soon become a measurable part of the heritage and practice of a good proportion of the human race.

For Chinese food and cooking have become, at first perhaps imperceptibly, and now during the past decade or two quite dramatically, easily the most universally accepted cuisine throughout the world. Soon it might be that all those who can afford to eat will be at one time or another during the week devouring Chinese food!

The Complete Chinese Cookbook

Before that time comes, it is as well that we should take a closer look at Chinese food and cooking, and decipher the sources of their strength and meaning, instead of merely branding them as exotic.

In the many lectures I have given on this subject, I have used the title 'The Sources and Strength of Chinese Gastronomic Imperialism'! Whether the strength is derived from the materials used, from the technique of cooking, or from the conception of the completed dish, it is for us to investigate and determine. With the world growing smaller every day, we will all be living out of one another's pockets soon; therefore whatever any country or people has of significance to contribute will soon become the common possession of all of us and a part of everyone's common inheritance. What then is our common inheritance, or legacy from the Chinese, in the line of food and cooking which we are about to embrace and claim as our own? In what way will this help in contributing to the enrichment of our daily lives? To answer this question, one has to take a look at the situation at closer quarters and examine it against a wider background.

First of all, the basic purpose of cooking is primarily to render food edible, and secondly to render it more enjoyable to eat. To achieve these purposes, two methods are generally employed: heating and flavouring. These two methods or processes are commonly used by people all over the world. The difference between one type of cookery and another, where differences exist, can really only lie in the degree of refinement and sophistication which is conceived or employed within each category of methods.

If refinement means the minuteness of adjustments, the delicacy of touch required in flavouring and heating, and the recognition and mastery of all the wide variety of interrelated factors which combine to produce the desired effect, then Chinese cooking must rank as one of the most refined and sophisticated in the world. For in ultimate refinement and sophistication, to outsiders at least, there is something which resembles the proverbial 'Chinese Puzzle' in Chinese cooking!

Perhaps it is only natural that it should be so, for refinement and sophistication have been the natural style and expression of the Chinese artistic instinct in more than one aspect of her culture and civilization. Here one can easily compare Chinese cooking with Chinese painting and calligraphy, where the aim is to achieve a very high degree of delicacy and refinement within a traditional and

Introduction

sometimes stylized framework, but at the same time never lose sight of the need for character, quality, and meaning which should be the foundation of every artistic expression.

Indeed, for Chinese cooking to have attained any style or character of its own, it is likely that it followed this broad stream of Chinese inclination and artistic tradition. It could hardly have been otherwise.

Take the heating of food, which is basically capable of only a limited number of variations, such as heating by air (roasting, baking), heating by fire or radiation (grilling, barbecuing), heating through the medium of water (steaming, boiling, stewing), heating by oil (frying), or heating by contact (any heating on or against a dry surface or object – such as a stone or a griddle). By combining the different methods, by varying the pace of heating (what we Chinese call 'fire-power'), by the speed or lengthiness of treatment, the stability or mobility (as in stir-frying) of food while being heated, we Chinese have developed some forty different accepted heating methods, each with its well-defined and established terms of reference and conception. These terms are used, more or less, as terms are used in ballet movements, to indicate some precise stylized execution, the purpose and details of which are well-known, accepted, and established. In the sphere of flavouring, the Chinese have perhaps developed and advanced even further than in heating. This is probably due to the normal Chinese practice of cross-cooking different types of foods, which results in the large-scale cross-blending of flavours, arising from the blending of different basic constituents of the dish.

Although not all Chinese dishes are 'mixed' dishes – some consist of only one ingredient cooked in the simplest way, such as by long, slow boiling – many more are mixed, usually consisting of one predominant ingredient which gives bulk and character to the dish, with one or two supplementary ingredients, supported by a few flavouring materials in small quantities, and further enriched by a range of seasoning materials and sauces. These seasoning materials and sauces are often applied at the last stage of cooking, when the heat is frequently turned up to a crescendo, thus creating a situation of 'explosive orchestration'.

The flavouring in Chinese cooking is, therefore, achieved through a multi-layer process; that is, through the use of supplementary ingredients for cross-cooking (to provide variety and difference in material and texture), the use of flavouring ingredients, seasonings, and sauces to further enhance taste and flavour, and finally through the serving of table condiments to provide the individual diners with the opportunity to do their own personal 'touch-ups' before consumption. Not that these categories or layers of flavouring can always be divided into clear-cut, water-tight stages – they are sometimes blurred and inter-merged – but in carrying out flavouring processes in the execution of Chinese cooking, the concept of the various stages of heating and flavouring should be quite clear in the chef's mind.

The fun and interest arise, therefore, when all the various different types and degrees of flavourings are being applied at different stages and by way of different methods of heating. In other words, it is when multi-angle flavouring is married to multi-phase heating, with all the possible variations involved, that possibilities multiply and add up to a degree of profundity (and occasionally absurdity). That is when Chinese cooking gets to take on the character of a Chinese puzzle!

Accepted Methods of Heating Food in Chinese Cooking

If one were to take into account all the differing provincial variations, there are probably twice as many verbs as the ones I have listed below indicating the different methods of heating food in Chinese cooking. The fact that even this short list contains more than three dozen distinct terms, each with its own accepted operative meaning, must be an indication of the refinement and importance which the Chinese attach to the art of heating – which is best described as 'fire control' 火候 He Hou – a term which we actually use to apply to the control of heating in our cooking.

In some Western cooking, the quality of the raw materials is the primary thing. In Chinese cooking three things are equally important: raw materials, 'fire control' in heating, and flavouring.

Heating or fire control has come to assume such importance in Chinese cooking partly because we often practise multi-phase heating, which involves much more change of 'pace', and partly because in the case of quick stir-frying the temperature is so high

Introduction

that timing has consequently to be as often in seconds as in minutes. This latter process can almost be more appropriately described as 'scorch-frying lubricated with oil'. Western readers who are attuned to reading Chinese recipe books in the original (in Chinese) would probably at first be surprised to note the frequent instruction: 'heat the pan red'. After such an instruction nobody would be surprised to find that cooking time is often just a matter of seconds!

Indeed, looking at Chinese cooking chemically, heating is so much a part of flavouring that they cannot be conceived separately. If you know heating, you will know flavouring, and that is two-thirds of mastering the business of cooking.

1. 煮 CHU

'Chu' is the usual Chinese verb to indicate the general process of cooking; more specifically, it indicates cooking in water by boiling. As a culinary method, it has to be a well-controlled and well-timed process. The boiling must not be too long or most of the flavour and juices of the ingredient cooked will go into the water (soup), nor must it be too short, resulting in undercooking. In the accepted Chinese practice, the boiling is controlled by bringing the water initially to a full-boil, and then either by introducing small amounts of cold water at intervals or by lowering the heat to such a point that the boiling will continue only at a simmer.

Boiling is a very popular and well-favoured method of food preparation, due primarily to the purity of flavour resulting from the plain cooking of the ingredients, which tend to retain more of their original tastes and flavours. The use of highly-seasoned dips allows the individual diners to flavour the food according to personal taste.

2. 燙 T'ANG OR 湯爆 T'ANG P'AO

This process can perhaps be described as 'steeping' or 'quick-boiling'. It is really a variation of the previous process of plain boiling. The method used here is to bring the soup, stock, or water to a high pitch of boiling; then the ingredients to be cooked are dipped into the hot liquid. The food is usually sliced or cut into suitably thin pieces and dipped into the hot liquid for the momentary process of quick-boiling. Alternatively, the hot liquid can be poured on to the food arranged in a serving bowl. The heat of the liquid seals and cooks the food quickly. Again, food cooked in this way is eaten by dipping into dips and mixes. The method is sometimes also called 'He'. 焓

3. 涮 SHUAN

When the previous method of cooking is carried out in a charcoal-burning, or methylated spirit-heated Hot-Pot placed on the dining table itself (a sight which is particularly warming on a winter's evening), it is called 'Shuan'. The ingredients cooked are usually thinly-sliced meats, such as beef, lamb, kidney, liver, and chicken. The best known of them all is Peking Mongolian Sliced Lamb Hot-Pot. This dish has a Chinese Moslem background, originating from the Central Asian grasslands and prairies.

4. 浸 CH'IN

'Ch'in' is the process of cooking in water by gradual reduction in temperature – that is, controlled heating achieved through natural reduction in temperature by removing the heated container from the source of heat.

The usual procedure followed in this process is first of all to bring the heating liquid (usually water) to the boil, immerse the food to be cooked, and after a very short period of boiling, remove the pan from the heat, allowing the rest of the cooking to be done by the remaining heat in the liquid.

'Ch'in' is applicable not only to heating in water, but also in stock and oil. Hence the terms 'cooking in stock-receding-heat' and 'cooking in oil-receding-heat'.

5. 川 CH'UAN

'Ch'uan' is another process of water-heating or stock-heating which is allied to 'Ch'in'. Here the technique is to use re-boiling as the measure of the length or extent of the heating. Stock or water is brought to a rolling boil, and the food to be cooked is then introduced.

At the next re-boil, or the following re-boil (after a short period when the container is removed from the heat), or else at the third re-boil, the food will be cooked and ready. Again, only young and tender fresh food can be cooked in this manner. For thicker or larger cuts of meat, two or three, or even four re-boils might be necessary before the food is well-cooked.

6. 煲 PAO

'Pao' is the process of deep-boiling, the equivalent of deep-frying. The quantity of water used should be at least three to four times greater than the amount of food cooked. As a rule, the heat applied is low, and the process is one of 'time-cooking' – a long-term affair. In this connection, it might be mentioned that although the Chinese are renowned for high-heat cooking, as in 'Chow' (quick-stir-frying), 'Cha' (deep-frying), and 'Pao' (high-heat stir-frying), they also possess extensive methods of low-heat cooking.

7. 燜 MEN

'Men' is very similar to the Western process of stewing. The procedure is to fry the main ingredient first in a little oil, together with various seasonings and supplementary ingredients and materials. A reasonable quantity of water or stock is then added, and the contents brought to the boil. The heat is then reduced, and a long period of slow-simmering follows.

The apparent difference between 'Men' and Western stewing lies in the fact that the Chinese concept involves somewhat lower heat and a longer period of cooking. Hence anything which is 'Men' tends to be cooked to almost jelly-like tenderness, and because of the use of soya sauce, an ingredient which does not seem to change character whatever amount of cooking it is subjected to, the chances of success here are much greater.

8. 燒 SHAO

'Shao' is one of the most commonly-employed terms in Chinese cooking. The process is very similar to the preceding 'Men' in that it involves frying first in a little oil, then continuing by cooking and simmering in stock or water.

The difference lies in that in the second phase in the process of 'Shao', there is a period of conscious reduction of liquid (as in French cooking), when small amounts of fresh ingredients and seasonings are often added, leaving ultimately only a small amount of thickened gravy to go with the meat. In 'Men' there is usually more gravy.

9. 义燒 CANTONESE CHA SHAO (SPIT-ROAST)

In the Cantonese 'Cha Shao' method, there is not only a process of reduction of liquid at the last phase, but in addition, the meat is placed over a fire or in the oven for a period of barbecuing or roasting. Often the 'Cha Shao' process involves cutting the meat (usually pork) into strips, then thoroughly marinating them before 'hang-roasting' them in the oven. The strips of meat are brushed with a specially prepared marinade at regular intervals until cooked.

10. 滷 LU

'Lu' is a process of cooking food (usually meat, liver, kidney, other entrails, poultry, eggs, and sometimes fish) in a strong, aromatic soya-herbal stock. The stock is initially prepared by simmering meat in broth with quantities of rock sugar, soya sauce, sherry, dried tangerine peel, ginger, garlic, and five spice powder (a mixture of cinnamon, fennel, cloves, anise, and star anise). The first stock produced is called the 'original stock' and as more meats and food are simmered in it the stock assumes the name of 'master stock'.

The master stock is used again and again, and every three to four times it is used more fresh herbs have to be added and boiled in it. The herbal strength of the stock, as well as the strength of the other ingredients, can be varied according to taste or requirement.

The master stock is further enriched each time fresh materials are cooked in it; it is not only enriched but renewed. So long as the stock is used with some frequency, and its herbs strengthened and renewed, it can be used more or less forever. Some master stocks can be ranked as living antiques!

11. 蒸 CH'ENG

'Ch'eng' is a form of steaming. There are two accepted forms of steaming in China: steaming in an open bowl or plate and steaming in a closed receptacle.

Introduction

'Ch'eng' is 'open steaming' – here the bowl, plate, or basin is usually placed on a wire or bamboo rack, mounted inside a boiler, with the water kept at a rolling boil some inches below. Or the process can be carried out in multi-layer baskets with enclosed sides which fit on top of one another in a top-hat fashion, and which are placed on top of the rice-boiler. Thus the dishes can be cooked while the rice is being steamed or boiled.

In 'Ch'eng' the food to be cooked is usually pre-marinated or treated with all the necessary seasonings, garnishes and decorations before being placed in a steamer. Sometimes the food is given only a short blast of vigorous steaming. 'Ch'eng' is most often used when the food to be cooked does not require prolonged cooking – indeed, a short, sharp blast of steam is one of the few ways that certain foods may be cooked in order to retain their original freshness, flavour and juiciness. Fish, being usually tender in flesh, is most often and best cooked in this manner. Because of the prevalence of 'Ch'eng', we Chinese have been recognized as expert fish and seafood cooks.

12. 燉 OR 炖 TUN

In contrast to 'Ch'eng', 'Tun' is closed steaming, that is, steaming in a closed receptacle; and in China the mouth of the receptacle is often sealed with paper which is stuck down or glued on. In the West this can be done by covering with a piece of tinfoil, but with so many different types of casseroles with lids available, it is rarely necessary to have to resort to this.

Again in contrast to 'Ch'eng', 'Tun' is, as a rule, a lengthy process – 30–40 minutes upwards to 3–6 hours. Another cooking process called 'Kao', which is very long simmering over a low heat, produces very nearly the same results. In this process, as in 'Tun', the food is subjected to a short, sharp boil, followed by rinsing in cold water, before the actual cooking starts.

13. 烹 P'ENG

'P'eng' is a process which involves frying the foodstuff on either side until brown, then introducing a limited amount of stock or water and supplementary ingredients. The cooking is then continued over a low heat until all the liquid has been reduced to dryness. This is, in a way, fairly akin to 'Cantonese Ch'a Shao', except that in the latter process the complete drying of the food is achieved through barbecue-roasting.

14. 燴 HUI

'Hui' can perhaps be described as 'hot assembly in thickened soup' (the soup is usually thickened with cornflour or water chestnut flour).

15. 拌 PAN

'Pan' can be described as 'hot toss-and-scramble', except when cold is expressly indicated, resulting in the production of a composite dish which can almost be described as a 'hot salad'. It is a process of cooking which is very similar to 'Hui'. They differ in that 'Pan' is a dry process – no soup is added; the different strip-foods (or foods reduced to strips) are tossed and scrambled together in flavour-impregnated oil, which is used almost as a savoury lubricant.

In conception, and as a process, it differs from the Italian idea of how pasta foods should be produced in that a much greater range of constituent ingredients is incorporated. These ingredients generally fall into two distinct categories: cooked ingredients and uncooked or fresh ingredients. Because of the juxtaposition and incorporation of both cooked and uncooked foods, each with their prior treatment, flavouring, or cooking, the resultant 'hot salad' has a very distinctive quality of its own. As in the process of 'Hui', a little sesame oil is generally used as a final flavouring.

16. 炸 CHA

'Cha', as a form of cooking, is much the same thing as Western deep-frying, where food is first of all battered, and then given a period of deep-frying until it is ready for serving.

But as often as not in China, 'Cha' is only one of two or three stages of heating in the cooking of a given dish. In Crispy and Aromatic Duck the duck is first marinated and steamed before it is finally deep-fried to give it that final crispiness; or in the case of Crackling Wun Tun, the thin-skinned ravioli with meat filling is steamed or simmered first before being finally deep-fried, again to achieve that final crispiness.

Introduction

In general, in the Chinese process of deep-frying, the food often requires two or three immersions in hot oil to complete the cooking, and the oil in these cases is divided into three degrees of heat-temperature: 'hot oil', 'very hot oil' and 'fierce oil'. In many cases it is necessary to break up the deep-frying process into several phases, as the food could easily burn if the frying were to be maintained as one continuous process. Besides, the intermission (when the food is given a chance to cook in its own heat) can often provide an opportunity for the food to be treated with additional flavouring.

Deep-frying in China is conventionally divided into three categories: 'plain-fried', when the food material is cooked or deep-fried on its own, 'soft-fried' when sauces and seasonings are added to the food, especially during the latter part of the frying, when the excess oil has been drained away, and 'dry-fried' when the food is rolled in flour or cornflour or battered before being fried.

17. 永 YUNG

'Yung' is cooking in one continuous deep-frying process or deep-frying in one phase. The oil used in this one-phase deep-frying is usually 'just hot'. Because the heat of the oil is not too fierce, and the sizzling noise after the food is introduced is just barely audible, the food can be cooked for 10–15 minutes without burning. In 'Yung' the food must be suitable for cooking in one continuous process.

18. 炒 CHOW (OR CH'AO)

'Chow' is distinguished from 'Cha' in that it is stir-frying and only a small amount of oil is used in the cooking (almost as a lubricant). The ingredients being fried are kept in more or less continuous movement throughout the process of cooking. A metal spoon (ordinary or perforated), or a pair of chopsticks, is used to keep the food in motion.

The materials to be cooked are usually cut into strips or small pieces, so that more of their surfaces come into contact with the pan, and are exposed to the heating-oil and seasonings. 'Chow' is usually a quick process (often translated as 'quick-frying'), and is probably one of the fastest cooking methods for a tasty dish. The process seldom takes more than 2–3 minutes – often only a few seconds.

The Complete Chinese Cookbook

19. 爆 PAO

'Pao' is a term employed to indicate rapid cooking over a high heat, either in oil or in stock. 'Yiu Pao' means oil-rapid-cooked and 'Tang Pao' means stock-rapid-cooked.

When oil is used, the method differs from the ordinary 'Chow' or quick-frying in that the cooking is for a shorter period of time, and over a higher heat. Besides, 'Pao' is always the finale in any multi-stage cooking process, while 'Chow' or 'Cha' quick-frying and deep-frying can take place at an earlier stage. In China, the term 'Pao' is the same word used to describe an explosion. The process can, therefore, be described as 'explosive-frying'.

A well-known example of the process of 'Pao' is Quick-Fried Diced Chicken in Soya Jam. In this case the chicken meat is first of all diced into cubes, and semi-deep-fried until almost cooked. It is then 'explosively-fried' in a boiling marinade of soya jam with sugar, wine, and vinegar for about 15 seconds to one minute to complete the cooking.

20. 煎 CHIEN

'Chien' is a process of cooking in oil, in which only a small amount of oil is used, and the cooking is static for a period of time (usually longer than 'Chow' and much longer than 'Pao'). The food to be cooked can be in larger chunks or pieces than in the case of 'Chow' or 'Pao', hence more time is required for them to cook through. A typical case of 'Chien' in Western cooking is fried bread. 'Chien' can be used as one phase in a multi-phase cooking process. The gravy or sauce used in the dish can be prepared separately and poured over the food afterwards.

21. 淋 LING

This is a process which might be called 'splash-frying'. In other words, the food is not actually immersed in the oil during the frying; instead it is suspended above the oil, and a ladle is used to pour and splash the food with hot oil which is then allowed to run down into the pan containing the oil. A well-known dish cooked in this manner is 'Yiu Ling Chi' or Splash-Fried Chicken. Here the

Introduction

chicken can be suspended over the oil in a wire-basket and ladles of oil are poured steadily over the chicken until the bird is brown and well-cooked.

22. 溜 LIU

'Liu' is a form of wet-frying in which a thickened sauce (invariably involving cornflour, sugar, and vinegar) is made or introduced during the middle or later stage of frying.

In 'Liu', the frying is comparatively static compared to 'Chow' or 'Pao': the food is not subjected to a rapid movement of stirring and scrambling and over modest heat. Hence in 'Liu' a flat, wide pan is favoured, so that more of the foodstuff being cooked can be in direct contact with the metal of the hot pan, without continual movement. Movements are confined to the steadier, gentler type of turning over of ingredients, without too much violence or overheating.

The sauce mixture used in 'Liu' is usually prepared beforehand in a separate bowl, and added into the frying pan soon after both sides of the food have been fried, or during the final phase of the cooking. 'Liu' is one of the favourite methods of cooking sliced fish, in which case some wine or spirit is often introduced into the sauce mixture, and the fish-slices themselves are initially fried in oil with a little garlic, ginger, and onion to heighten the flavour.

23. 貼 T'IEH

'T'ieh' resembles 'Chien' in that it is a static, non-scramble form of frying, in which not too much oil is used. It is different from 'Chien' in that normally only one side of the food is fried – the food is not turned over as in the frying of bread. In fact, it is quite often the practice to sprinkle the top side of the food with water or stock whilst the frying is going on, to keep it soft on top. Thus in the case of 'Kuo T'ieh' (Peking Pot-Stuck Ravioli), the aim is to produce something which is crispy underneath, soft on top, and juicy inside.

24.  PIEN

'Pien' is a type of frying which is used mostly in vegetable cooking; about 10–15% of oil is used in relation to the weight of the vegetables being cooked.

The Complete Chinese Cookbook

It is the practice to first of all fry a small quantity of onion, garlic, and ginger or pickles, so that the oil will be impregnated with their strong taste and aromatic flavour. The main vegetable is then fried in the oil, to take on the same appealing taste and flavour, enhanced by the heat of the frying.

After 2-3 minutes of continued frying, and when the vegetable is thoroughly oil-impregnated, a small amount of water or stock is introduced. This has the effect of preventing burning, and also provides quick-steaming. Furthermore, flavouring is added when a good stock is used. The result is tender, glistening vegetables which have in fact been cooked primarily in their own juices; and if some seasonings (such as soya sauce, flavour powder, sesame oil, chicken fat, wine, or sugar) are added, it should make an extremely palatable dish. 'Pien' is the usual way in which most vegetables are cooked in China.

25.  AO

'Ao' is really a compressed form of 'Pien'. It starts with the food or vegetable being fried in a small amount of oil, with the addition of some ingredients and seasonings. When partly-cooked and well-covered and impregnated with oil, a little water or stock is introduced. Thereafter the cooking is finished or rounded off with both a 'high-boil' and 'high-fry' over a high heat, resulting in the food being part fried and part steamed. Here the steam is, however, of special quality, being impregnated with the flavour and aroma of the strong-tasting vegetables.

26. 炆 WEN

In timing and method, 'Wen' is the cooking process which is nearest to the Western concept of braising. The food material is here first of all fried in oil with the addition of a few seasonings and other ingredients. After the initial quick stir-frying, a small amount of water or stock is introduced. The cooking pan is then moved to a low heat, to cook for 10-15 minutes with some gentle stirring. Just before serving, a small amount of cornflour and a dash of flavour powder (both mixed in water and wine) are introduced for a final fry-up to thicken the gravy and accentuate the flavour.

27. 烳 CHÜEH

'Chüeh' is a variation of 'Wen' in that some supplementary ingredients (usually garlic, ginger, and onion or chilli) are fried in oil first before the introduction of the main material. Once the latter is cooked or browned, the seasonings and stock are added. The contents of the pan are then simmered over a low heat for 10–20 minutes. Thereupon the solid food is removed and placed on a well-heated serving plate, to await the sauce. The sauce is produced by the addition of a little cornflour mixed in water, a dash of flavour powder, and some wine to the remaining liquid in the pan, which is then heated for 1 minute. When the sauce is ready it is then poured over the main ingredients in the dish or plate. The only difference between this method and the previous one is that in 'Chüeh' the gravy or sauce is produced at the last moment, separately from the main ingredients of the dish.

28. 焗 CHÜ

'Chü' is another variation on the braising theme. It involves an initial frying of the main and supplementary ingredients over a high heat, followed by the addition of further ingredients and the introduction of water, soup, or wine. The process is then continued along one of two lines, both involving a reduction of the liquid: prolonged simmering over a very low heat, and controlled braising over a somewhat higher heat, so that the liquid can be reduced visually to the desired thickness and quantity.

Another meaning of the term 'Chü' denotes pot-roasting or casserole cooking, where only a minimal amount of liquid is used.

29. 熗 TS'ANG

'Ts'ang' is a term generally applied to the method of frying and braising in which the ingredients are stir-fried in the usual manner and placed on a serving dish. A sauce is then made from a previously prepared mixture which is quickly heated in the pan. The sauce is poured over the food in the serving dish and left to cool. The dish is served cold.

'Ts'ang' is a term which is also used to describe the process of

The Complete Chinese Cookbook

treatment, seasoning, and marinating involved in 'cold mixing' or 'cold tossing' (as in salad making). Here the customary seasonings and ingredients are used: sesame oil, vinegar, soya sauce, good stock, chopped spring onions, ginger, and garlic. 'Cold mixing' in China generally applies not to the preparing of a vegetable dish, but to a pasta dish (noodles), involving both cooked and uncooked ingredients and supplementary materials, which are all seasoned and marinated, together or separately, prior to being served cold.

30. 塌 T"A

'T"a' (as in 'Kuo T"a') means deep-frying food in batter, then draining it of oil and cooking and braising it with various supplementary ingredients. 'T"a' is also used to describe the same process with an additional phase of initial steaming, before the deep-frying and braising.

31. 烤 K'AO

'K'ao' is a term which indicates exactly the same process as in Western roasting. However, in China, without the modern oven, fire control is much more difficult. A great deal of art and skill has to go into fire-building and timing. Usually a large pile-up of wood is first of all burnt in a stove, like a bonfire. The resulting smouldering wood and charcoal are then scraped and piled up on the sides, and the food to be cooked is hung up in the middle of the stove for roasting – as in the cooking of Peking Duck.

In denoting the process of roasting, 'K'ao' differs from the term 'Shao' in that the latter word when used in this sense denotes the type of roasting where the heat is applied entirely from below, such as barbecue roasting where the food is generally turned on a spit over the fire; or it can also indicate pot-roasting. In 'K'ao' the cooking is effected largely through air-heating (convection), or direct-level radiation.

32. 烘 HUNG

'Hung' indicates open barbecue-roasting. It involves the frequent turning of raw food on a spit over an open fire. The term 'Shao' sometimes indicates the same thing, but 'Hung' is the more specific term. It means heating mainly by radiation.

33. 煨 WEI

'Wei' is the process of cooking by 'burial', that is the burying of food in hot solids, such as charcoal, smouldering coal, heated stones, sand, salt, or lime (heat evolved by the addition of water). Foods cooked in this manner are generally of the type with a thick crust or skin, or foods which can easily be wrapped in a cover – such as in lotus leaves, a mud-pack, or a sheet of suet. (Sweet potato baked in its jacket by burying in hot coal and earth is a typical case.)

Without the modern oven, we Chinese resort to cooking by burial much more frequently than in the West. 'Chiao Hua Chicken' from Amoy is a case of heating by burial in lime, over which water is then poured.

34. 燻 HSÜN

'Hsün' is to smoke. In Chinese smoking, the food material used has usually been cooked beforehand. It is often previously seasoned in salt, wine, onion, and ginger.

The food is suspended over the smoke/fire on a wire rack. A few pieces of red, smouldering coal or charcoal are first placed under the rack inside a pan or tin fitted with a cover or in a proper Kilu. The coal or charcoal is then covered with a handful of sawdust, sugar, or dried tea leaves. This immediately creates a heavy smoke. The lid is then closed and the food left to smoke for 15–20 minutes, depending upon the degree of smokiness required. In Cantonese cooking, smoking with tea leaves is called 'Hsüng', and with sawdust 'Yen'.

35. 和 K'OU

'K'ou' is a double process – usually frying first and steaming afterwards, and the food is then turned out from the steaming bowl on to a plate (like a pudding).

The main ingredient to be cooked is usually fried first, then sliced into smaller pieces. It is then neatly packed with several supplementary and flavouring materials in a heatproof basin or steam-bowl.

The Complete Chinese Cookbook

The ingredients are arranged in layers, and placed in a steamer for a period of prolonged steaming. When the foods are cooked, they are then turned out on a serving plate. The term 'K'ou' in Chinese actually means 'turn out': the result is usually a 'meat-pudding'.

36. 扒 PA

'Pa' is just the reverse process of 'K'ou', in that here the food is steamed first, then fried. In the final frying the food is often given a last flavouring by the addition of supplementary materials, ingredients, and seasonings. This last 'treatment' has the effect of sharpening and livening up the flavour of the food.

37. 醉 TSUI

'Tsui' is the process of marinating fresh or cooked food in wine or liqueur before serving, thus giving it a 'drunken' effect, as in Drunken Chicken. Food treated in this way in China is usually only lightly cooked (often by the process of 'Chien' or poaching) and then subjected to a period of marinating in wine, liqueur, spring onions, ginger, and garlic. Meat, fish, and seafood can all be prepared in this manner. But when meat is used it is usually poultry-meat; and in a majority of cases the marinating needs only to be for a short length of time (although several days is more usual).

38. 醬 CHIANG AND 糟 CHIAOW

'Chiang' and 'Chiaow' are processes of food preparation which are closely related in method to 'Tsui'; the difference lies mainly in the difference between the marinating ingredients used. In 'Tsui', as already pointed out, the marinade is composed principally of wine or liqueur. In 'Chiang' the main ingredients are soya sauce and soya jam. In 'Chiaow' the principal ingredient used in the marinade is a paste made from wine-sediment (the dregs or lees from the bottom of a wine jar), which is called 'wine-sediment paste'. These pastes exist in different colours such as red, purple, brown, and cream. When these ingredients are used to marinate, a small amount of ground ginger and salt are often added. The foods are usually first of all lightly cooked, then placed in an earthen jar, where the marinating is carried out, often lasting several days or weeks.

Introduction

39. 醃 YIEN

'Yien' is the general term for salting and marinating, but more specifically, 'Yien' is the process of salting – usually with coarse salt.

The food to be salted is rubbed with coarse salt and a little saltpetre and placed in an earthen jar. It is turned over once every three days. After nine days a heavy weight (usually a stone) is placed on it to squeeze out any remaining liquid. Meat thus treated is capable of keeping for a good length of time and even inferior meat can become flavoursome after a period. Heating in one form or another usually precedes or follows the salting.

40. 風 FENG

'Feng' is the above process when it is carried out by drying in the wind, instead of by compressed marinating in a jar. Although these preserved meats and fish have very distinctive tastes and are very appealing to many, they are often used in conjunction with fresh food, to impart to the latter their distinctive flavour.

There are many more cooking terms in China than the foregoing forty. Every province and region has its own expressions and peculiarities. Some of the cooking terms are related to the material and ingredients used. But forty is a round number, and the various local terms and expressions, although they may run into dozens more, are really only variations of these principal, basic terms.

Cutting

Too much can be easily made of cutting, as too much can be made of carving. Over-elaboration only creates a mystique, which dissuades interested people from undertaking what are, in fact, only simple and logical procedures in tackling specific jobs. Chinese cooking is too big to need to cloud itself over with any mystique to command reverence.

However, something has to be said about cutting, as it is more of an integral part of Chinese cooking than of Western cooking. A good part of the necessary cutting of Western food is done on the dining table, for example, carving. In Chinese cooking, practically all the cutting is done in the kitchen. This is due to the fact that we Chinese use chopsticks, and that the most widely used form of Chinese cooking is quick stir-frying, which necessitates reducing different types of foods to uniform sizes before cooking commences. In the main, the following are the principal shapes and sizes to which the foods and materials have to be reduced through cutting: chunks, slices, strips, shreds, dice (cubes), grains, mince.

Chunks are further divided into mahjong-pieces, triangular (or water nut) pieces, and miniature chops (spare-ribs cut into 1 inch (2½ cm) lengths).

Slices are divided into autumn-leaf slices, willow-leaf slices (or slivers), nail-piece slices, long-oblong slices (about 3 inches (7½ cm) thick) slices, and very thin slices (for rapid dip-boiling in stock).

Strips are usually about the thickness of chopsticks or matchsticks, and shreds are thinner and more thread-like in size.

Diced cubes usually vary in size from the size of an average sugar lump to half that size.

The larger type of mince is about the size of grains, and the smaller is what we call 'velvet mince'. In neither case would we Chinese resort to the use of the grinder or mincing machine, as we feel that through the latter's squeezing action, most of the valuable meat-juices are squeezed out and lost. We prefer to do it with two choppers at a drum-beat!

In order to perform Chinese cutting and chopping efficiently, it has to be done on a chopping board (or rather block) which is at least 6 inches (15 cm) thick and 12–15 inches (30–37 cm) in diameter – usually a hardwood block from a tree-trunk. Since the Chinese kitchen chopper is a razor sharp implement, it has to be used on a very firm and steady base.

Although the Chinese kitchen chopper is able to perform all the functions which a knife or chopper is expected to do, the professionals in China use three weights of knife: the thin knife, heavy knife, and bone knife. The thin knife is used for slicing, dicing, shredding, and cutting into strips. This knife is used more frequently than any other knife. The thick or heavy knife is used for graining or mincing. Here the sides and top of the knife (opposite to the side of the blade) are constantly used for beating, hammering, flattening, and mashing, and the weight of the knife provides that additional

Introduction

gravitational power to each chop. The bone knife is, of course, used for cutting through the bone, as well as pushing through the joints. Bone chopping or cutting has to be done far more frequently in Chinese cooking than in Western cooking – with chopped chicken, or duck, or Chinese spare-ribs (which are cut into ¾–1½ inch (1½–3½ cm) lengths) the bones have to be chopped through at least a score of times even in the preparation of a single dish. Although it is a Western saying 'The nearer the bone, the sweeter the meat', it is the Chinese who eat the meat with its bone. The bone knife is also the implement used for de-boning, at which Chinese chefs are masters. All these knives – thin, heavy, and bone – are curiously shaped, like rectangular choppers.

As a rule, the shape and size of cutting follows upon the original size and shape of the principal ingredients, or the sizes or shapes into which they have been cut. Diced pork or chicken will be cooked with diced vegetables; shredded beef will have shredded vegetables or bean sprouts to go with it. Noodles always have meat and vegetables sliced into strips to go with them. It is only occasionally that supplementary materials in different shapes from the principal ingredients are cooked together; a fact which only proves the rule.

Variation is found or allowed to exist in cutting only when a shorter-cooking food is sliced into somewhat thicker pieces to cook with a food which requires longer cooking time, and which is cut into thinner or smaller pieces. It is all a matter of logical timing and harmony.

Texture in Chinese Food

It is a popular thing to talk about texture in food and cooking these days. But it is in Chinese food and cooking that texture suddenly takes on a fresh meaning and reality. This is for two reasons. First of all, because a Chinese meal consists of many dishes, whether served at once (as at home), or one after another (as at a party or banquet), the contrast between the texture of dishes is more of a concrete reality which has to be taken into account in the planning of the menu. It is only at a Chinese meal that you can have two or three soups, two or three casseroles, stews, and steamed dishes, a couple of semi-soup dishes, three or four or even half a dozen quick-fried dishes (of which one or two will be dry-fried in contrast to wet-fried, that is, frying with the addition of sauce), and several cold dishes as starters. Perhaps there will also be a sweet dish or two – one of which will probably be a sweet soup.

People have sometimes wondered why we Chinese have sweet soups. If you have had the experience of half a dozen or more highly savoury dishes, one following the other, you will understand what a welcome and refreshing thing it is to have something so very different in taste and texture from what has been served previously, especially if it is chilled. Savoury soups are generally used for breaking up the run of drier, quick-fried or deep-fried dishes, in addition to their function of washing down morsels of food, as table water is used in Western meals. The same applies to China's many semi-soup dishes – which are generally clear-simmered or long-steamed dishes, with meat or poultry cooked to jelly-like tenderness, sitting in clear consommé, perhaps supported by a small choice of vegetables added during the last stage of cooking. Here all the items which make up the dishes stand out in great purity and clarity. Such dishes act as an excellent contrast to the quick stir-fried dishes, which usually make up the bulk of the dishes in a Chinese meal.

Amongst the quick stir-fried dishes themselves, there is contrast and variation in the tastes and textures of the principal and supplementary ingredients used, and also in the way in which the foods are cut or shaped – whether diced into cubes, cut into matchstick strips, shredded into threads, left in chunks, or shaped into balls – like deep-fried prawn balls or meat balls. After a wet-fried dish, which in Chinese we call 'Lü', we would have a dry-fried dish, which we call 'Gan Shao'. The taste and texture of these two types of dish are entirely different; one is smooth and soft and should melt in the mouth, and the other is usually hot, spicy, and crispy and needs to be bitten or chewed before it can be swallowed. These dishes are excellent accompaniments to wine, or to the blandness of plain-cooked (boiled) rice.

Another excellent type of dish to follow a 'Lü' dish is the aromatic and crackling type – for example, Aromatic and Crackling Duck or Four Great Crispies – where the crackling qualities are used to provide contrast with the soft smoothness of the 'Lü'.

Crunchiness is another very important quality in the Chinese conception of texture. I have often suspected that the reason for bamboo shoots being used so extensively in Chinese dishes is entirely related to their crunchy texture – since bamboo shoots, although subtle to taste, have, in fact, very little flavour of their own. However, they possess an undeniable and inimitable crunchiness, whether in soup, fried, or in stews: a quality which is hard for them to lose in any combination, hence their popularity in all kinds of cross-cooked dishes.

Another popular way in which we Chinese introduce the quality of crunchiness into a dish is to use various raw vegetables, including cucumber, spring onions, carrots, turnips, and celery which are either cut into matchstick strips, or diced into small cubes and cooked for an instant, usually by quick-frying with the other materials which constitute the bulk of the dish. An example of this is the very popular northern dish, Quick-Fried Sliced Lamb with Spring Onions, which was as popular with the coolies as with the Emperors. Here the spring onions are given only a very short time in the oil and gravy with the sliced lamb.

The concept of texture of food applies not only in the difference between the textures of different dishes, but also to differences and contrasts in the feel of the different constituents within a single dish. Here, because of the extensive Chinese practice of cross-cooking different types of foods and materials, texture has a reality and meaning, which give it greater interest and significance than are generally apparent in other styles of cooking.

Chinese Flavourings and Food Materials

The flavourings in Chinese food, and their numerous variations, appear to be derived from five main sources, and are applied at different stages of the cooking and eating. It is the orchestration of this multi-stage flavouring with multi-stage heating, which in many instances acts to solder together the flavours, that gives the preparation of Chinese food its mystery and sophistication.

The five main sources of flavouring in Chinese cooking are:

(i) the principal food on which a dish is based, which always provides the main source of flavour in any style of cooking. Often it is the very purpose of the cooking to bring out the distinctive flavour of the main ingredient in a dish.

(ii) the supplementary materials, with which the principal ingredients are cooked or cross-cooked. In Chinese cooking, the use of supplementary materials is practised to a point where, in many instances, it is difficult to say which is the principal ingredient and which are supplementary materials. In such cases, there is usually a great deal of cross-blending of flavours, and here the supplementary ingredients are present not only to enrich and vary the taste of the dish, but also to provide additional substance. They often also contribute to the variations of texture and colour in the dish.

(iii) the flavouring ingredients, which are small amounts of materials, either fresh, prepared, or preserved, are introduced in limited quantities purely to enhance or vary the taste of the food. We Chinese are not inclined to use a great many herbs (although there are innumerable medicinal herbs which sometimes wander into the dishes), but we command a good range of preserved and dried foods, which are used extensively for this purpose.

(iv) seasonings and sauces – the seasonings used in Chinese cooking are quite conventional, and we do not go in a great deal for made-up sauces, as the French do. Chinese sauces might be called 'natural sauces', as they are the natural by-products of the process of cooking. They are usually concocted during the very last stage of cooking, when the ingredients of a dish are frequently heated up to a crescendo, with the addition of a little savoury, but neutral stock, and small quantities of seasonings and basic sauces.

(v) Chinese table condiments, or 'dips' and 'mixes', are probably more numerous than those customarily used in the West. They are often made-up condiments which are traditional in origin and are an essential part of the dishes which they accompany. They are usually concocted just before they are served, and are invariably served in small dishes or saucers – never in bottles – and arranged strategically on the dining table.

PRINCIPAL MATERIALS

One of the reasons why Chinese cooking is so easily acceptable in the Western world is because the principal materials used are almost identical to those used in Western cooking, except for dairy produce which is seldom used in China.

We use the same fish, flesh, and fowl, as well as the whole range of vegetables which are used in Western cooking, and perhaps a few more. If there is any difference in the principal materials used it is only a question of emphasis. We use pork more than any other type of meat, probably because pigs are difficult to use otherwise – for

Introduction

example, as beasts of burden. We eat and value fresh-water fish more than salt-water fish (except in coastal areas), because China is in the main a continental country, and Chinese farmers are habitual fish-farmers: the countryside is littered with millions of ponds and lakes in which fish are kept, fed, and grown. In addition, there are thousands of rivers, streams, canals, and tributaries from which fresh fish and other water-food can be obtained.

Although duck is one of the favourite fowls, chicken easily leads as the most popular of all poultry used. Next to pork, it is probably the most extensively used meat in China, even before the era of battery-produced chickens. Indeed, even in China today, battery-raised chickens are still probably unknown. As free-range chickens are used exclusively, Chinese chicken dishes are much more tasty than those we are now used to in the West.

In meat and poultry dishes we use bacon, beef, chicken, duck, ham, lamb, pigeon, pork, turkey, and venison.

In fish dishes we use abalone (or awabi), bass, bêche de mer, bream, carp, clams, cod, crab, eel, flounder, haddock, halibut, herring, jellyfish, lobster, mackerel, mullet, oyster, perch, pike, prawns, rock salmon, sardines, shad, sharks' fins, shrimps, sole, squid, sturgeon, trout, tuna, turbot, and whitefish.

In vegetable dishes we use asparagus, bamboo shoots, beans (and their various products), bean sprouts, bitter melon, broccoli, cabbage, celery cabbage, mustard cabbage, carrots, cauliflower, celery, chives, corn, cucumber, egg-plant, leeks, lettuce, lily buds, lotus roots, melon, mushrooms, onions, parsley, potatoes, pea-pods, peas, pepper, radishes, snow peas, spinach, squash, string beans, tomatoes, turnips, water chestnuts, and watercress.

In addition, we also use numerous variants and allied foods of the above principal materials. As far as food is concerned, the economically advanced countries are more amply supplied than China, therefore the Westerner taking up Chinese cookery should concentrate more on the treatment and cooking of the materials than on the materials themselves since they have the principal ingredients in plenty. Let not the mystique of Chinese cooking give the impression that we Chinese eat differently from you. We eat almost precisely the same things. If there is any mystery it is in the cooking, cross-cooking, flavouring, and heating.

SUPPLEMENTARY MATERIALS

Because of the extensive Chinese practice of cross-cooking different foods (especially those of different genre and texture), supplementary materials play a much bigger role in Chinese cooking than in Western food preparation. Indeed, as already said, there are situations where the materials used are so evenly balanced that it is difficult to decide which is the principal material and which are supplementary ones.

As a rule, the principal material is the one which lends the dominant bulk, flavour, or character to the dish; all the other materials which are cooked in conjunction with it, to provide a difference or balance in flavour, colour, and texture, are the supplementary materials. Sharks' fins generally represent only a small proportion of the bulk of a dish, but since they give it its character, they are the principal ingredient.

When one investigates the importance of supplementary materials, one comes to the conclusion that their presence in a dish serves two principal purposes: in the case of flavoursome principal materials such as meat or fish, supplementary materials add variety and interest to the general flavour; in the case of bland or neutral principal materials such as rice or noodles, supplementary ingredients provide some appealing taste and flavour. Of the two functions, the latter is probably the more important. For in any economically underdeveloped country, where meat and fish are not in plentiful supply, the need for making bulk-food tasty is of paramount importance. The Chinese ability and expertise in doing this is one of the high points in Chinese culinary art, and is what makes Chinese cooking so economical – and incidentally – so profitable!

To achieve this general purpose with greater effect, Chinese cooking advances one stage further from supplementary materials to the use of flavouring ingredients both fresh and dried.

FLAVOURING INGREDIENTS

The one thing which is common to both Chinese fish and vegetable cooking is that supplementary materials are seldom employed to any great extent in their cooking, and when they are used, it is as garnishing. Fish and vegetables are usually cooked with a selection of flavouring ingredients, either to enhance their interest and flavour, or to reduce or eliminate their inherent but less appealing tastes (such as fishiness in fish), or for both purposes. These flavouring ingredients are, of course, also used for the same purposes in the cooking of meat, rice, and pasta.

The most popular dried flavouring materials of animal origin include dried shrimps, dried scallop (stem muscle), dried oyster, dried mussels, dried squid, dried abalone, clam, salted duck, duck feet, duck liver, salted egg, salted fish, smoked or cured ham, small Cantonese salami sausage, and Fukien 'meat wool'.

Those of vegetable origin are far more numerous. The most popular of these are: dried mushrooms, dried tree fungus (wood ears and cloud ears – used more for texture than taste), dried tangerine peel, golden needles (lily bud stems), a whole variety of preserved cabbages (such as Szechuan cabbage, Shanghai cabbage, or Winter cabbage), preserved turnips, parsnips, dried chilli peppers, pickled mustard green, lotus seeds, lotus roots, melon seeds, dried lychees, longans (or dragon eyes), dried kumquats (tiny oval-shaped oranges), dried dates, cinnamon bark, black beans (salted and fermented), anise, star anise, and all the varieties of herbs which are often used in a combination called five spice powder, which is a ground powder made from anise, star anise, pepper, fennel, cloves, and cinnamon. It is used very frequently in meat cooking, especially with beef.

When fresh flavouring materials are used in conjunction with dried, preserved, or salted ingredients of both animal and vegetable origin, and when these are further combined with the principal ingredient and the various supplementary materials, great avenues of flavour-blending are opened to us. Indeed, the possibilities are exciting, intriguing, and almost fathomless! This is what prompted a French scientist to remark to me that Chinese cooking is not cooking, but alchemy!

SEASONINGS AND SAUCES

Chinese seasonings and sauces can be subdivided according to their order of application into marinades, seasonings, sauces, dressings, and table condiments in the form of dips and mixes.

Except for the frequent use of sugar as an ingredient in the preparation of savoury dishes, all the other basic seasonings used in Chinese cooking are much the same as those employed in Western cooking, namely, salt, pepper, vinegar, mustard, and chilli, which is usually in the form of dried chilli or chilli oil, rather than in powdered form.

The Complete Chinese Cookbook

The main difference between Chinese cooking and Western cooking in the area of food seasoning arises in the use of soya beans and their various by-products. First of all, there is soya sauce, which is already well known in the West and which comes crudely in light, dark, and heavy forms. It is, of course, capable of much finer gradations. Then there are fermented, salted, black beans, soya bean jam or paste (usually made from mashed brown beans, mixed with salt, sugar, garlic, and soya sauce), and 'soya cheese'. When these four soya bean products are combined in varying quantities with varying amounts of wine, sugar, and flavour powder (monosodium glutamate), the combination makes almost anything highly tasty. I have often called this mixture the Chinese gastronomic gunpowder!

Whatever there is in soya beans, we Chinese have certainly employed it and exploited it fully. The use of soya beans and their by-products has certainly accounted for the biggest difference between Chinese and Western cooking.

Apart from soya beans, the Chinese also make extensive use of oyster sauce, fish gravy, and red wine-sediment paste (also in other colours) to vary and enhance taste and flavour. We also use sesame oil and paste to provide an earthy smoothness and an appealing aroma, and this practice appears to have something in common with Middle Eastern cooking, which has been largely ignored by the French. In addition, there are the fruit-based and vegetable sauces such as plum sauce and hoisin sauce.

Except for fish gravy sauce, wine-sediment paste, and fermented, salted, black beans, which can only be applied to food during the cooking process, all the other basic sauces and seasonings can be used as ingredients for marinades, as seasonings during cooking, or even as table condiments in the form of dips and mixes.

The following are some of the basic sauces and seasonings generally employed in Chinese cooking. They do not include the natural sauces which are produced during cooking, or the sauces which are made up for special dishes and preparations.

SAUCES

Taking all in all, we Chinese do not appear to approach sauces in the grand manner of the French. Nor is there as much mystique about Chinese sauces, except for what is carried over from the Western reverence for the French sauces.

Introduction

As a rule, sauces are produced in Chinese cooking almost as a matter of course, as we proceed with our cooking – usually through the addition of stock (mostly chicken, meat, or bone stock) to the food we are preparing, often towards the last stages of its heating. Seasonings, thickenings (cornflour or water chestnut flour), and perhaps wine are also added at the same time.

Chinese chefs generally proceed with their cooking, producing the sauces as they go along, without giving them a second thought. To them, sauces are just a small cog in the large wheel of the exercise of cooking as a whole. They assume that anyone who knows the arts of cutting and the proportioning of supplementary materials, who has a sense of flavour-blending and the use of flavouring materials, and who has mastered the difficult art of heat control, must therefore be able to make the sauces, which after all are only a small part of the flavour orchestration.

Since sauces are not usually applied to wet, soupy dishes such as casseroles, steamed dishes, long-simmered dishes, and the numerous Chinese semi-soup dishes, their use is mainly confined to plain-cooked dishes, deep-fried dishes, quick stir-fried dishes, and bland rice and pasta dishes, which need additional flavouring to heighten their appeal.

Since the number of plain-cooked or deep-fried dishes is not quite so great as the quick stir-fried dishes, the larger proportion of sauces in Chinese cooking results from the process of quick stir-frying. Hence, although there are probably a vast number of sauces which are actually produced in the normal course of Chinese cooking (running probably into hundreds), they are so closely related to the main ingredients and supplementary materials of the dishes that they are seldom awarded an independent name, or, for that matter, given individual consideration. They are so much an integral part of the dishes themselves that they are seldom regarded as having a separate identity. Because of this lack of identity, the Chinese are much less preoccupied with sauces than the French. In actual fact, we probably produce as many sauces as the French, possibly many more. However, as the famous saying goes: 'We have it, but we don't talk about it!'

In one area, however, the French must possess a far bigger repertoire of sauces than the Chinese: these are the cold sauces, the mayonnaises, vinaigrettes, and dressings. This is probably only because, except for a very few dishes, the Chinese hardly eat cold food at all. They are obsessed with the fear of getting a chill in the stomach!

A quick survey of the Chinese cookery landscape will reveal that the majority of Chinese dishes which result from the cross-cooking of a number of ingredients usually generate ample gravy or natural sauce in themselves, and are therefore not in need of any additional made-up sauces to go with them. In the production of these natural sauces, those with wine, vinegar, and ginger content are usually used to counteract and balance the qualities of fish, and those made from preserves or fermented beans, and having a sharp piquant saltiness, are used to give a distinctive savouriness to meats. In the main, Chinese sauces consist of these natural sauces which are distilled out of the foods during the process of cooking, through the addition of a limited quantity of stock, seasoning, and flavouring ingredients.

On the other hand, the use of made-up sauces is therefore confined to plain-cooked meat and chicken dishes, to plain deep-fried dishes, to egg or Fu-Yung dishes and to some fish dishes, where some contrast and a garnish are essential. Above all, made-up sauces are used to contrast with the neutrality of rice and noodle dishes, particularly with noodle dishes which in China are served in four principal forms: fried, in soup, tossed with chopped scallion, garlic, bean paste, and sesame oil or paste (or both), or finally in thickened gravy, or sauces. These identifiable, made-up sauces are, in fact, not many. The recipes for the majority of them are provided below in this chapter. What gives capacity and potential to Chinese sauces is their liberal tradition which is the possibility of cross-blending natural sauces, and cross-blending of natural sauces with made-up sauces. It is these possibilities which give Chinese sauces something of the character of savoury cocktails and allow for their almost limitless repertoire.

The following recipes for sauces, dressings, dips, and mixes are sufficient for four to eight people, depending on how many other condiments are served.

Sauces for Noodles or Rice

Although the sauces in this section may be served with either noodles or rice, the Chinese themselves prefer to eat rice plain.

Introduction

Basic Pork Gravy Sauce for Noodles

8 oz (200 g) streaky pork
2 tablespoons peanut *or* corn oil
2 tablespoons chopped onion *or* spring onion
½ teaspoon salt
2 tablespoons soya sauce
¼ pint (125 ml) stock
1 teaspoon sugar
½ teaspoon flavour powder
½ tablespoon cornflour

Preparation Chop the pork coarsely.
Cooking Heat the oil in a frying pan. Add the pork, onion, and salt, and stir-fry for 4–5 minutes over a medium heat. Add the soya sauce, stock, sugar, and flavour powder. Bring the mixture to a gentle boil and cook for 4–5 minutes, then stir in the cornflour, blended with 4 tablespoons water. Stir until the mixture thickens.
Serving Pour over noodles in individual bowls.

Beef and Tomato Sauce for Noodles

6 oz (150 g) beef
4 medium-sized tomatoes
2 oz (50 g) onion
2 slices root ginger
1 clove garlic
2 tablespoons vegetable oil
½ teaspoon salt
2 tablespoons soya sauce
1½ teaspoons sugar
1 tablespoon sherry
¼ pint (125 ml) stock
½ tablespoon cornflour

Preparation Shred the beef, onion, and root ginger. Peel and quarter the tomatoes. Crush the garlic.
Cooking Stir-fry the onion, garlic, and ginger in hot oil for 30 seconds. Add the beef, salt, and tomatoes and stir-fry over a medium heat for 3 minutes. Add the soya sauce, sugar, sherry, and stock, bring to a gentle boil, and cook for a further 3 minutes. Stir in the cornflour, blended with 4 tablespoons water, and continue stirring until the mixture thickens.
Serving Pour the sauce over the noodles in individual bowls.

Plain Chicken Sauce for Noodles

1 pint (500 ml) chicken stock
1½ tablespoons cornflour
1 teaspoon salt
pepper to taste
½ teaspoon flavour powder
1½ tablespoons vegetable oil *or* lard

The Complete Chinese Cookbook

Cooking Blend the stock with the cornflour, salt, pepper, and flavour powder. Heat the oil or lard in a saucepan and pour in the stock mixture. Heat, stirring, until the liquid thickens and is smooth; then serve.

Peking Soya-Meat Sauce for Noodles

8 oz (200 g) lean pork
2 tablespoons soya sauce
1 tablespoon sherry
2 oz (50 g) spring onions
2 cloves garlic
2 tablespoons vegetable oil
2 tablespoons brown bean paste
1 tablespoon hoisin sauce
1 teaspoon cornflour

Preparation Mince the pork and marinate it in the sherry for 15 minutes. Chop the spring onions and crush the garlic.

Cooking Heat the oil in a pan. Add the spring onions, garlic, and pork and stir-fry for 4 minutes over a high heat. Combine the bean paste with the soya sauce and hoisin sauce, and mix into a smooth paste. Stir-fry this paste with the onions, garlic, and pork for 4 minutes over a gentle heat. Blend the cornflour with 6 tablespoons water and pour into the pan. Stir-fry until the mixture is well-blended and smooth, then cook gently for another $1\frac{1}{2}$–2 minutes until the sauce thickens.

Serving Do not pour this sauce over the noodles, but serve it in a bowl so that each person can dab 1–2 tablespoons of it on top of his own bowl of noodles.

Peking Soya-Meat Sauce Noodles are usually eaten accompanied by a variety of shredded raw vegetables, such as radishes, cucumber, spring onions, blanched bean sprouts, and spinach. It is very much a native Peking dish.

Master Sauce

Makes 2 pints (scant litre)

$1\frac{1}{2}$ lb (600 g) piece of boiling fowl *or* beef
$\frac{1}{4}$ pint (125 ml) soya sauce
$\frac{1}{4}$ pint (125 ml) red wine *or* sherry
2 small onions, finely chopped
3 cloves garlic, minced
4 tablespoons rock sugar
1 teaspoon salt
1 small piece tangerine peel
pinch of each of the following:
 anise, star anise, five spice powder

The term 'Lu' is used in China to indicate foods which have been cooked or braised in Master Sauce.

Introduction

Preparation Simmer meat or poultry in 2 pints (scant litre) water and remaining ingredients for 1 hour. Any kind of meat or innards of animals, including heart, kidneys, liver, tripe, or intestines, which are to be cooked in the sauce, should be simmered in it for a further 30 minutes to 1½ hours. Remove, drain, and cool, then slice thinly, and serve interleaved on an attractive platter. This makes a particularly good cold *hors d'œuvre*. Hard-boiled eggs simmered in Master Sauce are known as Soya Eggs. When cold, they are sliced and served with the other Lu items.

The Master Sauce is kept 'alive' by topping it up daily with water and fresh meat, and replenishing the herbal ingredients every two to three days.

Sauces for Fish

Meat and Vegetable Sauce for Fish

3 oz (75 g) lean pork
2 oz (50 g) Chinese dried mushrooms
6 golden needles (lily bud stems)
2 oz (50 g) bamboo shoots
3 slices root ginger
3 oz (75 g) leeks
¼ teaspoon salt
2 tablespoons vegetable oil
6 tablespoons water
1 teaspoon sugar
1 tablespoon soya sauce
1 tablespoon sherry
2 teaspoons cornflour

Preparation Soak the mushrooms and golden needles separately. Slice the mushrooms into matchstick strips and cut the golden needles into 1 inch (2½ cm) segments. Shred the pork, bamboo shoots, and ginger. Cut the leeks into 1 inch (2½ cm) pieces.
Cooking Stir-fry the pork, leeks, ginger, bamboo shoots, mushrooms, and salt in hot oil for 3 minutes. Add the golden needles, water, sugar, soya sauce, and sherry; then simmer for 5 minutes. Stir in the cornflour, blended with 2 tablespoons water, and stir until the sauce thickens.
Serving Pour the sauce over steamed or deep-fried fish. Arrange the vegetables on top as a garnish.

The Complete Chinese Cookbook
Five Willow Sauce for Fish

- 2 oz (50 g) green pepper
- 3 oz (75 g) cucumber
- 2 oz (50 g) carrot
- 2 medium-sized tomatoes
- 2 cloves garlic
- 2 spring onion stalks
- 2 slices root ginger
- 2 tablespoons vegetable oil

- 1 tablespoon mixed sweet pickles
- ½ teaspoon salt
- 1 tablespoon sugar
- 2 tablespoons vinegar
- 1 tablespoon soya sauce
- 1½ tablespoons sherry
- 5 tablespoons water
- 1 tablespoon cornflour

Preparation Shred the green pepper, cucumber, and carrot. Peel and slice the tomatoes. Crush the garlic, and cut the spring onions into ½ inch (1 cm) segments.
Cooking Stir-fry the ginger, garlic, and spring onions in hot oil for 1 minute over a medium heat. Add all the other vegetables, the pickles, and the salt; then stir-fry for 2 minutes over a high heat. Add the sugar, vinegar, soya sauce, sherry, and water and continue to stir. As the mixture comes to the boil, stir in the cornflour, blended with 6 tablespoons water, and continue to stir until the sauce thickens.
Serving Pour the sauce over the fish and arrange the vegetables on top as a garnish.

Hot Five Willow Sauce for Fish

Preparation Repeat the recipe for Five Willow Sauce, adding 1 tablespoon red chilli pepper or 1 teaspoon dried chilli pepper to the ginger, garlic, and spring onions during the initial stir-frying.

Egg Sauce for Lobster, Crab, or Giant Prawns

- 2 eggs
- 3 teaspoons fermented, salted black beans
- 1 clove garlic
- 2 slices root ginger
- 2 spring onion stalks
- 1 tablespoon soya sauce

- 1 teaspoon sugar
- 1 tablespoon sherry
- 6 tablespoons water *or* stock
- 1½ tablespoons vegetable oil
- 3 tablespoons minced lean pork
- ½ tablespoon cornflour

Preparation Soak and mash the black beans. Crush the garlic, mince the ginger, and chop spring onions into 1 inch (2½ cm) segments. Mix together the black beans, garlic, and ginger. Blend together the soya sauce, sugar,

sherry, and water; then add the spring onions. Beat the eggs.
Cooking Heat the oil in a pan and stir-fry the black bean mixture for 30 seconds. Add the pork and stir-fry for 2 minutes. Pour in the soya sauce mixture, bring to the boil quickly and simmer for 2 minutes. Stir in the cornflour, blended with 2 tablespoons water. Pour in the beaten eggs slowly in a thin stream along the prongs of a fork, and stir into the sauce.
Serving Pour it over lobster, crab, or giant prawns; then serve.

Sauces for Chicken

Soya-Vinegar Sauce for Deep-Fried Chicken

2 tablespoons soya sauce
2 tablespoons vinegar
2 spring onion stalks
1 clove garlic
1 slice root ginger
1 tablespoon vegetable oil
4 tablespoons water
½ tablespoon sugar

Preparation Chop the spring onions, crush the garlic, and shred the root ginger.
Cooking Stir-fry the spring onions, garlic, and ginger in the oil for 1 minute over a medium heat. Add the soya sauce, vinegar, water, and sugar. Simmer gently for 2 minutes.
Serving Pour over the pieces of chicken, and serve immediately.

Sauces for Boiled or Steamed Chicken

Soya-Stock Sauce for Boiled, White-Cut, or Sliced Chicken

1 tablespoon soya sauce
6 tablespoons good stock
¼ teaspoon salt
1 teaspoon sherry
¼ teaspoon flavour powder
½ tablespoon cornflour

Preparation Blend the soya sauce, stock, salt, sherry, and flavour powder together in a basin.
Cooking Pour the sauce mixture into a small pan and bring to the boil. Blend the cornflour with 3 tablespoons water and stir into the pan. Heat until the sauce thickens.
Serving Pour over pieces of chicken arranged on a dish.

Egg Sauce for Boiled White-Cut Chicken

2 eggs
2 spring onion stalks
7 tablespoons water
½ tablespoon cornflour

1½ tablespoons vegetable oil
½ teaspoon salt
1 tablespoon sherry

Preparation Cut the spring onions into 1 inch (2½ cm) segments. Beat the eggs lightly with 4 tablespoons of the water. Blend the cornflour with the remaining water.
Cooking Heat the oil in a small saucepan. Stir-fry the spring onions for 30 seconds. Add the cornflour mixture, salt, and sherry. Stir until the mixture is smooth and bubbling. Slowly stir in the beaten egg mixture, pouring it along the prongs of a fork. Continue to stir until the sauce is smooth and creamy.
Serving Pour over pieces of chicken arranged on a serving dish.

Sweet and Sour Sauces

Basic Sweet and Sour Sauce

4 tablespoons water
1 tablespoon sugar
1 tablespoon soya sauce

1 tablespoon tomato purée
2 tablespoons vinegar
¾ tablespoon cornflour

This is the Sweet and Sour Sauce which has found so much favour in the West. In China, it is used in both the north and the south, with slight variations.
Cooking Heat the water in a small pan. Add the sugar, soya sauce, and tomato purée. Stir until the sugar has dissolved; then add the vinegar. Finally, stir in the cornflour, blended with 3 tablespoons water. Continue to stir until the sauce thickens.

Strengthened Sweet and Sour Sauce

2 cloves garlic
2 slices root ginger
1 tablespoon vegetable oil
1 tablespoon chopped spring onions
2 tablespoons sugar
3 tablespoons vinegar

2 tablespoons tomato purée
2 tablespoons soya sauce
2 tablespoons sherry
4 tablespoons orange juice
4 tablespoons water
1 tablespoon cornflour

Preparation Crush the garlic and chop the ginger.
Cooking Heat the vegetable oil in a small saucepan or frying pan. Fry the garlic, ginger, and spring onions for 1½ minutes over a medium heat. Pour in the sugar, vinegar, tomato purée, soya sauce, sherry, orange juice, and water. Stir until the mixture is smooth and the sugar has dissolved, then increase the heat slightly, and stir in the cornflour, blended with 4 tablespoons water. Stir until the sauce thickens.

Hot Sweet and Sour Sauce

Cooking Add 1 or 2 chopped chilli peppers or 1 teaspoon dried chilli pepper to the recipe for Strengthened Sweet and Sour Sauce. Alternatively, add 2 teaspoons of chilli sauce to the sugar/vinegar mixture.

Marinades

In China marinating is extensively practised for dishes which are steamed, deep-fried, or quick-fried. In steamed dishes, the flavouring of the principal ingredient to be cooked has to be complete or almost complete before the steaming starts. Because of the use of a large quantity of boiling oil for deep-fried dishes, little flavouring can be added to them during the cooking process, and consequently, much of it has to be imparted by marinating beforehand. In the case of quick-fried dishes, the flavours of some of the participating ingredients have to be kept as distinct as possible from the others, and therefore if the application of seasonings, sauces, and flavouring ingredients was effected during the final stir-fry, all the different tastes might intermingle to such an extent that they would become indistinguishable. This results in dishes of no character. For the constituent ingredients to maintain their distinctive characters, they often have to be marinated separately and combined together in a final hot assembly only in the stir-frying.

Since the ingredients for Chinese marinades are fairly flexible, various types of purées and fruit juices can be added to the following recipes to give further variation. Fruit juices are used more extensively in the south than in the north.

Basic Marinade for Roast Pork, Barbecued Pork, Spare Ribs, or Fish

3 oz (75 g) spring onions
1 tablespoon soya paste
4 tablespoons soya sauce
1½ tablespoons sugar

4 tablespoons sherry
½ teaspoon flavour powder
dash of pepper

Preparation Chop the spring onions into ½–1 inch (1–2½ cm) segments. Blend all the ingredients together and use the mixture to marinate pork, ribs, or fish for 1–2 hours before cooking. Afterwards, use the remaining marinade to baste the meat during cooking.

As an alternative to soya paste, ¼ tablespoon fermented, salted black beans can be used. They should be soaked for 30 minutes, then drained before use.

Ginger-Garlic Marinade

Preparation Repeat the recipe for the Basic Marinade, adding 4–5 slices of root ginger, coarsely chopped, and 2 crushed cloves of garlic. This variation of the marinade is particularly suitable for fish.

Marinade for Pork or Spare Ribs with Hoisin Sauce and Five Spice Powder

2 tablespoons hoisin sauce
1½ tablespoons sherry
¼ teaspoon five spice powder

2 tablespoons soya sauce
1 tablespoon sugar *or* honey

Preparation Blend all the ingredients together. Marinate the pork or spare ribs in the mixture for 1–1½ hours.

There are two ways of varying this recipe. The first is to add 2 crushed cloves of garlic and 2 oz (50 g) spring onions, chopped into ½ inch (1 cm) segments, to the basic recipe. The second method of varying the marinade is to add 1 tablespoon chilli sauce to the basic recipe; or to chop 2 dried chilli peppers and fry them in 1½ tablespoons oil until slightly burnt; then add the mixture of oil and pepper to the marinade.

Soya-Red Bean Cheese Marinade for Pork or Spare Ribs

2 tablespoons soya sauce
1 tablespoon red bean cheese
1 clove garlic
1 teaspoon salt
1 teaspoon sugar
1 tablespoon sherry

Preparation Crush the garlic and combine it with the bean cheese. Mix in the soya sauce, salt, sugar, and sherry. Rub the mixture on the pork or spare ribs and leave to marinate for 1 hour.

Dressings

Dressings are mainly used, on foods which had been lightly cooked, smoked, or at least blanched, steeped, or parboiled. In other words, they were served with cold, cooked dishes, such as the different drunken dishes and *hors d'œuvres*. The Chinese 'tapestry *hors d'œuvres*' and similar dishes are a considerable contribution to the world of cold foods and their presentation. The Chinese use of wine, liqueur, sesame oil, sesame paste, and wine-sediment paste adds a great deal of interest to this sector of food preparation and to the culinary art. Since dressings in the Chinese tradition can be extremely good with Western salads and other dishes, I have included here the following selection of recipes.

Basic Soya-Vinegar Dressing

2 tablespoons soya sauce
2 tablespoons vinegar
½ tablespoon shredded ginger
2 tablespoons strong chicken stock
2 tablespoons vegetable oil

Preparation Mix together the soya sauce, vinegar, ginger, and stock. Stir in the oil gradually, blending the mixture well. Pour over prepared vegetables.

Soya-Sesame Dressing

2½ tablespoons soya sauce
2 teaspoons sesame oil
1 tablespoon sesame paste
1 tablespoon vegetable oil
2 tablespoons chicken *or* meat stock

Preparation Mix all the ingredients together in a basin, blending well. Use on cold meat or fish, or on cold, boiled noodles with blanched vegetables and shredded cold meats.

The Complete Chinese Cookbook

Hot Soya Dressing

2 red chilli peppers
3 tablespoons soya sauce
1 slice root ginger
2 tablespoons vegetable oil
1½ tablespoons vinegar
3 tablespoons chicken *or* meat stock

Preparation Chop the peppers and discard the pips. Chop the root ginger.
Cooking Stir-fry the peppers in oil until they begin to turn black. Add the ginger, then stir in the soya sauce, vinegar, and stock, and blend well. Leave to cool.
Serving When cold, use the dressing on meat, cold cooked fish, or vegetables.

Mustard Dressing

1 tablespoon powdered mustard
2 tablespoons soya sauce
2 tablespoons water
⅛ teaspoon pepper
1 tablespoon vinegar
1 teaspoon sugar
1 tablespoon vegetable oil
1 tablespoon sherry

Preparation Combine all the ingredients in a basin. Blend well. Leave to stand in a cool place or in a refrigerator for 2 hours to mature and develop. Use on cold cooked chicken, meat, or blanched vegetables.

Egg Dressing

3 eggs
1 clove garlic
2 slices root ginger
1 tablespoon soya sauce
¼ teaspoon flavour powder
3 tablespoons chicken *or* meat stock
½ teaspoon salt
2 tablespoons sherry
dash of pepper
4 tablespoons vegetable oil

This is a kind of Chinese mayonnaise.

Preparation Hard-boil the eggs. Crush the garlic, and shred the ginger. Mash the hard-boiled eggs; then mix them together with the garlic and ginger. Combine with all the other ingredients; blend well. Use on vegetables or blanched vegetables.

Introduction

Table Condiments, Dips, and Mixes

Table condiments, dips, and mixes constitute the final phase in the multi-phase flavouring of Chinese food. As with Western food, dips and mixes are placed on the dining table for the diners themselves to add to the food. The main difference in presentation of Chinese and European condiments is that the Chinese ones are normally placed in small, open, saucer-like dishes into which the food is dipped; never in bottles for shaking over the food on the individual's plate. A second difference is that we Chinese blend the basic condiments into various mixes for the many types of dishes. Hence, although there are in fact only a limited number of basic sauces and condiments, there exists quite a variety of blended dips and mixes which are brought to the table to be eaten with different types of food. It is the cross-blending which increases and accounts for the large Chinese variety.

The Chinese attitude towards the use of dips and mixes, as towards cooking in general, is a liberal one; there is a high flexibility in practice. Although there are conventional condiments and mixes for different traditional dishes, there is no rule against using whatever one is inclined to use. Hence it is a frequent practice to arrange on the dinner table a number of basic dips and condiments, such as plain soya sauce, hoisin sauce, hot chilli sauce, mustard, tomato sauce, and Salt and Pepper Mix, in addition to the few made-up mixes specially prepared for the dishes included on the menu, so that the diners will have a chance to follow their own inclinations. Besides, since many of the basic sauces are of contrasting colours, they provide an attractive colour display on the dining table, which should be particularly appealing to the colour-conscious world of today.

When eating a range of Chinese dishes (e.g. Mongolian Barbecue of Meats) in a typical Peking restaurant, each diner is provided with two empty bowls, one for beaten egg, and the other to enable him to mix his own dip or sauce from the variety of basic sauces and condiments provided on the table. It gives the diners great satisfaction to mix their own dips after they have settled down at the dining table. They also have the anticipation of the barbecuing ahead, as a flaming earthenware brazier will be brought in and placed at the

The Complete Chinese Cookbook

centre of the table. To eat such a meal in Peking is one of the most interesting culinary experiences in the world.

Basic Condiments

The basic Chinese condiments are, in the main, the same as in the West: salt, pepper, vinegar, mustard, and tomato, with a few additions such as soya sauce, plum sauce, sesame paste, oyster sauce, shrimp sauce, chilli oil, and hoisin sauce (a vegetable sauce, dark in colour, available canned).

Soya sauce and hoisin sauce usually come ready-made, and nobody in China tries to make them. The other sauces, however, are sometimes home-made, and in the West will frequently have to be made at home, since not all Western towns and cities have Chinese provision shops. Both hoisin and soya sauce should be a boon for vegetarian and meat cooking alike when adopted for Western use.

SOYA SAUCE

Soya sauce comes in many grades, especially in sauce-producing areas such as Foochow, where I was brought up, but in the main it is available in three grades, light, dark, and heavy. The heavy type is generally used for cooking materials such as beef and spare ribs, which require a strong, full-bodied sauce; however, it can also be used as a tasty dip for large chunks of white-cooked meat. Good quality, heavy soya sauce has a flavour of its own which is not unlike Marmite, but with a more universal palatability, and therefore it is very useful for any type of food which is not in itself highly savoury or salty. The taste of soya sauce can perhaps be defined as the epitome of savoury-saltiness.

For foods which are already fairly salty and savoury, or for mixing with other condiments in cooking, the light and dark varieties are generally used, as they are not too thick to serve as table condiments.

The lighter types are more delicate, and therefore more suitable for mixing when preparing dips. They are invariably used in the preparation of soups, the various semi-soup dishes, and the numerous vegetable dishes; even if only to avoid colourization and the blanketing of taste. Shrimp sauce is also often used in dishes where there is a good proportion of soup.

Introduction

HOISIN SAUCE

Hoisin sauce normally comes in a much thicker form than soya sauce: it is almost a paste or jam, and is brownish-red in colour, with a pungent sweet-spiciness. It is made from soya beans, garlic, chilli, and spices, and looks almost like raspberry jam. It is used in cooking shellfish, spare ribs, pork, duck, chicken, and vegetables, and can be used as a table condiment for plain cooked food, such as pork and poultry, as well as roasted and deep-fried foods. It is sometimes called 'red vegetable sauce' or 'sweet vegetable paste'. I have found it very useful in frying vegetables, and as a dip in place of plum sauce. Hoisin sauce is very easily acceptable to the Western palate and can be used almost like tomato ketchup, although since it is much stronger it should be used more sparingly.

Hot Chilli Oil

8–10 red chilli peppers *or*
  2 tablespoons dried chilli
pepper
6 tablespoons peanut *or* corn oil

This is a basic constituent ingredient for making up all the hot sauces in China, and can almost be classified as one of the basic sauces, although more often than not it is made in the kitchen. The red colour in Kung-Po dishes and in a majority of all the hot dishes of Szechuan is attained by the use of hot chilli oil.

Preparation Remove the pips from the chilli peppers.
Cooking Heat the oil in a small saucepan. Add the peppers and cook gently over a low heat, stirring occasionally, until the oil turns dark red. Cool and strain. Use sparingly as it is extremely hot!

Plum Sauce

8 oz (200 g) plums
2 tablespoons brown bean paste
3 tablespoons chutney
3 tablespoons apple sauce
2 tablespoons soya sauce

4 tablespoons sugar
¼ pint (125 ml) water
2 tablespoons vinegar
1 teaspoon salt

Preparation Peel, stone, and chop the plums. Blend all the ingredients in an electric mixer for 30 seconds.
Cooking Pour the mixture into a saucepan and bring to the boil. Cover, and

simmer very gently for 30 minutes, stirring occasionally. Store in a jar for 1 month to mature.
Serving Use for Peking Duck (to spread on the pancake) or with roast pork.

Hot Mustard Sauce

1 tablespoon powdered mustard
½ teaspoon salt
1 teaspoon chilli sauce

1 teaspoon vinegar
6 tablespoons water

Cooking Add the salt, chilli sauce, and vinegar to the water. Bring to the boil and boil for 1 minute; then allow to cool. Stir the liquid very slowly into the mustard until the mixture becomes smooth and creamy.

Mustard is served as a dip with more or less the same types of food as it is used in the West.

Salt and Pepper Mix

2 tablespoons sea salt

2 teaspoons freshly milled pepper

Cooking Heat the salt and pepper in a small, dry frying pan over a gentle heat for 3–4 minutes, stirring constantly, until there is a strong smell of pepper.

Salt and Pepper Mix is best prepared fresh, otherwise it must be kept in a stoppered jar. It is a widely-used dip for many deep-fried dishes and for roasted food, such as prawn balls, crackling chicken, or ordinary deep-fried chicken.

Salt-Cinnamon Mix

2 tablespoons salt
1 teaspoon ground cinnamon

dash of five spice powder

Cooking Heat the salt in a dry pan over a gentle heat until it starts to brown. Allow it to cool slightly, then stir in the cinnamon and add the five spice powder. This mix is best freshly prepared, otherwise it must be kept in a stoppered jar. Use it in the same way as Salt and Pepper Mix.

Introduction

Various Dips for Chicken

The following dip-sauces or basic sauces should be placed on the dining table for the diners to use at their own discretion. They can make their own choice of dips to blend together, or they can dip their pieces of chicken in any one or several of the mixes. Salt and Pepper Mix, Hot Mustard Sauce, soya sauce, tomato sauce, shrimp sauce, Soya-Oil Dip, Soya-Oil-Garlic Dip, Soya-Oil-Ginger Dip, and Soya-Sherry Dip should all be served. Such an array should satisfy even the connoisseurs.

Soya-Oil Dip for Chicken

3 tablespoons soya sauce   2 tablespoons vegetable oil

Cooking Heat the oil until it is about to smoke. Let it cool, then stir in the soya sauce.

This dip gives added smoothness to white-cooked chicken. The Chinese often use oil to give extra smoothness to the surface of foods which have been boiled or simmered.

Soya-Oil-Garlic Dip

3 cloves garlic   3 tablespoons peanut *or* corn oil
6 tablespoons soya sauce   ¼ teaspoon sugar

Preparation Crush the garlic. Mix all the ingredients together, using an electric blender if possible.

This mix can be used as a dip for clear-simmered, white-cooked chicken or for roast chicken. The same dip, using 3 tablespoons vinegar instead of oil can be served with white-cooked pork. (As pork is fatter than chicken, it requires no oil.) The quantity in this recipe can be divided among three or four small sauce dishes and is sufficient for a table of ten.

Soya-Oil-Ginger Dip

3 slices root ginger   3 tablespoons vegetable oil
6 tablespoons soya sauce   ½ teaspoon vinegar

Preparation Shred and chop the root ginger. Mix all the ingredients together and blend well, using an electric blender, if available.

The Complete Chinese Cookbook

Use the dip with clear-simmered, white-cooked chicken or with roast chicken. When serving it with white-cooked pork, substitute vinegar for the oil.

Soya-Ginger-Garlic Dip

1½ cloves garlic
1½ slices root ginger
12 tablespoons soya sauce

6 tablespoons peanut *or* corn oil
¼ teaspoon sugar
½ tablespoon vinegar

Preparation Crush the garlic. Shred and chop the root ginger. Mix all the ingredients together, using a blender if available. Use with chicken or pork.

Soya-Oil-Onion Dip

3 spring onion stalks
6 tablespoons soya sauce

3 tablespoons vegetable oil
½ tablespoon vinegar

Preparation Chop the spring onions finely, then mix them with the other ingredients, using a blender if possible.
Serving Divide the dip among three sauce dishes. Serve with chicken or pork, but substitute vinegar for the oil if using with pork.

Soya-Mustard Dip

3 tablespoons soya sauce
1 tablespoon mustard powder
2 tablespoons stock

½ teaspoon salt
1 teaspoon sesame oil

Preparation Blend all the ingredients together, using a blender if available. Use as a dip for white-cooked or roast chicken and pork.

Hot Soya-Oil Dip

Preparation Add 1 teaspoon Hot Chilli Oil (see page 49) to every 3 tablespoons soya sauce in any of the preceding Soya-Oil Dips. Use with chicken or pork.

Hoisin or Plum Sauce for Pork

8 tablespoons hoisin *or* plum sauce

1–2 teaspoons sesame oil

Introduction

This dip appeals to those who like a sugary-sweet quality to contrast with the fatness of the pork. It serves the same function as redcurrant jam or jelly in European food, except that the Chinese sauce is slightly spicier.

Preparation Blend the sesame oil with the hoisin sauce or plum sauce, and serve as a dip with white-cooked, boiled, simmered, or roast pork.

Plum Dip for Duck

4 tablespoons plum sauce
2 tablespoons soya sauce
2 teaspoons chilli oil

Preparation Combine all the ingredients, blending well. Serve in three sauce dishes.

Soya-Sesame Dip for Pork

4 tablespoons soya sauce
2 teaspoons sesame oil
2 tablespoons sesame paste *or* peanut butter
1 tablespoon vegetable oil
1 tablespoon sherry
2 teaspoons minced root ginger

Preparation Combine all the ingredients in an electric blender for 15 seconds. Divide the dip between two dishes.

Various Dips for Pork

Arrange the following dips on the table: plain, heavy soya sauce, hoisin sauce, Hot Mustard Sauce, Chilli Sauce, tomato sauce, Salt and Pepper Mix. You can also serve Vinegar-Garlic Dip (2 teaspoons crushed garlic with 3 tablespoons vinegar) and Vinegar-Ginger Dip (3 teaspoons chopped ginger in 3 tablespoons vinegar). The diners can use whichever dips they choose, or dip the food into several sauces at the same time, if so desired.

Basic Dip for Seafoods

4 slices root ginger
4 tablespoons vinegar
2 tablespoons soya sauce

Preparation Shred or mince the root ginger. Combine all the ingredients, blending well. Divide the mixture among three sauce dishes.

Dip for Crab

Preparation Repeat the previous recipe, doubling the quantity of soya sauce.

As crabs are steamed, boiled, or fried with a light sauce, a saltier, heavier condiment is required to attune them to the average palate. Hence, a larger proportion of soya sauce compared with the previous recipe should be introduced.

Dip for Prawns

2 cloves garlic
4 slices root ginger
4 tablespoons soya sauce
2 tablespoons sherry
1 tablespoon hoisin sauce
1 tablespoon tomato purée
1 teaspoon hot chilli oil

Preparation Crush the garlic and shred the root ginger. Combine all the ingredients, blending well. Serve in four sauce dishes.

Dip for Clams

3 slices root ginger
2 spring onion stalks
2 tablespoons soya sauce
1 tablespoon sherry
1 tablespoon vinegar
1 tablespoon tomato sauce
1 tablespoon vegetable oil
1 teaspoon sesame oil

Preparation Shred and chop the root ginger and chop the spring onions. Combine all the ingredients, blending well. Serve in three sauce dishes.

Soup

湯

Chinese soups, like Western soups, are mainly either thick or clear. We Chinese tend to have fewer thick soups than you do in the West, but, on the other hand, the Chinese range of clear soups is immense.

Our variety is probably due to the Chinese concept of cross-cooking. A great many Chinese clear soups are only partly consommés in the Western sense, for they are clear soups with various meats and vegetables, in different sizes and shapes, floating or immersed in them. But the Chinese concept of soups provides that so long as the consommé is pure and crystal-clear, despite the many items in it, the soup can be classified as clear.

In other words, some Chinese soups are really big dishes in the Western sense. But these soups are never heavy, because although there is a variety of solids, these contrast with the light, clear purity of the broth in which they are immersed. The idea is of a clear, deep, mountain pool (albeit a hot savoury one!), with many intriguing items of 'nature' in it, contributing to its form, colour, and flavour.

The consommé of these Chinese clear soups consists mainly of chicken stock, meat stock, bone stock, a mixture of the two, or all three, in different proportions. The variety of flavours, colours, shapes, and appearances occurs only when other materials are added to the soups. Since these other materials can be fresh or cooked, dried, salted, or hotted meats, fish, or vegetables, the number of possible combinations rises into the sphere of permutations.

Take the basic chicken stock. If one were to add to it a few slices of abalone, smoked ham, or dried mushrooms or scallops, a few lengths of meaty pork ribs, or a tablespoonful or two of shelled prawns or crab-meat, the resulting soup, after a short period of simmering, would have changed and achieved a distinctive flavour of its own, even without the addition of any further types of flavourers or ingredients.

If even more ingredients are added, perhaps in different stages of the preparation, the flavour of the stock undergoes a further subtle transformation. This is how the subtlety and differentiation in the flavour or taste of the stocks is gradually advanced and achieved in China – usually in stages, until each soup has a complete individuality and tradition of its own. It is this unique blending of *flavour* which the Chinese hanker for in their soups, when they look for traditional authenticity in their foods.

Texture also enters into the preparation and character of Chinese soups – not so much in the body of the soup itself, but in the texture of the various materials and ingredients which are added to it.

For example, there is a well-known and popular soup called the Triple Shred Soup, which consists of ham, white chicken meat, and bamboo shoots, all sliced into matchstick strips, and simmered for a while in good stock. If the strips are not cooked overlong in the stock they should retain their own colour and texture, and at the same time contribute something to the flavour of the soup; the bamboo shoots should be ivory and crunchy, the ham, pink and salty, and the chicken, white and flavoursome. The combination of the three gives the soup its unique character, and although it is by no means a great soup, it can be very appealing and evocative to a Chinese when it is really well made. Like tea, the quality is all a question of the care taken in its preparation.

When any meat is used in thinly sliced pieces in soup, it is usually first salted, then dredged in cornflour. The latter treatment gives the slices a very smooth texture after a short period of simmering; this quality provides the added satisfaction of eating meat while one is drinking soup. Without such treatment all meats tend to become dry and fibrous after a period of cooking.

SUPERIOR STOCK

The traditional Superior Stock is usually produced in quantity in China, and is a long and stylized process. When dining in a restaurant in Peking, one can usually call for Superior Stock to be served as soup free of charge.

In its simplified and shortened form it can be made as follows: Remove the breast meat and 2 drumsticks from a 3 lb (1¼ kg) chicken, and boil the rest of the chicken for 15 minutes with 2 lb

Soup

(1 kg) pork, 2 lb (1 kg) spare ribs, 2 lb (1 kg) pork bones, 1 lb (400 g) bacon bones, and 1 lb (400 g) ham in 8–9 pints (4½ litres) of water, skimming off all scum and extraneous matter. Lift out the chicken and pork, then the bacon and pork bones, and place them all in a basin containing 3 pints (1½ litres) of cold water. After turning the chicken and bones around in the water, pour half of it into the stock, in which the chicken, etc., has been boiled. The sudden coolness of the water coagulates and precipitates more of the grease and impurities in the stock, and these can easily be skimmed off. Before returning the chicken, pork, and bacon bones to the pan for a further period of boiling and simmering, pour a quarter of the now augmented stock into a separate bowl or basin to cool. This cooling stock will be used later on in the same way as the cold water was used to precipitate and coagulate grease and impurities. After the chicken, etc., has been returned to the main boiler, bring the contents to boil and simmer gently for 1 hour. The materials are again lifted out, and the cooled broth water poured in, again precipitating and coagulating more grease, impurities, and extraneous matter which are once more removed.

The above process is repeated twice more over a period of 3 hours, after which the broth will have become much stronger as well as more purified.

The final phase of the preparation consists of some seasoning and double dredging. The seasoning is done by the addition of a small amount of ginger, onion, and soya sauce (according to your own taste). Mince the breast meat and the meat from the drumsticks of the chicken, keeping them separate. The minced darker drumstick meat is used for the first 'dredge', and the minced white breast meat is then used as the second 'dredge'. The dredging is achieved in each case by simmering the minced chicken in the stock for 10–12 minutes, then straining it. The important thing is not allowing the stock to come to a full boil at any time, thus creating what we call a stewed stock. The simmering has to be kept very gentle throughout to produce clear stock.

For making larger quantities of this Superior Stock a duck, where available, can be added to every 2 chickens used. But only chicken meat should be used for dredging. For the lighter and most refined stocks, the frog-and-chicken combination (in the ratio of 1:2) is considered the best.

A fascinating and established way of conducting the process of dredging in restaurants is to place only a quarter of the boiler over the open fire, and a filter at the opposite end just below the surface of the broth. Because of the heat, the stock at the fire-end of the boiler rises rapidly carrying all the dredger with it. As the liquid reaches the top and pours over to the opposite end, the dredger is caught by the filter. As the process is circular and continuous, the stock becomes progressively and increasingly purified; and within the 10–12 minutes that the dredger is working, the stock will become crystal-clear.

Superior Stock is an essential in the preparation of soups and sauces if these are to be of the highest quality.

A note concerning quantity – 10 lb (4½–5 kg) of bones, chicken, pork, and ham should produce approximately 10–12 pints (5–6 litres) of stock.

CLEAR STOCK
Clear Stock is a term sometimes used for Superior Stock, but sometimes it indicates a stock which has a little less bone content than the normal Superior Stock. That is, instead of 2:1 ratio between bone and chicken, the ratio is reduced to 1:1.

CHICKEN STOCK
Chicken Stock is a clear stock used for certain dishes such as Bird's Nest and Shark's Fin soups, and in making some sauces. It is produced by long, slow simmering of chicken, unadulterated by the addition of pork or bone, except perhaps a small amount of best ham. The stock is purified by the dredging method, described above – that is, by the use of minced chicken meat as a 'dredger' during the last stage of the cooking.

SECONDARY STOCK
In the preparation of Secondary Stock, the only materials used are bones: chicken bones or carcase, pork bones, and bacon bones in the ratio of 2:2:1, simmered slowly for 3½–4 hours, starting with twice as much water as material. Necks of chicken or ducks may be added if available.

WHITE SOUP OR MILKY STOCK
The White Soup or Milky Stock is made simply by boiling up all the remnants of the raw materials (bones) used in producing Superior

Soup

Stock, with the addition of about 25% of fresh bones. The boiling should be vigorous, although not too vigorous, otherwise it might produce a burnt taste, and it should be continued for 2 hours, until the liquid is reduced to just under half. The stock will then have become white. Filter carefully through a sieve and muslin and you have milky stock.

Casserole of Chinese Cabbage Soup

Serves 4–6, with other dishes

- 2 lb (1 kg) Chinese celery cabbage *or* Savoy cabbage
- 4 oz (100 g) lean pork
- 1½ pints (750 ml) water *or* stock
- 2 oz (50 g) transparent noodles
- 1 tablespoon dried shrimps
- 2 slices root ginger
- 2 teaspoons salt
- 2 teaspoons cornflour
- 1 tablespoon lard
- 1½ tablespoons light-coloured soya sauce
- 2 tablespoons white wine *or* sherry
- ½ teaspoon flavour powder *or* 1 chicken stock cube

Preparation Clean the cabbage thoroughly and cut into 2 inch (5 cm) pieces. Soak the noodles and dried shrimps in warm water for 15 minutes, then discard the water. Slice the pork into thin 1 × 1½ inch (2½ × 3½ cm) pieces. Rub with half of the salt and all of the cornflour. Shred the ginger.

Cooking Heat the lard in a large saucepan. Add the pork, shrimps, and ginger and stir-fry together over a medium heat for 2 minutes. Add the cabbage and soya sauce. Stir them together with the other ingredients for 2 minutes. Add the noodles, and pour in 1½ pints (750 ml) of water or stock. Finally, when the contents come to the boil again, add the remaining salt and the wine and flavour powder (or chicken stock cube). Place the casserole in a preheated oven to simmer for 30 minutes at 375°F (190°C or Gas Mark 5). Serve in the casserole.

Since the principal attractions of this soup to the Chinese are its purity and the dominating flavour of the cabbage, it is equally acceptable whether made with water or stock.

Spare Rib and Chinese Celery Cabbage Soup

Serves 4–6, with other dishes

- 1 lb (400 g) meaty spare ribs
- 1¼ lb (600 g) celery cabbage *or* Savoy cabbage
- 2 pints (generous litre) superior *or* secondary stock *or* water
- 2 teaspoons salt
- pepper to taste
- 2 tablespoons sherry
- ½ teaspoon flavour powder *or* 1 chicken stock cube

Preparation Trim any excess fat from the spare ribs and chop them into 2 inch (5 cm) pieces. Boil in water for 5 minutes, then pour away the water. Clean and chop the cabbage into 2 inch (5 cm) slices.
Cooking Place the ribs in a large saucepan. Add 2 pints (generous litre) water or stock. Bring to the boil, reduce the heat, and simmer for 30 minutes. Add the cabbage, salt, pepper, sherry, and flavour powder. Simmer over a low heat for the next 20-25 minutes; then serve in a large soup bowl or tureen.

After 50 minutes of cooking, the meat on the spare ribs will have become sufficiently detachable from the bone to be easily dipped into table dips, mixes, and condiments for eating.

Spare Rib and Sliced Cucumber Soup

Serves 4-6, with other dishes

Repeat the recipe for Pork Spare Rib and Chinese Celery Cabbage Soup (see above), using 1 lb (400 g) cucumber instead of cabbage. Cut the cucumber into 2-3 inch (5-7½ cm) pieces, then slice it vertically into thin matchstick strips (without peeling). Cucumber requires very little cooking, and should be added to the spare ribs in the soup only 5 minutes before serving.

Meat Balls and Chinese Celery Cabbage Soup

Serves 4-6, with other dishes

5-6 oz (125-150 g) streaky pork
1 medium-sized onion
2 tablespoons water chestnuts
1 medium-sized Chinese celery cabbage *or* Savoy cabbage
1½ pints (750 ml) good stock
1 egg white
2 tablespoons cornflour
½ tablespoon soya sauce
2 teaspoons salt
2 tablespoons sherry
¼ teaspoon flavour powder *or* 1 chicken stock cube
pepper to taste

Preparation Mince the pork, and chop the onion and water chestnuts finely. Mix them all in a basin with the egg white, cornflour, and soya sauce. Blend into a paste and form into meat balls half the size of ping-pong balls. Clean the cabbage and cut into 2 inch (5 cm) pieces.
Cooking Boil the cabbage in water for 3 minutes. Pour away the water and place the cabbage in a casserole. Place the meat balls on top of the cabbage. Pour in the stock and sprinkle with seasonings. Cover the casserole and place it in an oven preheated to 375°F (190°C or Gas Mark 5) for 30 minutes.
Serving Remove from the oven, test the meat balls to make sure that they are cooked through, adjust the seasonings, and serve in the casserole.

Sliced Pork and Mushroom Soup

Serves 4–6, with other dishes

8 oz (200 g) streaky pork
8 oz (200 g) mushrooms
1½ pints (750 ml) good stock
1 teaspoon salt
1 tablespoon cornflour
2 tablespoons soya sauce
pepper to taste
½ teaspoon flavour powder

Preparation Slice the pork thinly into 1½ × 1 inch (3½ × 2½ cm) pieces. Rub with salt and cornflour, discarding any excess cornflour. Clean the mushrooms thoroughly and remove stalks. Cut the stalks into very thin slices.
Cooking Bring stock to the boil in a saucepan. Add pork and mushrooms. Simmer gently for 10 minutes. Add soya sauce, pepper, and flavour powder. Simmer for a further 5–6 minutes. Adjust seasonings, and serve.

Sliced Pork and Egg-Flower Soup

Serves 4–6, with other dishes

8 oz (200 g) streaky pork
2 eggs
2 pints (generous litre) good stock
1 teaspoon salt
1 tablespoon cornflour
2 tablespoons soya sauce
pepper to taste
½ teaspoon flavour powder
1 teaspoon sesame oil
½ tablespoon chopped chives *or* spring onions

Preparation Slice the pork into 1½ × 1 inch (3½ × 2½ cm) thin slices. Beat the eggs lightly in a bowl for about 10 seconds. Rub pork with salt and cornflour.
Cooking Bring the stock to the boil in a saucepan. Add the pork, and simmer gently for 15 minutes. Trail the beaten egg into the soup in a fine stream along the prongs of a fork. Add soya sauce, pepper, and flavour powder. Stir the soup gently, and pour it into a large soup bowl or tureen. Sprinkle with sesame oil and chives or spring onions; then serve.

Tripe and Green Pea Soup

Serves 4–6, with other dishes

8 oz (200 g) pork tripe
8 oz (200 g) green peas
1½ pints (750 ml) superior stock
1 medium-sized onion
3 teaspoons salt
1½ tablespoons cornflour
1 tablespoon chicken fat *or* lard
1 tablespoon chopped chives
½ teaspoon flavour powder
2 tablespoons sherry
1 teaspoon chilli sauce

The Complete Chinese Cookbook

Preparation Cut sheet of tripe into four to six pieces. Chop the onion. Simmer the tripe in 1 pint (500 ml) water, together with the chopped onion and 2 teaspoons of the salt for 30 minutes. Pour away onion and water, allow tripe to cool and slice into very thin matchstick strips. Thaw the peas (if frozen) and cream them in a liquidizer. Blend the cornflour with 3 tablespoons water.

Cooking Heat 1 tablespoon fat in a saucepan. Add creamed peas and stir-fry gently over medium heat for 2 minutes. Add the remaining salt, and stock, and bring to the boil. Add tripe and chopped chives, and simmer for 10 minutes. Add flavour powder, cornflour mixture, sherry, and chilli sauce. Adjust the seasonings, simmer for a further 5 minutes; then serve.

The tripe adds to the smoothness of the texture of this rich soup.

Basic Beef Broth

It is the general belief in China that beef broth is extremely nutritious and excellent for convalescence. The traditional way of preparing it is as follows.

Take 2 lb (1 kg) lean beef (1 lb (400 g) stewing and 1 lb (400 g) shin). Cut beef into 1 inch (2½ cm) square pieces. Clean and soak in 3 pints (1½ litres) cold water for 2 hours. Drain, and divide beef into three portions.

Place one portion of beef in 3 pints (1½ litres) water. Bring to the boil, skim away impurities, and simmer very gently for 2 hours (with the aid of an asbestos sheet under the pan, or use double-boiler if available).

Place the second portion of beef in a saucepan with 1 pint (500 ml) of water. Boil for 3 minutes and pour away the water. Add this portion of beef to the first, and continue to simmer for 30 minutes.

Repeat with the third portion of beef. After it has been added to the first two portions, continue to simmer for another 30 minutes, together with 3 slices of root ginger, and 1½ teaspoons of salt. The resultant beef broth will be suitable for various beef broth soups. The following are a selection.

Beef Broth and Spring Green Soup

Serves 4-6, with other dishes

Remove the outer leaves of three spring greens, using only the more tender stems and leaves. Cut each of these hearts into four pieces. Plunge them into boiling water for 3 minutes, and drain. Add them to 2 pints (generous litre) of beef broth. Simmer for 20 minutes. Add 1 teaspoon melted lard, 1½ teaspoons salt, and ½ teaspoon flavour powder. Stir, and serve.

Beef Broth and Marrow Soup

Serves 4–6, with other dishes

Peel the tough outer skin from 1 lb (400 g) marrow, and cut into pieces 1 inch (2½ cm) wide and 2 inches (5 cm) long. Heat 2 pints (generous litre) of beef broth in a saucepan, adding 1 tablespoon dried shrimps. Allow them to simmer for 10 minutes. Add the marrow, along with 2 oz (50 g) bean sprouts. Simmer them together for 6–7 minutes. Add the usual melted lard, salt, soya sauce, flavour powder, and pepper before serving.

In many cases the beef broth soups are made more interesting by the addition of a small amount of thinly sliced beef. In these cases the beef, sliced into razor-thin slices measuring 1 × ¾ inches (2½ × 1½ cm) should be salted with ¼ teaspoon salt, rubbed with 2 teaspoons cornflour, and added to the soup only 2 minutes before serving. The purpose behind the addition of beef here is not so much to enhance the taste, but to increase interest and variety. The following are some of the recipes where sliced beef is added to beef broth.

Sliced Beef and Cucumber Soup

Serves 4–6, with other dishes

6 inch (15 cm) piece of a thick cucumber
3 oz (75 g) fillet of beef
2 pints (generous litre) beef broth

1 teaspoon salt
1 tablespoon cornflour
1 teaspoon lard
1 tablespoon soya sauce
½ teaspoon flavour powder *or* 1 chicken stock cube
pepper to taste

Preparation Scrape, but do not peel cucumber. Slice lengthwise into 1 × ½ inch (2½ × 1 cm) thin pieces. Slice beef into pieces about the same size. Rub with salt and cornflour, discarding any excess.
Cooking Bring broth to the boil in a saucepan. Add beef and cucumber. When contents come to the boil again, simmer for 3 minutes. Add lard, soya sauce, and flavour powder or stock cube. Add pepper to taste; then serve.

The Complete Chinese Cookbook

Sliced Beef and Watercress Soup

Serves 4-6, with other dishes

4-5 oz (100-125 g) fillet of beef
1 bunch of watercress
1½ pints (750 ml) beef broth
2 spring onion stalks
1 teaspoon salt

1 tablespoon cornflour
1 tablespoon soya sauce
½ teaspoon flavour powder *or*
 1 chicken stock cube
1 teaspoon lard
pepper to taste

Preparation Clean the cress thoroughly; cut off and discard roots. Cut cress into 1 inch (2½ cm) lengths. Cut the spring onions into pieces of similar length, including green parts. Slice beef into very thin slices, 1 × ½ inch (2½ × 1 cm) in size. Rub with salt and cornflour, discarding excess.
Cooking Bring broth to the boil in a saucepan. Add soya sauce, cress, and beef. Simmer for 2 minutes. Add spring onions, flavour powder or stock cube, lard, and pepper. Simmer for 1 minute more; then serve.

Cream of Pork Tripe Soup

Serves 6-8, with other dishes

6 oz (150 g) cooked pork tripe
1 pint (500 ml) white stock
4 oz (100 g) broccoli
1 large onion
4 small slices ham

1½ tablespoons lard
¼ pint (125 ml) top of the milk
1½ teaspoons salt
6 bamboo shoots
½ teaspoon flavour powder
1½ tablespoons cornflour

Preparation Place the tripe in boiling water and simmer for 5 minutes. Drain; then soak in fresh water for 30 minutes, and slice into matchstick strips. Break the broccoli into six to eight branches, place in boiling water and simmer for 3 minutes; then drain. Chop the onion into eight to ten slices, and chop the ham.
Cooking Fry the onion in the lard over medium heat for 3-4 minutes. Remove the onion, and add the stock, top of the milk, salt, bamboo shoots, broccoli, ham, tripe, and flavour powder. Bring to the boil and simmer gently for 5-6 minutes, then add the cornflour blended with 3 tablespoons water, and stir until the soup thickens.

The use of milk here is definitely a Western influence, but as mentioned elsewhere, Chinese cuisine is adventurous and always ready to borrow other culinary practices.

Soup

Crackling Cream of Fish Soup

Serves 6–8, with other dishes

- 4 oz (100 g) white fish (cod, haddock, sole, turbot, carp, *or* bass)
- 1 pint (500 ml) white stock
- 2 oz (50 g) bread *or* Chinese steamed buns
- 1 oz (25 g) Chinese dried mushrooms
- 1 oz (25 g) peeled firm tomato
- 1 teaspoon melted chicken fat
- 1 teaspoon sesame oil
- 1 oz (25 g) green peas
- 3 tablespoons white wine
- 1½ teaspoons salt
- pepper to taste
- ¼ pint (125 ml) top of the milk
- 1½ tablespoons cornflour
- 4–5 tablespoons cold chicken stock
- oil for deep-frying

From Peking

Preparation Dice the bread into ¼ inch (½ cm) cubes. Boil the fish, drain, and mince it to a paste. Soak the mushrooms in warm water for 30 minutes; then drain, discard the stems, and slice the caps into pieces the size of peas. Chop the tomato. Blend the melted chicken fat with the sesame oil.

Cooking Bring stock to boil in a saucepan. Add the minced fish, tomato, mushrooms, peas, wine, salt, and pepper, and simmer for 2 minutes; then add the top of the milk, the cornflour blended with 4–5 tablespoons of cold chicken stock, and the chicken fat/sesame oil mixture, and stir until the contents of the pan come to the boil. Turn the heat to low. Deep-fry the bread cubes in very hot oil until golden brown. Place the croûtons, while still sizzling, at the bottom of a large, warmed, heat-proof bowl or tureen. Immediately pour in the soup which has been simmering gently, and the croûtons will start to crackle. The soup should be served and eaten before the croûtons become soft.

First Rank Hot-Pot

Serves 10–12, with other dishes

- 4 oz (100 g) bêche de mer
- 1 lb (400 g) Chinese celery cabbage
- 1 small cauliflower
- 8 oz (200 g) ham
- 2–3 lb (1–1¼ kg) knuckle of pork
- 2 oz (50 g) Chinese dried mushrooms
- 1–1½ lb (400–600 g) chicken
- 1–1½ lb (400–600 g) duck
- 2 slices root ginger
- 4 hard-boiled eggs
- 6 tablespoons white wine
- salt to taste

The Complete Chinese Cookbook

Preparation Soak the bêche de mer overnight, and drain. Discard the coarse outer leaves of the cabbage; clean and cut the heart into four pieces. Clean the cauliflower, and break into individual branches. Boil the ham and pork knuckle in water for 40 minutes; then drain. Soak the mushrooms in warm water for 30 minutes, remove the stalks, and drain. Chop the chicken and the duck into manageable pieces, place in a boiler with 5 pints (generous 2½ litres) water and boil for 40 minutes. Remove the chicken and duck, place them in a large, heat-proof basin, and strain and filter the stock until it is crystal clear.

Cooking Add the vegetables (cabbage, cauliflower, and mushrooms), the ginger, ham, pork knuckle, and bêche de mer to the chicken and duck. Place the basin in a steamer, and steam for 30 minutes. Arrange all the solid materials, including the eggs, in layers in the moat of a charcoal burning hot-pot. Pour in the stock and wine, and add the salt. Light the hot-pot (by adding a few pieces of burning charcoal to the unburnt charcoal in the funnel), and fan until the soup starts to boil; then boil for 5–6 minutes.

Serving Bring the hot-pot to the table; its arrival will be a heart warming sight in winter.

Hot-pots are available in many Chinese food-stores and supermarkets.

Bird's Nest Soup

Serves 6–8, with other dishes

4 oz (100 g) bird's nest
1½ pints (750 ml) freshly prepared, high quality chicken stock
2 oz (50 g) chicken breast meat

2 egg whites
1 teaspoon salt
½ teaspoon flavour powder
1 tablespoon water chestnut flour *or* cornflour
2 tablespoons minced ham

Bird's nest itself has a faint subtle flavour, the appreciation of which is largely a cultivated taste. In the main, the total flavour of the soup is derived from the chicken and chicken stock – these must be first class if the soup is to be good. Birds' nests are generally available in small boxes from Chinese provision stores – they come in a porous and brittle form, ground down from the original pieces of birds' nests. They are not, by the way, the branches and twigs which make up an average bird's nest, but what is left by the birds in their nests, probably for their young ones, after eating or part eating the fishes and seaweeds they live on. They are obtained from a species of sea swallow which inhabits the South Seas, and they also come in small nestlet shapes or as curved chips called Dragons' Teeth. The latter are rather rare and expensive.

Preparation Simmer bird's nest in 1 pint (500 ml) water for 1 hour. Let it cool, and drain. (If Dragons' Teeth or nestlets are used, they must be soaked overnight first.) Cut the chicken meat into small pieces, and then mince. Beat the egg whites lightly with a fork.

Cooking and Serving Heat the chicken stock in a heavy pan, and add half of the minced chicken. After 10 minutes, add the bird's nest and the remaining chicken, and simmer for 15 minutes. Add the salt and flavour powder, and thicken the soup with the water chestnut flour or cornflour, blended with 3 tablespoons water. Slowly stream in the beaten egg whites along the prongs of a fork, trailing it evenly over the soup – thus producing a white cloud effect. Garnish the soup with the minced ham, and serve in a high quality ceramic bowl, worthy of the quality of the soup.

Shark's Fin and Crab-Egg Soup

Serves 8–10, with other dishes

6 oz (150 g) shark's fin
4 tablespoons crab-eggs
1½ pints (750 ml) first quality chicken stock
2 slices root ginger
2 oz (50 g) Chinese dried mushrooms
4 oz (100 g) chicken breast meat
4 oz (100 g) Chinese celery cabbage
3 spring onion stalks
3 tablespoons lard
1 teaspoon sugar
1 teaspoon salt
4 tablespoons crab-meat
1½ tablespoons cornflour
3 tablespoons white wine

Preparation Soak the shark's fin in water overnight; then simmer in 1 pint (500 ml) fresh water, with 2 slices root ginger, for 1 hour. Rinse several times in cold water; then repeat the simmering and rinsing once. Cut the fin into eight pieces. Soak the mushrooms for 30 minutes, remove the stalks, and shred the caps. Shred the chicken, and cut the cabbage and spring onions into 1 inch (2½ cm) pieces.

Cooking Fry the spring onions in 2 tablespoons of the lard over medium heat for 2 minutes. Add stock and sugar and bring to a gentle boil; then add the chicken, salt, shark's fin, crab-meat, mushrooms, and cabbage, and continue to simmer for 25 minutes. Thicken with the cornflour mixed with 3 tablespoons water, and pour in the crab-eggs, wine, and the remaining lard. Simmer for a further 5 minutes, and serve.

Some Miscellaneous, Regional, and Well-Known Soups

Hot and Sour Soup

Serves 8–12, with other dishes

- 4 oz (100 g) lean pork
- 2 oz (50 g) Chinese dried mushrooms
- 1 oz (25 g) bamboo shoots
- 2 cakes bean curd
- 2 eggs
- 1 tablespoon dried prawns *or* 2 tablespoons peeled prawns
- 2 pints (generous litre) superior stock
- ½ teaspoon flavour powder *or* 1 chicken stock cube

Hot and Sour Mixture
- 2 tablespoons soya sauce
- 2 tablespoons vinegar
- 2 tablespoons cornflour, blended with 4 tablespoons cold stock
- ¼ teaspoon black pepper

This is a thick soup, more popular in north China than in the south. It can actually be made almost ad lib from various bits and pieces of meat, fish, shrimps, or crab which are available. The classical version requires cooked, solidified chicken blood. A useful ingredient is bean curd, and Chinese dried mushrooms are essential. But first of all, you will need a good savoury stock.

Preparation Shred pork into matchstick strips. Soak mushrooms in warm water for 30 minutes and drain, retaining 3 tablespoons mushroom water. Cut bamboo shoots into 1–2 inch (2½–5 cm) segments, and bean curd into ½ inch (1 cm) cubes. Beat the eggs lightly for 10 seconds. Prepare the Hot and Sour mixture by blending the ingredients together until smooth.

Cooking Prepare the soup by simmering pork, prawns, mushrooms, and bamboo shoots in the stock for 30 minutes. Add the bean curd, mushroom water, and flavour powder, and simmer for a further 5 minutes. Now stream in the Hot and Sour mixture and stir – this should thicken the soup. Trail the beaten egg into the soup along the prongs of a fork – the egg will coagulate almost immediately – and the soup is ready to serve.

Because of its heat, and the solid ingredients used, this soup is very popular in winter.

Whole Chicken Soup

Serves 10–12, with other dishes

5–6 lb (2–2½ kg) capon
6 spring onion stalks
3 teaspoons salt
2 slices root ginger

4 oz (100 g) ham
1 lb (400 g) Chinese celery cabbage
4 oz (100 g) abalone
4 tablespoons sherry

Preparation Clean capon thoroughly. Cut the spring onions into 2–3 inch (5–7½ cm) pieces. Place capon and spring onions in 6–7 pints (3½ litres) water in a heavy metal or earthenware pot and bring to the boil. After 7–8 minutes boiling, skim away all impurities, and pour away ½ pint (250 ml) of the top stock. Add the salt, ginger, and ham, and after a further 5 minutes simmering, skim away any further impurities, and remove the ham. Slice the cabbage into 1 inch (2½ cm) slices, and the ham and abalone into thin slices; return the ham to the pot.

Cooking Insert an asbestos sheet under the pot, reduce the heat, and simmer for 2 hours. Put the cabbage under the chicken, and continue to simmer for 30 minutes. Add the abalone and sherry, and simmer for 5 minutes more.

The soup should be both rich and refreshing (owing to the late addition of the cabbage), and it should now be possible to take most of the chicken apart with a pair of chopsticks. The dish can be the central point of a big home dinner, or a major course during a banquet.

Whole Duck Soup

Serves 10–12, with other dishes

4–5 lb (1¾–2 kg) duck
6 oz (150 g) bamboo shoots
8 oz (200 g) spring onion stalks
2 slices root ginger

2 teaspoons salt
1 lb (400 g) Chinese celery cabbage
4 oz (100 g) Chinese dried mushrooms
8 oz (200 g) best ham

This recipe is similar to the recipe for Whole Chicken Soup, but as ducks are usually fatter than chickens, they require longer boiling to remove the excess fat. No abalone is added, but a greater quantity of ham and onion is used.

Preparation Clean the duck thoroughly, and remove tail and oil sacs. Place in a heavy metal pot with 5–6 pints (3 litres) water and bring to the boil. After 10 minutes, skim away impurities; boil for 10 minutes more, and skim off any more impurities. Slice the bamboo shoots thinly, and cut the spring onions into 2–3 inch (5–7½ cm) pieces. Stuff the duck with the bamboo shoots, onions, and the ginger, and replace in the soup, with the salt. Cut the cabbage into 1 inch (2½ cm) thick slices, and the mushrooms and ham into strips.

Cooking Insert an asbestos sheet under the pot, reduce heat, and simmer for 2 hours. Put cabbage underneath duck in the pan, and place ham and mushrooms on top. Simmer for a further 30 minutes and serve in a very large tureen.

The large quantity of cabbage should absorb most of the fat in the duck and provide a final freshening. The black and red garnish of mushrooms and ham provides added interest. Because of the very slow cooking, the soup should be very rich and crystal clear.

Painted Soup

This soup makes an occasional appearance on Chinese banquet tables, usually when the cook preparing the meal is a chef/artist, and likes to present something intriguing: however, Painted Soup does not involve actually painting the surface of a liquid! The preparation of a solid surface to place a design on is made simply by beating up 2–3 egg whites with a rotary-beater for 3 or more minutes (until quite stiff), then spreading the egg white thickly over the soup (usually the soup bowl or tureen is filled only up to two thirds full) and smoothing over carefully with a spatula or large spoon. When the surface of the egg white is smooth, all kinds of designs can be placed on it. The Chinese chef/artist usually creates a rural scene, where the brownish yellow strips of golden needles (lily bud stems) are used to illustrate branches or trunks of trees; any green vegetables thinly sliced or in leaves can be used to illustrate foliage or leaves, or a fresh carrot can be cut into a disc with thin strips radiating from all sides to simulate the sun. Tomato skins are cut into all shapes of bright red flowers. All these can be lightly pressed into the malleable surface of the egg white. The more ambitious chef/artist would create and add pictures of human beings and animals to further liven the scene.

The actual soup used in the Painted Soup can be prepared from virtually any recipe in this section, according to taste. When the soup is ready to serve, the host or hostess would break up the picture in the common tureen or soup bowl, and ladle the soup and a part of the picture intact into each individual's soup bowl.

Rice

米

Rice is the main bulk-food of China and is eaten just as bread and potatoes are eaten in the West. It is eaten with every meal: soft rice (or congee) for breakfast in the morning, and boiled or steamed rice for lunch as well as dinner. The only time when rice is not eaten is at a party dinner or banquet, for during such occasions so many courses are served that the customary bulk intake of rice might hinder the enjoyment and progress of the dozen or more dishes. Not infrequently, however, at the end of a banquet, four emphatically plain dishes with a soup or two and rice are served to settle the stomach.

So in China you just cannot get away from rice altogether. It gives unity to the multi-dish or multi-course meal. Its absorbent softness enables it to set off both dry, crackling foods as well as the stews and dishes with sauce. Its neutral blandness enables it to act as an ideal absorbent for all the spicy, savoury, rich, and hot dishes which are often served to the diners at a Chinese dinner. For foods which are fresh, light, and refreshing, rice can act as an essential complement which helps to smooth their progress, thus giving more time for the palate to enjoy them. Rice, therefore, has an all-purpose function in the context of a Chinese meal, quite apart from such considerations as calorific value.

Although we often talk about rice existing as a complement to various dishes, it is in fact equally true that a great many dishes exist to complement rice. Without rice, much of their significance and appeal would be lost. There must be hundreds of Chinese dishes which belong to this category, but we Chinese tend to forget that rice is not merely a complement to other dishes simply because we are so used to eating it. An example of a rice-complementing dish is Red-Cooked Pork Knuckle. Indeed, if the diners are not used to eating large quantities of rice, some other bulk-food such as steamed

The Complete Chinese Cookbook

buns or toasted hot-cakes could be provided as a substitute, since quantities of Red-Cooked Pork would be too rich for people unaccustomed to rice.

Since rice takes two or three times as long to steam as it does to boil, and since the end product is much the same boiling is the most common way of cooking it for ordinary day to day requirements, particularly in the West.

BOILED RICE

The problem of cooking boiled rice is that one can so easily make it too watery; but on the other hand it is all too easy to use too little water and burn it. Great care is therefore necessary when boiling rice, as it should be dry, flaky, and well-cooked. There are many methods of achieving this result. The following is a method which I have found simple and fool-proof, and which I have used many hundreds of times:

Quantity For Europeans a pound of rice should be sufficient for 6–8 persons. When cooking rice one should add to it $1\frac{1}{4}$ times its volume in water, i.e. for a cup or bowl of rice one should use $1\frac{1}{4}$ cups or $1\frac{1}{4}$ bowls of water as the case may be.

Washing Before cooking, rice must be washed and rinsed until the water runs clear. This has the effect of washing away the starch and helps to prevent the grains from sticking to one another, thus assuring that the rice will be flaky when cooked.

Cooking Before beginning to cook the rice, boil a kettle of water and leave it simmering for later use. Place the rice in a saucepan, add the required quantity of water and bring to the boil. Leave to boil for 2 minutes. Reduce to a low heat and continue to boil very gently under cover for 7–8 minutes. By this time the surface of the rice will have become dry (if not, replace the lid and wait until it dries). Once the top layer of the rice is dry, pour in sufficient boiling water to cover the top of the rice by about $\frac{1}{4}$ inch ($\frac{1}{2}$ cm). Replace the cover, insert an asbestos sheet under the pan and leave the contents to simmer for another 5 minutes. Turn off the heat and leave the rice to stand in the pan to cook in its own heat and steam for the next 7–8 minutes (do not open the lid). By this time, after a total of just over 20 minutes cooking time, the rice should be ready; well-cooked and flaky, but not soggy.

Cooked, boiled rice which has not been used can be re-heated again when required, or it can be made into fried rice by frying with various other ingredients. It can also be made into soft rice by further boiling with additional water.

To keep left-over rice for further use it is best to loosen it from the pan and break up any large lumps so that they do not become hard and encrusted. Rice which has been loosened can best be prepared for use again simply by placing it in a fresh saucepan and heating it up again with a small quantity of water, approximately two tablespoons of water to every bowl of rice.

STEAMED RICE

There are two traditional ways of steaming rice. In both cases the rice has to be boiled first in ample water for five minutes, then drained.

(a) Divide the partly-boiled rice into the number of portions required. Place each portion in a heat-proof bowl and cover with $\frac{1}{4}$ inch ($\frac{1}{2}$ cm) of hot or boiling water. (Leave space in each bowl for rice to double its size.) Place the bowl or bowls in a steamer and steam for $\frac{3}{4}$ hour. Alternatively, place the bowls on a rack inside a large saucepan in which $1\frac{1}{2}$–2 inches ($3\frac{1}{2}$–5 cm) of water has been brought to the boil. Boiling water should be added at intervals when required. Under the cover of the closed lid of the saucepan, the rice should be steamed and well-cooked in approximately 30–40 minutes. This method of steaming is often employed in restaurants as the heated bowls help to keep the rice very warm when served.

(b) The second method of steaming, which is more often employed at home in China, depends on the use of a flat, round, tray-like, bamboo steamer, which is placed on top of a cauldron of boiling water. There is a bamboo cover which fits over the top of the steamer. When the water in the cauldron boils, the rising steam passes through the steamer – frequently, there are several layers of steamer in use for one meal. A layer of cheese-cloth is spread at the bottom of the steamer, and the drained boiled rice is spread on top to not more than 1 inch ($2\frac{1}{2}$ cm) thickness. The rice is then pierced at numerous points with a pair of chopsticks to allow the steam to pass through. It should be cooked for just under one hour. Rice can also be steamed this way wrapped in a lotus leaf.

The advantage of steaming rice over boiling it is that steamed rice never gets burnt, but it requires much more time and many more

The Complete Chinese Cookbook

elaborate utensils. For cooking in the average Western kitchen boiling is much simpler, and to be recommended.

FRIED RICE

As rice is not an independent dish for eating on its own (as is the case of bread and potatoes), it is usually served to complement other dishes, and therefore in its native state (cooked, of course). When it is cooked or cross-cooked with other foods and ingredients, it is usually as Fried Rice, which is regarded as a snack, or is served when there are very few other items available on the dining table. It should never be served at a full dinner or a banquet. (Just as you do not serve bubble and squeak at the Lord Mayor's Banquet.)

There are no rules as to what can be fried with rice. In fact, almost any fryable item can be fried with rice, and made into Fried Rice. However, there are a few traditional ones, which seem to bring out the best orchestration.

Some of the points to aim at in the frying or in this orchestration are:

(a) Aromatic – hence some onion is always introduced in the earlier stages of the frying.

(b) Tastiness –
   (1) By providing some direct contrast to the blandness of rice, some chopped ham or bacon is often used.
   (2) By providing savouriness as a contrast in texture and taste – hence chopped, cooked pork, chicken, beef, lobster, shrimps, or prawns are frequently used.

(c) A Variation in Texture and Colour – this is achieved by the inclusion of chopped vegetables which are lightly cooked (fried), such as celery, cucumber, peas, or bamboo shoots.

(d) The unity and basic background tastiness in Fried Rice is provided by the beaten eggs, which should always be stir-fried and well-scrambled in the pan before the rice is introduced. The eggs have to be set before the rice is added, otherwise a messiness will soon become apparent.

The following are a few of the more traditional Fried Rice Dishes.

Basic Fried Rice

Serves 4

8–12 oz (200–300 g) cooked rice
1 medium-sized onion
3 oz (75 g) ham *or* bacon
4 tablespoons diced celery,
cucumber, *or* greens
4 tablespoons green peas
3 eggs
1 teaspoon salt
4 tablespoons vegetable oil
1 tablespoon soya sauce

Preparation Chop the onion finely. Slice the ham or bacon into small pieces. Dice the celery, cucumber, or greens into small pea-size pieces. Thaw the peas if the frozen variety is used. Beat the eggs lightly with ½ teaspoon of the salt.

Cooking Heat the oil in a frying pan or saucepan. Add the onion, the bacon or ham, and remaining salt. Stir-fry over a high heat for 1½ minutes. Reduce the heat to low and pour in the egg. Allow the eggs to set and then scramble. Add the peas and celery. Continue to stir and scramble for 1 minute. Pour in the rice and continue to turn, mix, and stir for 2 minutes. Sprinkle with soya sauce. Turn and mix once more; then serve.

Fried rice should be eaten as soon as possible after it leaves the pan, otherwise it will no longer be aromatic and it might become greasy.

Chicken Fried Rice

Serves 4

This is one of the favourites among the fried rice dishes served in restaurants, probably because many parts of the chicken meat come in bits and pieces and this is one of the best ways of using them up.

The chicken used in this dish is usually cooked beforehand. The ingredients and method of preparation for this dish are the same as for Basic Fried Rice, with two exceptions: 4–6 oz (100–150 g) of chicken meat should be added to the pan 30 seconds after the onion, and an extra ½ teaspoon of salt will be needed.

Shrimp, Prawn, or Lobster Fried Rice

Serves 4

Seafoods such as shrimps, prawns, and lobsters are favourites for frying with rice, mainly because of their savoury flavour. When lobsters and prawns are used, the meat should be diced to about the same size as peas. A clove or two of garlic (crushed and chopped) could be added to the pan, together with the chopped onion. This will make the dish even more aromatic. If root ginger is available, a thin slice or two, finely chopped, could also be added at the same time as the garlic and onion. This will reduce the fishy taste of the seafoods. Otherwise, the procedure is precisely the same as in the previous recipes for fried rice.

Cooked Rice with Other Ingredients

Rice may be cooked with many types of ingredients, but this practice is more popular in Europe than in China. Spanish paellas and Italian risottos are examples of dishes in which the rice and savoury ingredients are cooked together. In China, rice is most often used as an accompaniment to several other dishes, and the Chinese prefer making their own selection from these dishes to having the rice served already mixed with other ingredients. The following recipes are for a few Chinese dishes in which the rice is cooked along with the other ingredients.

Vegetable Rice

Serves 6–8

1 lb (400 g) rice
1 lb (400 g) spring greens

2 tablespoons lard
1 tablespoon butter
2 teaspoons salt

This is one of Shanghai's native dishes.

Preparation Clean the rice in two changes of water and drain. Discard the coarse outer leaves of the greens, and chop into 1½ × 2 inch (3½ × 5 cm) pieces.
Cooking Heat the lard and butter in a saucepan. Add the greens and salt. Stir-fry over a medium heat for 3 minutes. Add the rice and 1¼ pints (750 ml) water. Bring quickly to the boil. Reduce heat to a minimum, and insert an asbestos sheet under the pan. Simmer gently, covered, for 15 minutes. Turn the heat off altogether, keep covered, and allow the rice and greens to steam in their own heat for another 15 minutes before serving.
Serving Serve on a well-heated dish.

The rice should be well-cooked and impregnated with the fresh vegetable flavour of the greens after 30 minutes of cooking together. It should be eaten as an accompaniment to any savoury dish or dishes, and is very often served with hot or cold red-cooked meat dishes.

Rice

Vegetable rice need not always be made with spring greens. Various other cooked vegetables may be substituted.

Rice Cooked with Chinese Sausages

This is often served in middle-class homes and even occasionally in restaurants. Chinese sausage has the appearance and flavour of salami: it is salty, spicy, and rich. As it is an ideal complement to the neutral blandness of rice, they are often eaten together and occasionally cooked together. The usual point at which to add the sausages to the rice is when the surface of the steamed or boiled rice has dried during the cooking. Pieces of sausage are pushed into the rice and buried as deeply as possible, then allowed to steam in the pan with the rice for at least 15-20 minutes, to allow the characteristic flavour and aroma of the cooked sausage to impregnate the rice. The flavour and aroma have a peculiar Chinese quality, recognizable to all who have any experience of Chinese food. The sausage and rice mixture should be accompanied by all the other savoury foods normally served with rice. As these sausages are pinkish-red in colour, they contrast with the whiteness of the rice, giving the dish a colourful and attractive appearance.

Topped Rice, or Cooked Rice with Toppings

Topped rice is not often served in China as it is a dish most suitable for a person dining alone. Since a Chinese meal is a communal meal, all the dishes accompanying the rice are set on the table for the diners to share. This means that a far greater variety of dishes can be sampled than would be practical in preparing a meal for one person.

However, as people nowadays are more mobile than in the past, the practice of dining alone has increased. Furthermore, the mushrooming of Chinese restaurants abroad, where life is lived in a more individualistic manner than in China, has resulted in an increasing demand for portions of rice to be served along with portions of the savoury foods which form the garnish, as a complete, self-contained dish.

It is probably true to say that plain cooked rice can be topped with almost any Chinese dish, especially those served with some sauce or gravy. A well-balanced dish of rice with topping should have two types of topping – meat and vegetable – and these, if possible, should be separate and distinct. They should not only present a contrast in colour, but also a difference in type, texture, and flavour. As a rule, if the meat for the topping is 'dry', such as roast pork, chicken, or duck, the vegetable or vegetables should be frybraised and sauce-covered, thus providing the necessary gravy.

For the less demanding, the topping for rice can be one of the many cross-cooked dishes where meat and vegetables are already blended in the cooking. There are countless cross-cooked Chinese dishes; the following list contains only a few.

Sliced Lamb Quick-Fried with Spring Onion (see page 153)
Shredded Lamb Quick-Fried with Ginger and Young Leeks (see page 153)

Red-Cooked Beef with Tomato (see page 141)

Steamed Beef Balls with Oyster Sauce (see page 143)
Diced Chicken in Soya Jam (see page 173)

Soft Rice or Congee

Soft rice is a traditional Chinese dish, unlike Topped Rice, as it is used throughout China for breakfast, and midnight suppers, or for invalids and the aged. It is usually eaten as an accompaniment to cold, salty, pickled, or highly savoury foods. Indeed, one of the tests for the quality of soya sauce is to take it with soft rice, the blandness of which provides a contrast with the mild, not too salty, savoury flavour of good soya sauce. This unique savoury flavour cannot be imitated by any chemical ingredient such as monosodium glutamate, which is not used in the original Chinese preparations.

Few Westerners have taken to soft rice at the first try. This is probably because there is no Western food with a corresponding function – it is as if one were asked to eat porridge with a cold savoury dish! However, by persisting, the Westerner would almost certainly find that there is a particular pleasure to be derived from every method of preparing and serving Chinese food.

Savoury soft rice is more readily appreciated than ordinary soft rice by the Westerner, as it has the appearance of a thick savoury soup. To the Chinese, however, it is simply a variation of soft rice or congee which is eaten only at certain times of the day, and not at any meal.

Basic Soft Rice

Serves 10   12 oz (300 g) long grain rice
                         4 oz (100 g) glutinous rice

Cooking Wash the rice thoroughly in three changes of water. Place it in a deep saucepan and add 8 pints (generous 4 litres) of water. (Note: soft rice boils over very easily.) Bring to the boil, immediately reduce heat to the minimum, and insert an asbestos sheet underneath the pan if available.

Leave to cook for 1½ hours, stirring occasionally. If it becomes too thick, add a little boiling water. Continue to cook gently for approximately 30 minutes.

Soft rice or congee should be about half as thick as the usual rice pudding, although some prefer it thinner. At breakfast time it is valued for its refreshing quality and for its warmth. At supper time it has a settling effect on the digestive system and it provides warmth throughout the night, like an internal hot water bottle.

Almost any kind of meat can be added to cook with soft rice to produce savoury soft rice. Often the meat is first of all marinated or previously cooked and added to the rice during the later stages of its cooking. Usually a drop or two of sesame oil is added to give it special appeal and flavour. The following recipes are a few of the more popular savoury soft rice dishes, some of which are served in the Cantonese Chinese restaurants abroad.

Chicken Soft Rice

Serves 6–10

10 oz (250 g) *or* 8 oz (200 g) chicken (see *Preparation*)
12 oz (300 g) long grain rice
4 oz (100 g) glutinous rice
1 teaspoon salt
2 tablespoons soya sauce
½ tablespoon sherry

2 slices chopped root ginger
2 spring onion stalks, chopped into ½ inch (1 cm) pieces
pepper to taste
1 tablespoon hoisin sauce
1 chicken stock cube
1 teaspoon sesame oil
soya sauce for dip

Preparation Chop 10 oz (250 g) chicken through the bones into 1½–2 inch (3½–5 cm) cubes. Many Westerners may prefer the chicken to be boned, in which case 8 oz (200 g) of chicken meat should be chopped into cubes. Marinate the chicken cubes for 1 hour in a mixture of salt, soya sauce, sherry, root ginger, spring onion, pepper, and hoisin sauce.

Cooking Follow the instructions given in the Basic Soft Rice recipe for cooking the rice, using 8 pints (generous 4 litres) water. When the rice has simmered for 1½ hours, the chicken and marinade should be stirred in, but the root ginger should be removed. Add a chicken stock cube to the saucepan. Simmer the rice and chicken together for 30–45 minutes. Add the sesame oil 3 minutes before serving.

Serving Divide the rice and chicken mixture among six to ten bowls as required. Ideally, this dish should be eaten with chopsticks. The pieces of chicken should either be dipped in high quality soya sauce or sprinkled with soya sauce. The savoury flavour of the sauce and the contrasting blandness of the rice combine to form a most enjoyable dish.

The Complete Chinese Cookbook
Pork Spare Rib Soft Rice
Serves 6–10

Repeat the recipe for Chicken Soft Rice, substituting 12–16 oz (300–400 g) spare ribs chopped into 1 inch (2½ cm) long pieces, for the chicken. Pork bones are easier for Westerners to handle than chicken bones, therefore it should not be necessary to bone the spare ribs. The rice and spare ribs should be cooked together for 45 minutes.

Roast Duck or Roast Pork Soft Rice
Serves 6–10

As roast duck or Cantonese Cha Shao roast pork are two of the more readily available cooked foods in a Chinese kitchen, they are often added to soft rice.

Use the recipe for Basic Soft Rice (see page 78) as the basis of this dish. Chop 10–16 oz (250–400 g) roast duck or pork into 1½ inch (3½ cm) pieces and add to the rice 15–20 minutes before serving. At the same time add 2–3 spring onions chopped into 1 inch (2½ cm) pieces, 2 slices of root ginger, 1 teaspoon salt, and 1 teaspoon sesame oil. Remove the pieces of ginger when serving.

Beef Soft Rice
Serves 6–10

This is probably the most suitable dish for Westerners, as it contains no bones. Use 8–12 oz (200–300 g) lean beef (rump or fillet). Cut into 1½ × 1 inch (3½ × 2½ cm) very thin slices, and marinate in the same manner as the chicken in the Chicken Soft Rice recipe (page 79). Add a chicken stock cube and 4 oz (100 g) green peas to the rice 30 minutes before serving. Add the beef to simmer in the rice for 10–12 minutes. Stir before serving.

Sampan Soft Rice

This is a typical Cantonese dish where various types of fish or seafoods are added to the rice. Most types of fish can be used (except those which are too bony) and every type of shellfish. When fish is used, it should be marinated in soya sauce, hoisin sauce, salt, ginger, onion, garlic, and a small amount of lard or vegetable oil. The ginger (2–3 pieces) should be removed before serving. Sprinkle a tablespoon of chopped spring onion or parsley and a teaspoon of sesame oil over the rice before serving.

Fish which has been sliced very thinly and marinated for one hour does not require much cooking. One practice is to place a few pieces of marinated fish at the bottom of the individual serving bowls and pour in the boiling hot soft rice until it almost reaches the rim of the bowl. Add 1 drop of sesame oil, 1 teaspoon chopped spring onion, and 1 teaspoon best quality soya sauce. Allow the rice to stand for 5 minutes before eating. As boiling soft rice is hotter than boiling water, the fish or seafood ingredients will cook in its heat in 5 minutes.

Noodles

麵

After rice, noodles and steamed buns, known as Man Tou, or unstuffed steamed breads rank as the most important bulk-foods of China. Steamed buns are eaten primarily in the north, whilst noodles are eaten both in the north and south at all times of the day and night except at breakfast. Noodles therefore seem to have beaten buns as a bulk-food by a short head.

It has been said that Italian pasta has its origin in Chinese noodles, which were first introduced to Europe in the fourteenth century by none other than Marco Polo, and which have now blossomed into all the familiar spaghettis, macaronis, and vermicellis. The main difference between Chinese noodles and Italian pasta does not lie in their shape or substance – there they are very similar – but in the way they are prepared and cooked. Because of the Chinese habits of cross-cooking, blending, and multi-phase heating, and because of the possibility of combining noodles with almost every variety of meat, fowl, seafood, or vegetable, there are probably many more Chinese noodle dishes than Italian pasta dishes. There is, in fact, an almost inexhaustible number of Chinese noodle dishes, and the majority of them are delicious and acceptable to the Western palate.

In the main, Chinese noodle dishes fall into the following categories:

1. Soup noodles
2. Noodles in thickened sauce and gravies
3. Cooked noodles
4. Fried noodles: soft-fried and crisp-fried noodles
5. Tossed noodles: hot-tossed and cold-tossed noodles
6. Pea-starch transparent noodles

Soup noodles are generally served as an appetizer to commence a social occasion, often to precede an evening of dining and banqueting. They are often served in the hall or reception room soon after

Noodles

the guests arrive. In China when there is a wedding, anniversary, funeral, or memorial of any sort, noodles are usually served in clear chicken stock and garnished with a few strands of cooked chicken meat or shredded ham. This dish is designed to heighten interest and improve sociability, but not to hamper the great expectations of the banquet to come.

However, should the occasion be a birthday, the noodles will be served in a thickened gravy-sauce called Lu Mein. There is a good range of gravy-sauce noodles prepared with a variety of ingredients and garnishes, which are without exception highly delicious and appetizing. In all these cases, the gravy-sauce, garnish, and noodles are prepared and cooked separately, then combined together in the serving bowl.

When the noodles, sauce, and other ingredients are cooked together in a large pan and served in a large tureen, garnished in profusion, the dish is called Cooked noodles or Wo Mein. Wo Mein is served mostly by restaurants where a wide range of ingredients is more easily available and where it is important to impress. The Cantonese often use seafoods such as prawns and crabs in the ingredients or as a garnish.

Fried noodles or Chow Mein are the best known Chinese noodles to Westerners. Chow Mein is a dish of soft-fried noodles, that is, boiled noodles which have been stir-fried in oil and gravy and then garnished with a good helping of shredded meats, vegetables, and seafoods. In Canton there is a special version of fried noodles where the noodles and other ingredients are pressed down flat into the frying pan until they are slightly scorched, and then turned over like a pancake and pressed down again to fry until slightly scorched on the other side. Noodles cooked in this manner are generally fried with ample oil or fat (about 4–5 tablespoons) and are not popular in other parts of China. This type of noodle dish quite often makes an appearance abroad, as the majority of Chinese restaurants abroad are Cantonese.

Tossed noodles or Pan Mein are boiled noodles which are served like a salad. They are boiled, drained, and placed in serving bowls. The diner helps himself to spoonfuls of soya jam (or soya jam and meat sauce), shredded cucumber, radishes, spring onions, and bean sprouts which he mixes and tosses with the noodles. Vinegar and sesame oil are frequently added to this type of noodles. This method of serving noodles is probably the nearest Chinese version to the

Italian spaghetti Bolognese or Milanese. A meat sauce prepared by stir-frying minced meat with soya jam in oil can be mixed with the noodles, making the dish very similar indeed to the Italian versions (except that the soya jam contributes an extra piquancy which the Italian dishes lack). But the use of crunchy vegetables, such as bean sprouts, cucumber, and radishes gives the Chinese sauce a texture which contrasts with the softness of the noodles.

Another method of preparing Tossed noodles is to add shredded meat – usually roast chicken or duck – seasoned with salt, pepper, mustard, soya sauce, and flavour powder to cold cooked noodles. Selected shredded raw vegetables, sesame oil, and vinegar should then be mixed and tossed with the noodles and meat. This grand conglomeration of ingredients, all with very different flavours and characteristics, results in what the Westerner might call a salad. This salad can be further hotted up with a small amount of chilli oil. It is a useful dish to serve as a starter to a meal. As Chinese Cold Tossed Noodles form a salad with bulk, the dish should complement the lighter Western salads to make an interesting summer meal, especially if served outdoors.

The principal noodles used in China are wheat-flour noodles, egg noodles, rice-flour noodles (often called rice-sticks) and pea-starch transparent noodles. The latter are used primarily in soups, or to cook with and complement meats and vegetables. They are never eaten as a bulk ingredient in themselves. Rice-flour noodles, which often come in straight strands or sticks, from which the name rice-sticks is derived, are popular in the south, where more rice is grown, and where rice is the principal diet. They are often cooked with seafoods, and when cooked with oysters, coupled with meats, their savouriness is devastating! Egg noodles usually come in small pads like the Western breakfast food Shredded Wheat; these have been partially pre-cooked by steaming. They generally require only a minimal amount of cooking (4–5 minutes of boiling and loosening in water). They can be made into various types of noodle dish in a very short time indeed.

Basic Noodles

All noodles have to be boiled or steamed before they are cooked in any other way. It is difficult to specify the exact length of time they should be boiled or steamed, as that depends partly upon the quality of the noodles themselves, and partly upon the length of time they are going to be subjected to further cooking with other ingredients in the later stages of preparation. The general rule is that noodles should never be cooked until they are soft, mushy, and on the point of breaking up. They should be cooked to a point where they are soft outside but still firm inside. This can be tested by taking out a strand and biting it, or pressing it between one's thumb and finger. The additional cooking in preparing the noodles as soup noodles, fried noodles, cooked noodles, or gravy noodles should provide sufficient further heating to cook them through.

Soup Noodles

Although soup noodles are often used as 'Noodles of Occasion' (that is when there is an occasion in the family and there is a crowd of guests and visitors to be entertained), they can also be eaten as between-meal snacks or as a full meal. The quantity of noodles and toppings or garnish used may be varied accordingly. After all, there are no limits to the size of the serving bowls which can be used or to the quantity of toppings added. It is always impressive to see people in China eating enormous soup bowls or tureens of soup noodles with great relish!

Soup Noodles with Cha Shao Roast Pork and Spinach Topping

Serves 4 or 5

- 1 lb (400 g) wheat-flour noodles
- 8 oz (200 g) spinach
- 8 oz (200 g) Cha Shao roast pork
- 1 small onion
- 2 tablespoons vegetable oil
- 1 teaspoon sugar
- 1½ tablespoons soya sauce
- ½ pint (250 ml) stock
- ½ teaspoon salt
- ½ teaspoon flavour powder
- 2 tablespoons sherry

Preparation Parboil the noodles for 11–12 minutes, drain, and divide among four or five bowls. Wash the spinach thoroughly, drain, and remove coarser stems. Slice Cha Shao pork and onion thinly.

The Complete Chinese Cookbook

Cooking Heat the oil in a large frying pan. Add the onion and spinach, and stir-fry over a high heat for 1 minute. Add sugar and soya sauce and stir-fry for another minute. Place the pork on top of the spinach and cook them together for 1 minute. Heat the stock in a saucepan. Add salt, flavour powder, and sherry. When the mixture comes to the boil, stir, and pour over the noodles in the individual bowls.
Serving Top the noodles first with spinach and then with the pork. This is a simple but satisfying dish, which provides a balanced meal.

Chinese Chicken and Ham Soup Noodles

Serves 4 or 5

8 oz (200 g) egg noodles
4 oz (100 g) cooked chicken breast
4 oz (100 g) cooked ham
2 pints (generous litre) superior stock
1 teaspoon salt
½ teaspoon flavour powder
1 slice root ginger

This is the usual style of light noodle snack served at receptions, social functions, and other occasions of that nature.

Preparation Parboil the noodles for 5–6 minutes if pre-cooked, and 12–14 minutes if uncooked. Drain and divide among four or five serving bowls. Slice the chicken meat and ham into very thin, thread-like strips. Sprinkle these chicken and ham strips evenly over the noodles in the bowls.
Cooking and Serving Heat the stock in a saucepan. Add the salt, flavour powder, and ginger. Allow to simmer gently for 4–5 minutes. Stir, then pour the stock into the bowls containing the noodles. Place the bowls on a saucer or plate with a pair of chopsticks and serve.

Soup Noodles with Red-Cooked Beef or Pork

Serves 4 or 5

Prepare noodles and stock as in the previous recipes for Soup Noodles. All red-cooked meats (pork, beef, lamb, etc.) can be used as toppings for soup noodles. These meats are often cut into large chunks, unlike the recipe for Soup Noodles with Cha Shao Roast Pork and Spinach Topping, where the pork is sliced thinly. To increase the appeal of the dish, and to provide a balanced meal, about 2 oz (50 g) of vegetables for each bowl are usually cooked and added to the noodles along with the meat. The meat can be added cold or hot. The vegetables – spinach, greens, cauliflower, leeks, pepper, celery, etc. – should be cut into 2 inch (5 cm) pieces, then stir-fried for a couple of minutes in 1½–2 tablespoons of oil, with salt and pepper to taste. Then add 2–3 tablespoons of stock, a pinch of flavour powder, and 2 tablespoons of gravy from the red-cooked meat. Cook over a high heat for 2 minutes, gently stirring and turning over the contents of the pan, then place the vegetable toppings on the noodles in the bowls. The meats should now be placed on top of the vegetables to complete this attractive dish. Some Chinese yellow wine or dry sherry may be sprinkled over the dish at the last moment to provide an appealing bouquet. Yellow wine is widely used in this manner in China even among the peasantry, who also sometimes break an egg into the soup to provide variety, added appeal, and nourishment when there is no meat available.

Lu Mein (or Noodles in Sauce)

'Lu' is the general Chinese word for sauce or herbal sauce. Hence Lu Mein means 'sauce noodles'. The noodles served on birthdays are usually sauce noodles. Lu Mein is composed of approximately the same amounts of noodles and sauce served in the same bowl. The sauce can vary a good deal in thickness and flavour; even fish sauce, which can be extremely appetizing, can be used in preparing sauce noodles, and they are often topped with a chunk of red-cooked fish and a few strands of spring onion tops or chives. The sauce or gravy used in preparing Lu Mein is usually thickened first with cornflour or water chestnut flour. This appetizing dish of noodles, covered with plenty of thick sauce, is particularly suitable for serving in winter as it generates inner warmth.

Noodles in Meat Sauce

Serves 4–6

1 lb (400 g) wheat-flour *or* egg noodles
8 oz (200 g) streaky pork
1 slice root ginger
2 spring onion stalks
1 oz (25 g) wood ears
3 oz (75 g) Chinese dried mushrooms
3 oz (75 g) bamboo shoots

1 pint (500 ml) chicken *or* superior stock
2 tablespoons soya sauce
¾ teaspoon flavour powder
2 tablespoons sherry
2 tablespoons cornflour
¼ pint (125 ml) cold stock
1½ tablespoons vegetable oil
4 tablespoons red-cooked meat gravy
½ teaspoon salt

Preparation Parboil and prepare the noodles in the same way as in the Soup Noodle recipes. Cut the pork into thin lean and fat strips. Shred the root

ginger. Cut the spring onions into 2 inch (5 cm) pieces. Soak the wood ears and mushrooms in warm water, and remove mushroom stalks. Reserve 4 tablespoons of the mushroom water. Cut the bamboo shoots into thin slices.
Cooking Heat 1 pint (500 ml) stock in a saucepan. Add soya sauce, flavour powder, sherry, and cornflour blended with ¼ pint (125 ml) cold stock. Stir until the liquid thickens into a sauce. Heat the oil in a frying pan, add the pork and ginger, and stir-fry for 3-4 minutes over a high heat. Add mushrooms, wood ears, bamboo shoots, and spring onions. Stir-fry them together for 2 minutes. Add the meat-gravy, salt, and mushroom water. Continue to stir-fry for 3 minutes.
Serving Serve by dividing noodles among four to six bowls. Pour a proportion of the thickened stock into each bowl, and top the noodles with the other ingredients fresh from the frying pan.

Long Life Noodles in Egg Sauce

Serves 4 or 5

12 oz (300 g) egg noodles
2 eggs
2-3 oz (50-75 g) cooked ham
1 pint (500 ml) superior stock
¼ pint (125 ml) red-cooked pork gravy
1½ tablespoons soya sauce
2 tablespoons sherry
½ teaspoon flavour powder
2 tablespoons cornflour
pepper to taste

Preparation Parboil the noodles for 5-6 minutes. Drain, and divide among four or five bowls. Shred the ham and beat the eggs lightly for about 10 seconds.
Cooking Heat the stock in a saucepan. Add gravy, soya sauce, and sherry. Blend the flavour powder and cornflour with 4 tablespoons of water. Pour the mixture into the simmering stock and stir until it thickens into a sauce. Trail the egg along the prongs of a fork into the soup in as thin a stream as possible. When the egg coagulates, which is almost immediately, give the soup a stir or two. Add pepper to taste.
Serving Pour a proportion of the soup over the noodles in each of the bowls. Sprinkle with shredded ham, and serve.

In China, eggs are associated with long life. Here we have egg noodles in egg sauce; it is not surprising that this dish is called Long Life Noodles, and is usually served on birthdays.

Noodles in Shrimp or Prawn Sauce

Serves 4–6

12 oz (300 g) egg noodles
5 oz (125 g) shrimp *or* prawn meat
1½ pints (almost 1 litre) superior stock
5 oz (125 g) lean pork
3 oz (75 g) cooked ham
3 oz (75 g) Chinese dried mushrooms
3 spring onion stalks
1 clove garlic
¾ teaspoon flavour powder
2 tablespoons cornflour
1½ tablespoons vegetable oil
2 slices root ginger
½ teaspoon salt
2 tablespoons soya sauce
2 tablespoons sherry

Preparation Parboil the noodles as in the recipe for Long Life Noodles in Egg Sauce. Shred the pork and ham. Soak the mushrooms in a cup of water for 30 minutes, remove stalks and slice caps into matchstick strips. Reserve the mushroom water. Cut the spring onions into ½ inch (1 cm) pieces. Crush and chop the garlic. Mix the flavour powder and cornflour with 6 tablespoons water.

Cooking Heat the oil in a large saucepan. Add garlic, ginger, pork, and salt. Stir-fry for 2 minutes over a high heat. Add spring onions and mushrooms and stir-fry for a further 2 minutes. Add shrimps, mushroom water, soya sauce, sherry, and finally the stock. Bring to the boil, reduce heat and simmer gently for 5 minutes. Pour the cornflour mixture into the stock. Stir until stock thickens into a sauce.

Serving Divide the noodles among four to six bowls. Pour the prepared sauce over the noodles, dividing the ingredients evenly among the individual bowls. Sprinkle with shredded ham and serve.

Chow Mein

Chow Mein is probably the best-known Chinese noodle dish in the West. It is also one of the fastest savoury noodle dishes which a restaurant cook can slap out when time is pressing, yet at the same time it has the advantage of having been freshly cooked. Chow Mein illustrates the principal difference between Chinese noodles and Italian pasta: Chinese noodle dishes are usually made in two basic steps, the flavouring of the noodles by frying them in oil and meat-gravy, and garnishing the dish with a mixture of ingredients, thus providing additional variety of textures, tastes, and colours. In short, there is rather more blending and cross-cooking in the Chinese version.

The cooking of Chow Mein is therefore a two-stage stir-frying process, apart from the parboiling of the noodles themselves. The ingredients for the topping are stir-fried together in rapid stages, and then removed from the pan and put aside. The cooked noodles are turned in the oil and gravy in the pan to achieve a savoury flavour. By adding more oil or gravy you can make the noodles crisper or more savoury. This early treatment gives the noodles a tasty flavour. Half of the topping is stir-fried into the noodles before they are placed on the serving dish. In the final phase the remainder of the topping is stir-fried, adjustments to the seasonings are made, and a spoonful or two of sherry and a pinch of flavour powder may be added. Then the topping is added to the noodles.

Thus Chow Mein is the product of a two-stage stir-frying treatment, with a two-tier presentation. For an efficient chef, with all the ingredients at his finger tips, the whole operation need not take more than 3 minutes (1½ minutes for the first stir-frying of the topping, 1 minute for the stir-frying of the noodles, and 30 seconds for the second frying of the topping). However, in the recipes included here, it has been done at a much more leisurely pace.

Fried Noodles with Pork and Vegetable Topping

Serves 5–6

1 lb (400 g) wheat-flour noodles
6 Chinese dried mushrooms
2 oz (50 g) golden needles (lily bud stems)
3 spring onion stalks
8 oz (200 g) streaky pork
3 oz (75 g) bean sprouts
3 tablespoons vegetable oil
½ teaspoon salt
2¼ tablespoons soya sauce
2 tablespoons sherry
1 teaspoon sugar
pepper to taste

Preparation Parboil the noodles in 3 pints (1½ litres) of water for 12–14 minutes, stirring occasionally. Soak the mushrooms and golden needles separately in warm water for 30 minutes. Cut the golden needles and spring onions into 2 inch (5 cm) pieces. Slice the pork and mushrooms into matchstick strips.

Cooking Heat 1½ tablespoons of the oil in a large frying pan. Add pork, salt, and golden needles, and stir-fry together for 3 minutes over a high heat. Add mushrooms, onions, and bean sprouts, and continue to stir-fry for 1½ minutes. Add half of the soya sauce, sherry, sugar, and pepper, and stir-fry for a further 1½ minutes. Remove vegetables with a spoon and keep hot. Add the remaining oil and soya sauce to the pan. Pour in the noodles and turn them over in the oil/soya gravy for 1½ minutes over medium heat, to heat well through. Add a quarter of the fried topping to the noodles, blend and stir-fry together for 1¼ minutes and remove to a well-heated serving dish. Return the remainder of the topping to the pan, adding a small quantity of oil, soya sauce, or sherry at this point if necessary. Stir-fry over a high heat for 30 seconds, then arrange the topping on the noodles.

This is a fairly standard way of cooking Chow Mein. Other meat ingredients can be substituted for pork, and other sliced vegetables such as leeks, cabbage, broccoli, celery, or greens can be substituted for bean sprouts, golden needles, etc., with equal success; however, dried mushrooms and spring onions are always essential.

Fried Noodles with Chicken and Vegetable Topping

Serves 4–6

Repeat the recipe for Fried Noodles with Pork and Vegetable Topping, substituting 4–5 oz (100–125 g) chicken breast meat for the pork, and 2 oz (50 g) of wood ears (soaked in two changes of water for 30 minutes) for the golden needles.

Fried Noodles with Beef Ribbons and Vegetable Topping

Serves 4–6

Repeat the recipe for Fried Noodles with Pork and Vegetable Topping, substituting the same quantity of beef (fillet, rump, etc.) for the pork, and 3–4 oz (75–100 g) celery and 2 oz (50 g) leeks for bean sprouts. Cut the leeks and celery into 1 inch (2½ cm) pieces and stir-fry them with the meat and 1 slice of root ginger. Remove the ginger, and put the meat/leek/celery mixture aside. Add a quarter of the vegetable ingredients when stir-frying the noodles; the remainder should be retained for the final stir-frying process and then placed on top of the noodles.

Fried Noodles with Fresh Shrimps or Prawns, or Crab-Meat and Vegetables

A feature of Chinese cooking is that seafoods are often combined with meat. Although these two quite different materials are sometimes blended together (in some prawn balls or fish balls), in the majority of cases they are usually prepared and cooked separately, and are combined only at a later stage of the cooking. This is because in the creation of Chinese dishes, one should always try to avoid making a mess and ingredients and flavours should remain recognizable and distinct.

The Complete Chinese Cookbook

This dish can be prepared by simply repeating any of the previous recipes, reducing the meat content to half, and adding an equal or slightly greater quantity of whatever seafood you have decided to use (shrimps, prawns, crab, and lobster are all suitable). The meat and seafood can be stir-fried together, but it is preferable to cook them separately. The same vegetables should be added to both; a slice or two of root ginger and a clove of crushed garlic should also be added to the seafood.

When meat and seafood have been stir-fried, a proportion of each can be stir-fried into the noodles. The balance is left to be stir-fried for use as a topping when the dish is almost ready to be served. Naturally some preparation of the seafood is needed; in the case of crab, the meat will have to be removed and flaked, and in the case of large prawns or lobsters, the larger pieces of meat will have to be cut into three or four smaller bite-sized pieces before cooking.

Pea-Starch Transparent Noodles with Stewed Meat and Vegetables

Serves 6–8

- 4 oz (100 g) transparent pea-starch noodles
- 8 oz (200 g) spring greens *or* broccoli
- 8 oz (200 g) red-cooked pork *or* beef (see Index)
- 1 pint (500 ml) superior stock
- 2 oz (50 g) Chinese dried mushrooms
- 2 tablespoons dried prawns
- ½ teaspoon flavour powder
- 1 tablespoon soya sauce
- 2 tablespoons sherry

Transparent noodles are not served in the same way as other noodles. They are not used as a bulk food, but are usually cooked with savoury foods in plenty of gravy, and eaten with rice. As transparent noodles have the unusual quality of never becoming soft and mushy through cooking, and since they are very useful as absorbers and conveyors of flavours, it is both traditional and convenient to cook them along with meats and other foods. To the connoisseurs they are a great boon as an aid to the consumption of rice; they serve almost as a savoury lubricant when eating quantities of rice and provide one of the basic pleasures in the enjoyment of Chinese food.

Preparation Soak the noodles in warm water and drain. Clean the greens or broccoli, discarding outer leaves. Cut into 1½ inch (3½ cm) pieces. Parboil for 2 minutes, then drain. Soak the mushrooms and dried prawns in a bowl of warm water for 30 minutes. Drain, retaining the mushroom water. Discard the mushroom stalks, and slice the caps into matchstick shreds. Cut the pork or beef into 1 inch (2½ cm) cubes.

Cooking Heat the stock in a saucepan. Add greens, mushrooms, prawns, flavour powder, soya sauce, and mushroom water. Simmer for 5–6 minutes. Add the noodles and mix with the vegetables. Continue to heat gently for another 7–8 minutes. Pour the mixture into a large oven-proof dish or casserole. Place the red-cooked pork or beef on top, pour in any gravy from the meat, and then add the sherry. Place the dish or casserole in a steamer and steam for 15 minutes, then serve.

Noodles in Lobster Sauce

Serves 4–6

12 oz (300 g) egg noodles
5 oz (125 g) lobster meat
1½ pints (almost 1 litre) superior stock
4 oz (125 g) lean pork
4 oz (75 g) cooked ham
3 oz (75 g) Chinese dried mushrooms
3 spring onion stalks
1 clove garlic
¾ teaspoon flavour powder
2 tablespoons cornflour
1½ tablespoons vegetable oil
2 slices root ginger
½ teaspoon salt
1½ tablespoons soya sauce
1½ tablespoons dry sherry

Preparation Prepare and parboil noodles as in recipe for Long Life Noodles in Egg Sauce. Slice pork and ham into matchstick strips. Soak mushrooms in a cupful of warm water for 30 minutes, remove the stems, and slice caps into matchstick strips. Reserve the mushroom water. Cut the spring onions into ½ inch (1 cm) segments. Crush and chop the garlic. Combine the flavour powder and cornflour with 6 tablespoons water.

Cooking and Serving Heat the oil in a large saucepan. Add the garlic, ginger, pork, and salt, and stir-fry for 2 minutes. Add the spring onions and mushrooms, stir-fry for a further 2 minutes; then add lobster meat, mushroom water, soya sauce, sherry, and finally the stock. Bring to the boil, and simmer gently for 5 minutes; then pour the cornflour mixture into the pan, and stir until it thickens into a sauce. Divide the noodles among four to six bowls. Pour the lobster sauce over the noodles, sprinkle with shredded ham, and serve.

Wo Mein (Pot-Cooked Noodles)

Wo Mein (or Pot Cooked Noodles) is really a variation of Noodles in Sauce. But because it is cooked in a pot, rather than having sauce poured over it in the serving bowl, it comes to be called 'cooked noodles' or 'pot-cooked noodles' (Wo being the Cantonese word for pot; hence pot-cooked). These noodles are frequently served in restaurants, where many different materials

The Complete Chinese Cookbook

for toppings and garnishes are usually available. Very often these noodles are served in a large tureen and brought to the table with quantities of garnish piled on top. The dish is rather more elaborate than Lu Mein. The soup or sauce in Wo Mein is likely to be thinner than in Lu Mein (sauce noodles), but since the noodles and soup have been cooked together with the various ingredients and a proportion of the garnish, it tends to be a more highly savoury dish. In Cantonese restaurants, a selection of seafoods, such as fresh shrimps, prawns, crabs, or lobsters are bound to have been added. Wo Mein is a larger dish with a greater variety of added ingredients than Lu Mein, and therefore gives the impression of being more sumptuous.

Vegetable and Vegetarian Dishes

蔬菜

There are three background factors in Chinese vegetable and vegetarian cooking which give them strength, tradition, and variety.

The first of these is the widespread use of soya beans and their by-products, which, as we have already seen, add a great deal of flavouring power to Chinese meat cooking, as well as the cooking of other foods. One must also recognize that the use of bean curds is of great importance – for sheer versatility they have few equals in the whole realm of food materials.

Vegetable and vegetarian dishes derive their tradition principally from Buddhist monastery and temple cooking. As many of these monasteries and temples are large communities of people with well-developed traditions and hierarchy like the Papal Court which go back to antiquity, or, at least, to medieval times, their kitchens were often institutions of their own, carrying within them traditions and methods of which many palace kitchens would be proud. It was in these kitchens that a great array of vegetarian dishes were invented and developed (much in the same manner as the Benedictine Monks developed their liqueur).

Stir-frying is the most frequent and popular method by which vegetables are cooked. The usual practice is to stir-fry the stronger vegetables first (the garlic, ginger, onions, etc.), and thus impregnate the oil with their flavours before it is used to cook the fresh vegetables. This practice of frying with impregnated oil, often with a small quantity of salt which has the salutary effect of making green vegetables greener, usually acts as the first-line of flavouring, and this is frequently followed and supplemented by other phases of further seasoning and flavouring. Furthermore, by taking advantage of the interplay of textures which results partly from the Chinese practice of blending the cooked with the un-cooked (or fresh), and partly from the throwing together of foods of widely different substance and texture, the 'tapestry of texture' in cooking, if one might invent an expression, is in this way brought to a new height in Chinese vegetarian cooking.

For these reasons, and probably for others, Chinese vegetable and vegetarian dishes can often be eaten on their own, as interesting savoury dishes. Once vegetable dishes were considered to be able to stand in their own right, more time and competence naturally came to be devoted to their cooking and preparation – resulting in their attaining a high degree of excellence and distinction.

Basic Vegetarian Stock

8 oz (200 g) fresh mushrooms
2 oz (50 g) dried mushrooms
2 oz (50 g) dried mushroom stalks
1 lb (400 g) fresh mushroom stalks
1½ lb (almost ¾ kg) yellow beans
2 teaspoons flavour powder

Cooking Boil the fresh and dried mushrooms, the mushroom stalks, and the yellow beans in 1 gallon (4½ litres) of water for 3 hours. Keep the quantity of liquid constant by adding small amounts of water whenever the level of the stock falls visibly. Add the flavour powder 5 minutes before the stock is ready. This stock is used in the same way as superior stock is used in normal cooking.

Pao T'Sai (White Hot Pickle)

Makes 3 pints (1½ litres)

1 medium-sized white cabbage
2 young carrots
1 turnip
2 oz (50 g) radishes
3 tablespoons salt
3 tablespoons gin
2 dried red chilli peppers

This plain pickle is used extensively in China to accompany soft rice; it is also used with other vegetables in Chinese salads.

Preparation Clean the cabbage thoroughly, breaking it up into individual leaves and discarding the coarse outer leaves. Cut the leaves into 1½–2 inch (3½–5 cm) pieces. Shake off any lingering water and put the cabbage leaves in a colander. Leave them in an airy place to dry for 1 day. Peel the carrots and turnip and cut them into thin slices. Remove the tops and roots from the radishes, quarter them, and wash and dry them. Dissolve the salt in 3 pints (1½ litres) of boiling water. When cold, add the gin and all the vege-

Vegetable and Vegetarian Dishes

tables. Put the mixture in a screw-top jar, close it firmly, and place it in a warm room for 1 week. The resultant pickles will be slightly hot, salty, and very crunchy.

Three Fairies Salad

Serves 4-6, with other dishes

1 large Chinese celery cabbage *or* Cos lettuce *or* Savoy cabbage
3 oz (75 g) radishes
2 teaspoons salt

1 oz (25 g) watercress
2 onions
2 fresh chilli peppers
3 tablespoons vegetable oil
2 tablespoons Pao T'Sai pickle
1 teaspoon sesame oil

Preparation Clean the cabbage or lettuce and cut the leaves into 2 × 1 inch (5 × 2½ cm) pieces. Shred the radishes, and mix with the cabbage or lettuce in a bowl. Add the salt and rub it into the vegetables. Leave to stand for 4 hours in a large colander. Clean the watercress thoroughly, discarding the roots, and cut the onions into thin slices. Chop the chilli peppers and discard the seeds.
Cooking Stir-fry the onion and chilli in the vegetable oil for 3 minutes; then remove from pan.
Serving Put the cabbage and radishes into a salad bowl, add the watercress and pickle, and pour in the onion/chilli-impregnated oil. Sprinkle with sesame oil. Toss and mix well; then serve.

Chinese Carrot Salad

Serves 6-8

10 young carrots
3 teaspoons salt
dash of pepper

3 tablespoons vinegar
1 tablespoon sugar
1½ tablespoons soya sauce
3 teaspoons sesame oil
2 tablespoons sherry

Preparation Scrape and clean the carrots; then slice them thinly by cutting downwards in a slanting, crosswise fashion. Soak in water for 15 minutes; then drain. Sprinkle with salt and pepper, and rub the seasonings into the carrots. Set them aside for 2 hours; then drain away all the liquid extracted from the carrots at the end of this time. Add the vinegar, sugar, soya sauce, sesame oil, and sherry. Toss and serve.

The Complete Chinese Cookbook
Eight Precious Hot Salad

Serves 6–8

4 golden needles (lily bud stems)
1 oz (25 g) wood ears
2 oz (50 g) bean curd skin
4 large Chinese dried mushrooms
2 oz (50 g) carrots
1½ oz (40 g) turnip
3 oz (75 g) bamboo shoots
4 oz (100 g) celery

4 oz (100 g) bean sprouts
4 tablespoons vegetable oil
1½ teaspoons salt
3 tablespoons vegetarian stock (see page 96)
2 tablespoons sesame oil
1¼ tablespoons soya sauce
1 tablespoon vinegar
1 teaspoon flavour powder

This salad can also be served cold.

Preparation Soak the golden needles for 1 hour in warm water; then cut them into 2 inch (5 cm) segments. Soak the wood ears for 1 hour, and rinse in two changes of water. Soak the bean curd skin for 1 hour in warm water and cut it into 2 inch (5 cm) segments. Soak the mushrooms for 30 minutes, discard the stalks and shred the caps. Shred the carrots, turnip, bamboo shoots, and celery.

Cooking Stir-fry the carrots, turnip, and bean sprouts in 2 tablespoons of vegetable oil for 2 minutes over a high heat; then for 2 minutes more over a low heat, adding 1 teaspoon of salt. Stir-fry the mushrooms, wood ears, celery, bean curd skin, and bamboo shoots in the remaining vegetable oil and salt over a medium heat for 3 minutes. Combine the two lots of vegetables and add the vegetarian stock, sesame oil, soya sauce, vinegar, and flavour powder. Toss and 'assemble' over a high heat for 1½ minutes; then serve.

Vegetarian Cold Salad

Serves 6–8, with other vegetarian dishes

4 oz (100 g) Savoy cabbage
4 oz (100 g) Cos lettuce
3 young carrots
2 oz (50 g) radishes
3 medium tomatoes
3 spring onion stalks
1 large onion
2 cloves garlic

4 tablespoons vegetable oil
2 slices root ginger
4 oz (100 g) bean sprouts
1 teaspoon salt
2 tablespoons soya sauce
2 tablespoons wine vinegar
½ teaspoon chilli oil
1 teaspoon flavour powder
3 teaspoons sesame oil
1 tablespoon chopped chives
1 tablespoon chopped coriander

Vegetable and Vegetarian Dishes

Preparation Shred the cabbage, lettuce, carrots, and radishes; skin and quarter the tomatoes. Chop the spring onions into 1 inch (2½ cm) segments. Slice the onion, and crush the cloves of garlic.

Cooking Heat the vegetable oil in a saucepan. Add the spring onions, onion, ginger, and garlic. Stir-fry over a medium heat for 3 minutes, discard the onions, ginger, and garlic, and allow the oil to cool. Clean and blanch the bean sprouts, drain them, and allow to cool.

Serving Place the shredded cabbage, lettuce, carrots, and radishes, the tomato quarters, and the bean sprouts in a large salad bowl. Add the impregnated oil with the salt, soya sauce, vinegar, and chilli oil. Toss well. Sprinkle with flavour powder, sesame oil, chives, and coriander; then serve.

Plain-Fried Spinach with Vegetarian Stock

Serves 6–8, with other vegetarian dishes

1¼ lb (600 g) spinach
3 tablespoons vegetarian stock (see page 96)
2 medium-sized onions
2 cloves garlic

4 tablespoons vegetable oil
1½ tablespoons lard
2 slices root ginger
½ teaspoon salt
1½ tablespoons soya sauce
1 tablespoon sherry
½ teaspoon flavour powder

Preparation Wash the spinach thoroughly, discarding all the coarse leaves and stems. Slice the onions thinly, and crush and chop the garlic.

Cooking Heat 4 tablespoons of oil in a large frying pan. Add the ginger, garlic, and onion, and stir-fry together for 2 minutes over a high heat. Remove the ginger, garlic, and onion. Add the spinach and stir-fry over a high heat for 2 minutes until it has been well-coated with oil. Add the salt, soya sauce, and vegetarian stock and stir-fry for a further minute. Sprinkle with sherry, lard, and flavour powder. Continue to stir-fry for another 30 seconds; serve and eat immediately.

Throughout the cooking, a high heat should be maintained. The glistening green of the resulting dish is one of the most appealing sights of Chinese vegetable cuisine.

Splash-Fried Bean Shoots

Serves 4–6, with other dishes

8 oz (200 g) bean shoots
1 oz (25 g) chives

oil for splash-frying
1 teaspoon salt
2 teaspoons sesame oil

The Complete Chinese Cookbook

This salad should be served hot. One of the best-known qualities of bean shoots is their crunchiness. Splash-frying is said to enhance this, but be very careful when using this method.

Preparation Select white bean shoots, all of about the same length. Lay them to an even depth, like a bed, on a wire basket. Clean and dry the chives thoroughly, and use a pair of scissors to cut them to about the same regular length as the bean shoots. Lay them down evenly on top of the bed of shoots.
Cooking Hold the wire basket over a pan of boiling oil, and use a large ladle to spoon the oil over the vegetables in the basket. Take your time when pouring the oil over; let it drain and drip through slowly. Spoon about 18 ladles of oil over the vegetables. After the last of the oil has drained through, pour the vegetables into a large, heat-proof glass or china bowl. Sprinkle with salt and sesame oil; then toss. This dish should be eaten while still very hot.

The interlacing of the green chives with the white bean shoots makes a most attractive colour combination.

Double-Fried Vegetarian Bamboo Shoots

Serves 6–8

1½ lb (600 g) fresh winter bamboo shoots (choose small ones)
2 tablespoons vegetarian stock (see page 96)
3 oz (75 g) red-in-snow
8 tablespoons oil
1 teaspoon brown sugar
1 tablespoon sherry
2 tablespoons soya sauce
¼ teaspoon flavour powder

This recipe uses red-in-snow, which is a type of Chinese pickle.

Preparation Clean the bamboo shoots and cut them slantwise into thin 1 inch (2½ cm) pieces, using only the inner, more tender parts. Chop the red-in-snow coarsely. Rinse them in hot water, and drain.
Cooking Heat 2 tablespoons oil in a frying pan, add the red-in-snow and stir-fry over a high heat for 2½–3 minutes until crispy. Remove the red-in-snow, drain, and put aside. Heat the remaining oil in a frying pan, add the bamboo shoots, and stir-fry gently over a medium heat for 2 minutes, until all the shoots are well-covered in hot oil. Simmer for a further 5 minutes, turning them over occasionally, until the shoots have turned golden-brown. Drain away all the oil, or as much of it as possible. Return the red-in-snow to the pan, with the brown sugar, sherry, soya sauce, flavour powder, and vegetarian stock. Turn the heat up to maximum, stir-fry quickly for 1 minute; then serve.

Vegetable and Vegetarian Dishes

This is a connoisseur's dish which should be served on a plain, but artistic bowl, such as a Sung piece (or imitation), rather than one from the Ming or Ching dynasties.

Sweet and Sour Chinese Celery Cabbage

Serves 4–6, with other dishes

1½ lb (600 g) Chinese celery cabbage *or* young celery *or* Savoy cabbage
1 dried chilli pepper
2 tablespoons vinegar
1 tablespoon soya sauce
2 tablespoons sherry
1½ tablespoons sugar
½ teaspoon flavour powder
3 tablespoons orange juice
1 tablespoon cornflour
3 tablespoons vegetable oil
4 tablespoons vegetarian stock (see page 96)
½ teaspoon salt

This is a vegetarian dish.

Preparation Remove the root and outer leaves from the cabbage. Cut the inner leaves crosswise into 1½ inch (3½ cm) pieces. Cut the pepper in two and discard the pips. Mix the vinegar, soya sauce, sherry, sugar, flavour powder, and orange juice in a bowl. Blend the cornflour with 3 tablespoons water and add to the mixture in the bowl.
Cooking Fry the pepper in the oil for 1 minute; then discard the pepper. Pour in the cabbage and stir-fry over a high heat for 2 minutes. Add the stock and salt. Reduce the heat to low and simmer for 5 minutes. Pour in the vinegar mixture. Stir-fry gently for 1–2 minutes, and serve in a deep dish or bowl.

Because of its sweet and sour quality, this is a good dish to serve with other rich foods. It is a favourite in Peking.

Red-Cooked Chinese Celery Cabbage

Serves 4–10, with other vegetarian dishes

2½–3 lb (about 1¼ kg) Chinese celery cabbage *or* young celery *or* Savoy cabbage
3 Chinese dried mushrooms
2½ tablespoons soya sauce
2 teaspoons sugar
½ teaspoon salt
3 tablespoons sherry
1 teaspoon flavour powder
4 tablespoons vegetarian stock (see page 96)
1 dried chilli pepper
2 spring onion stalks
4 tablespoons vegetable oil

The Complete Chinese Cookbook

This is a vegetarian dish. Although cabbage is a common vegetable, this dish, made by the common people, is one of the most highly-prized home-cooked dishes from Peking.

Preparation Soak the dried mushrooms; then shred them. Remove the coarser outer leaves from the cabbage. Cut the inner leaves crosswise into 1½ inch (3½ cm) pieces. Wash, drain, and dry well. Mix the soya sauce, sugar, salt, and sherry in a bowl. In another bowl, blend the flavour powder with the vegetarian stock. Chop the chilli pepper into four pieces, removing the seeds. Chop the spring onions into 1 inch (2½ cm) pieces.

Cooking Put the oil in a large frying pan over a medium heat. Stir-fry the pepper and onions in it for 1¼ minutes, then discard the pepper. Add the cabbage and mushrooms, and stir-fry over a medium heat for 5 minutes. Pour in the soya sauce mixture and stir-fry gently for 1 minute. Reduce the heat, and simmer gently for 10 minutes, turning the cabbage over a couple of times. Add the vegetarian stock mixture. Stir and turn over a few times more, allowing the gravy to thicken. Serve in a large bowl.

This is a dish which one does not tire of eating day after day.

Silk-Thread Bamboo Shoots in Cream of Chicken

Serves 4–8, with other dishes

1½ lb (600 g) fresh bamboo shoots *or* canned shoots
3 oz (75 g) chicken breast meat
½ pint (250 ml) chicken stock
1 oz (25 g) ham
1 oz (25 g) pork fat
2 egg whites
1 tablespoon cornflour
¼ teaspoon flavour powder
1 teaspoon salt
1 tablespoon lard

This is a non-vegetarian dish.

Preparation Remove the outer leaves and coarser parts of the bamboo shoots. Using only the more tender parts, slice them into very fine matchstick strips. Chop the ham into fine pieces. Mince the chicken meat and pork fat together twice. Beat the egg whites in a basin for 15 seconds. Add the cornflour, flavour powder, half of the salt, and half of the stock. Beat together for 15 seconds. Add the minced chicken and pork to the egg and cornflour mixture. Stir and beat until thoroughly blended.

Cooking Heat the remainder of the chicken stock in a saucepan. Add the bamboo shoots and cook over a medium heat until practically dry. Immediately add the lard and the remaining salt, and stir-fry gently for 1¼ minutes, until all the strips of bamboo shoot are well-covered with oil. Pour the egg and minced meat mixture into the saucepan. Stir-fry gently for 2¼

Vegetable and Vegetarian Dishes

minutes. Serve on a well-heated plate, garnished with chopped ham or Fukien meat wool, if available.

Fu-Yung Cauliflower

Serves 4–8, with other dishes

1 medium cauliflower
3 oz (75 g) chicken breast meat
2 egg whites
1 tablespoon cornflour
½ teaspoon flavour powder
1½ teaspoons salt
¼ pint (125 ml) chicken stock
2 tablespoons vegetable oil

This is a non-vegetarian dish. When minced chicken, egg white, and cornflour are mixed together, the resulting highly savoury, white, creamy mixture is called 'Fu-Yung' in north China. It is used extensively for cooking with various vegetables, including cauliflower.

Preparation Remove the root of the cauliflower and break it into small individual branches. Blanch them by dipping into boiling water for 5 minutes, drain, and put aside. Mince the chicken meat and mix it in a basin with the egg whites, cornflour, flavour powder, half of the salt, and the chicken stock. Blend together into a smooth mixture.

Cooking Heat the oil in a frying pan. Add the pieces of cauliflower and sprinkle with the remaining salt, stir-fry gently for 2 minutes and remove from the pan. Pour the minced chicken and egg white mixture into the pan. Mix and stir-fry for 2–3 minutes over a medium heat. As soon as the liquid thickens into a white sauce, return the cauliflower to the pan and stir-fry gently for a further 2 minutes. Serve on a well-heated dish, garnished with chopped ham.

Salt Beef with Heart of Spring Greens or Cabbage

Serves 4–8, with other dishes

6 oz (150 g) salt beef
1⅓ lb (600 g) spring greens *or* cabbage
2 tablespoons vegetable oil
6 tablespoons superior stock *or*
chicken stock
1 tablespoon soya sauce
1 teaspoon sugar
dash of pepper
½ teaspoon flavour powder
1 tablespoon lard

This is a non-vegetarian dish.

Preparation Cut the beef into very thin strips 1½ inches (3½ cm) long and ⅓ inch (1 cm) wide. Remove the root and outer leaves of the vegetable. Cut the hearts crosswise into 2 × 1½ inch (5 × 3½ cm) pieces. Blanch them by

The Complete Chinese Cookbook

dipping in boiling water for 2 minutes; then drain.
Cooking Heat the oil in a saucepan. Add the greens or cabbage and stir-fry over a high heat for 1 minute. Add the beef and stock. Sprinkle with soya sauce, sugar, pepper, and flavour powder. Stir-fry gently over a medium heat for 4 minutes. Add the lard, and continue to mix and stir-fry for 30 seconds; then serve.

Although a simple dish, this appeals to the common people and to connoisseurs alike. If greens are used, they will have a glistening appearance because of the short period of cooking and the amount of oil used.

Vegetarian Spring Rolls

Serves 6

- 1 oz (25 g) wood ears
- 4 Chinese dried mushrooms
- 2 cakes of bean curd
- 1 teaspoon bean curd cheese
- ½ teaspoon salt
- ½ tablespoon hoisin sauce
- 2 oz (50 g) bamboo shoots

Make the Vegetarian Spring Roll skins according to the instructions given in the recipes for egg roll or spring roll skins on pages 269 and 270. Alternatively, they can usually be bought nowadays from Chinese provision stores. The instructions given below are for the filling.

Preparation Soak the wood ears for 1 hour and rinse them in two changes of water. Soak the dried mushrooms for 30 minutes; then remove the stalks and shred the tops. Chop the bean curd into small pieces. Mash together the bean curd, bean curd cheese, salt, hoisin sauce, mushrooms, bamboo shoots, and wood ears. Use this mixture as a filling for the spring roll skins, rolling and sealing them in the manner described on page 270.
Cooking When the spring rolls are sealed, place them in a wire basket and deep-fry for 2 minutes over a high heat, followed by 2 minutes over a medium heat. They are usually served as snacks.

Pan-Fried Stuffed Cucumber

Serves 4–6, with other dishes

- 1 large cucumber
- 3 oz (75 g) belly of pork
- 3 oz (75 g) chicken breast meat
- 2 oz (50 g) peeled prawns *or* shrimps
- 1½ teaspoons salt
- 1 egg white
- 1 tablespoon white wine
- 1½ tablespoons cornflour
- 4 tablespoons vegetable oil
- ¼ pint (160 ml) chicken stock
- 4 tablespoons top of the milk
- ½ teaspoon flavour powder

Vegetable and Vegetarian Dishes

Preparation Cut the ends off the cucumber, and slice the middle part into 1 inch (2½ cm) segments. Scoop out ½ inch (1 cm) of each segment. Mince the pork, chicken, and prawns or shrimps, and mix them in a basin with 1 teaspoon salt, egg white, white wine, and ½ tablespoon cornflour. Blend into a smooth paste. Stuff 1 tablespoon of the paste into the excavated part of each piece of cucumber.

Cooking Heat the oil in a large, flat frying pan, ensuring that it is spread evenly over the surface. When it is hot, place all the pieces of cucumber, paste-side down, in the pan and fry for 4 minutes over a medium heat. Turn them over and fry the other side for 1 minute. Use a fish-slice to remove the pieces of stuffed cucumber from the pan. Arrange them on a well-heated serving plate. Heat the chicken stock in a small saucepan. Add the remaining salt, the remaining cornflour, blended with the milk, and the flavour powder. Stir until the liquid boils and thickens into a sauce. Pour this white sauce over the stuffed cucumbers, and serve.

Pork

猪 肉

Pork is even more important to the Chinese than beef is to the British. This is principally because of the greater versatility of pork – there is an almost inexhaustible number of ways in which it can be prepared in China.

Hence, while all other types of meat have to have the name of the animal affixed to them – such as bullock-meat (beef), sheep-meat (lamb or mutton), goat-meat, and deer-meat (venison) – pork is often just referred to as 'meat'. The amount of pork eaten in China probably outweighs all other meats several times over.

Because of the neutrality in the taste and flavour of pork, which is not unlike chicken (as opposed to the much stronger taste of lamb, beef, and venison), it can be successfully combined with an almost unlimited range of other materials and foodstuffs, whether they be vegetables, seafoods, other meats, or various salted or pickled ingredients. Hence, apart from being cooked whole, pork is often cooked diced into cubes, cut into thin slices, shredded into threads, or minced finely and made into cakes or balls. In all these latter forms (except the cakes and balls) the meat is usually cooked instantaneously by stir-frying – a process which is economical both in time and fuel consumption. With our Chinese propensity towards cross-cooking and cross-blending, and our natural sense of economy, the avenues which are opened to us here are many and inviting indeed.

Red-Cooked Leg of Pork

Serves 8–10, with other dishes

4–5 lb (1¾–2¼ kg) leg of pork
1 teaspoon salt
6 tablespoons soya sauce
6 tablespoons sherry
1 tablespoon sugar

Pork

Red-cooking usually means stewing with soya sauce at a slow simmer, with the addition of such ingredients and flavourers as sugar, ginger, sherry, and star anise. It is one of the simplest as well as one of the most effective ways of cooking meat, with almost foolproof results. So long as the heat is kept low during the slow-simmering (the placing of an asbestos sheet underneath the pan is recommended), one can hardly go wrong. There are so many ways and so many parts of the pig which can be red-cooked.

Preparation Score the skin of the leg of pork by cutting several slashes along both sides.

Cooking Choose a heavy saucepan, heat-proof casserole, or iron pot. Pour in 5–6 pints (3 litres) of water and bring to the boil. Place the leg of pork in the water and boil for 7–8 minutes; then pour away all of the water. Sprinkle the pork with salt, half of the soya sauce, and half of the sherry. Pour in ¼ pint (125 ml) water, down the side of the pan. Insert an asbestos sheet under the pan, or put the casserole into an oven preheated to 350°F (180°C or Gas Mark 4). Keep the liquid at a slow simmer for 1 hour. Turn the pork over once and baste it with the liquid at the bottom of the pan.

Sprinkle the pork with the remainder of the soya sauce and sherry; then add the sugar, with 6 tablespoons water, and continue to cook at a low simmer. Turn the meat over after 15 minutes, and then twice, each time after a 30 minute interval. Baste the pork with the gravy in the pan every time it is turned over.

Serving Carve and serve in thick oblong slices, 1½ × 2 inches (3½ × 5 cm). Alternatively, carve and serve in large, thin slices measuring 2 × 3 inches (5 × 7½ cm). In each case, leave the skin attached to the slices of pork.

Pork cooked in this manner is usually extremely tender and rich. Although the meat is white, the skin and outside of the pork should be brownish red, and almost jelly-like in tenderness. The gravy from pork cooked in this way is almost the tastiest thing in the whole repertoire of Chinese cooking, and is absolutely heavenly to eat with rice.

Red-Cooked Pork in Pieces

Serves 6–8

3–3½ lb (1¼–1½ kg) streaky pork (lean belly of pork)
2 spring onion stalks
2 slices root ginger
½ teaspoon salt
5 tablespoons soya sauce
4 tablespoons sherry
½ tablespoon sugar

Preparation Slice the pork through the skin into 2–3 inch (5–7½ cm) long pieces, making sure that each piece has about 1 square inch (2½ sq cm) of skin attached on the top, and that each piece is composed of alternate layers of lean and fat. Cut the spring onions into 1 inch (2½ cm) segments, and shred the ginger. Rub the pork with salt and 2 tablespoons of the soya sauce. Place in a heavy pan or casserole, skin side down, then pour in 6-8 tablespoons of water and half of the sherry. Sprinkle with the ginger and spring onions.

Cooking Bring the contents of the pan to the boil, insert an asbestos sheet beneath the pan, and reduce the heat to a low simmer. Simmer for 45 minutes, turning the pieces of pork once. Add another 6-8 tablespoons water. Sprinkle the pork with the remainder of the sherry, sugar, and finally the soya sauce. Cover and allow the pork to simmer for a further hour, turning the pieces of meat over every 20 minutes.

Serving After a total of 1¾ hours cooking, the pork and skin should be sufficiently tender to serve in a bowl or deep dish. It should be served skin side up. This is a favourite dish for a family meal.

Pork of Original Preciousness

Serves 6-8

3 lb (1¼ kg) streaky belly of pork, with skin attached
½ teaspoon salt
1 tablespoon soya paste
4 tablespoons soya sauce
3 tablespoons sherry
1 teaspoon red bean cheese
½ tablespoon brown sugar
2 slices root ginger
2 large onions
vegetable oil for deep-frying
3 eggs
¼ pint (125 ml) soya sauce

Preparation Boil the pork in water for 15 minutes. Drain away the water; then paint both sides of the piece of pork with a mixture of salt, soya paste, and 1 tablespoon of the soya sauce. Blend together the remainder of the soya sauce, the sherry, bean cheese, and sugar. Shred the ginger, and slice the onions very thinly.

Cooking Heat the oil until it is about to smoke. Fry the pork in it for 5-6 minutes. Remove from the oil and leave to cool. When cool, cut into fairly thick slices, 1 × 2 inch (2½ × 5 cm) each with some skin attached. Arrange the pork in a heat-proof dish, skin side down. Spoon half of the soya/sherry mixture over the pork, scatter the onion and ginger over, and then sprinkle with the remaining soya mixture. Cover the dish securely with the lid or tinfoil; then place in a steamer and steam for 1¼ hours. While the pork is steaming, hard-boil the eggs, shell them, and simmer them in ¼ pint (125 ml) soya sauce for 5 minutes. They will take on a brown colouring. Five minutes before serving, cut the eggs in half and arrange them on the slices of pork in the heat-proof dish. Steam for a further 3 minutes; then serve from the heat-proof dish.

Red-Cooked Round Knuckle of Pork with Spinach

Serves 6–8, with other dishes

3 lb (1¼ kg) large knuckle-end of pork with skin
1 lb (400 g) fresh spinach
½ teaspoon salt
5 tablespoons soya sauce
3 spring onion stalks
2 cloves garlic
2 slices root ginger
1 teaspoon soya bean cheese
4 tablespoons vegetable oil
2 tablespoons sherry
1 tablespoon sugar

Preparation Clean the skin of the pork and remove any hairs. Cut the knuckle-end open half-way lengthwise and remove the bone. Rub the pork with salt and 2 tablespoons of the soya sauce. Cut the spring onions into 1 inch (2½ cm) segments. Crush the garlic, and shred the ginger. Mix them in a basin with the soya bean cheese. Wash the spinach thoroughly, and drain.

Cooking Heat the oil in a frying pan. Turn and fry the knuckle in it for 5–6 minutes, until brown; then stuff the cavity with spring onions and the garlic/ginger mixture. Sit the knuckle vertically in a round pot or deep heat-proof dish or casserole. Add the remaining soya sauce, sherry, sugar, and whatever is left of the sauce at the bottom of the frying pan. Pour in sufficient boiling water to cover the meat. Cover the dish securely with a lid or tinfoil and place in an oven preheated to 400°F (205°C or Gas Mark 6) for 15 minutes. Reduce the heat to 350°F (180°C or Gas Mark 4), and simmer very gently for 3 hours, turning the knuckle over four times. It should finish with the smaller end pointing up. Five minutes before serving, pour 6–8 tablespoons of oil and gravy from the heat-proof dish into a large saucepan. Turn the heat up to full and when the liquid boils vigorously, add the spinach. Stir-fry for 4–5 minutes until well-cooked and glistening.

Serving Place the knuckle in a serving bowl or deep dish and arrange the spinach around it. Pour the remaining gravy over the knuckle. This small, brown mountain of glistening pork surrounded by a field of dark green is always one of the most appealing sights on a Chinese dinner table.

Red-Cooked Pork with Chestnuts

Serves 6–8

Preparation Repeat the recipe for Red-Cooked Pork in Pieces (see page 107), but with the addition of about 1 lb (400 g) shelled chestnuts. Skin the chestnuts and boil them for 15 minutes. Add them to the pan during the last 45 minutes of the simmering, with an additional 2 tablespoons of soya sauce. Use the chestnuts as a base or bed for the pork when serving.

Red-Cooked Pork with Bamboo Shoots

Serves 6-8

Preparation Repeat the recipe for Red-Cooked Pork in Pieces (see page 107), but with the addition of 8-12 oz (200-300 g) bamboo shoots. If you use canned bamboo shoots, drain away all the liquid. Cut the bamboo shoots into triangular wedges, similar in size to the pieces of pork, and add them to the pan during the last 45 minutes of simmering.

Red-Cooked Pork with Carrots

Serves 6-8

Preparation Repeat the recipe for Red-Cooked Pork in Pieces (see page 107) with the addition of 12 oz (300 g) well-scrubbed carrots. Cut them slantwise into triangular wedges about $1\frac{1}{2}$ inches ($3\frac{1}{2}$ cm) long. Add them to the pan during the last hour of simmering.

Red-Cooked Pork with Dried Squid and Golden Needles

Serves 6-8

Dried squid is used widely in Chinese cooking, particularly in red-cooked dishes, to flavour meat. It has a half-cheesy, half-smoked flavour. Golden needles are also a very typical Chinese dried vegetable ingredient, and are used in a wide number of dishes – both meat and vegetable. Appreciation of their taste, which can only be described as mouldy, is entirely acquired, and they generally have no appeal to the Western palate. They are regarded by the Chinese as an essential and traditional ingredient for many dishes.

Preparation Both golden needles and dried salted squid should be soaked in warm water for 45 minutes, before being added to the pork for the last 45 minutes simmering. Repeat the recipe for Red-Cooked Pork in Pieces (see page 107), with 3 oz (75 g) golden needles, and 4 oz (100 g) dried squid. They will produce a flavour and savouriness which are unique, and which are capable of inducing near-addiction if indulged in for any period of time, especially when eaten with quantities of rice and gravy.

Pork

White-Cooked Sliced Pork

Serves 8–10

3 lb (1¼ kg) streaky pork (belly or leg)
1 tablespoon salt
4 slices root ginger

Cooking Bring 4 pints (generous 2 litres) water to the boil in a heavy saucepan or casserole. Place the pork in the boiling water; add the salt and ginger. Cover the pan, insert an asbestos sheet under it, and simmer gently for 45 minutes. Remove the pork from the pan (reserve the stock for other uses) and cool for 2–3 hours. When cold, cut the meat into thin slices measuring 2 × 3 inches (5 × 7½ cm).
Serving Arrange the slices in tile-piece fashion, and serve with various table dips:
Soya sauce, soya paste, mustard powder, chilli oil, sesame oil, chopped chives (or spring onions), shredded root ginger, crushed and chopped garlic, vinegar, and sherry.

Barbecued Pork (Cantonese Roast Pork)

Serves 10–12, with other dishes

4 lb (1¾ kg) lean pork
2 teaspoons salt
¼ teaspoon freshly milled pepper
¼ teaspoon five spice powder
3 tablespoons vegetable oil
2 tablespoons soya sauce
1 tablespoon hoisin sauce
2 tablespoons sherry
1 tablespoon honey
½ teaspoon flavour powder

This dish is easily cooked, and should appeal to Westerners.

Preparation Slice the pork along the grain into 5 × 2 inch (12½ × 5 cm) strips. Sprinkle and rub with salt, pepper, and five spice powder; season for 2 hours.
Cooking Mix the oil, soya sauce, hoisin sauce, sherry, honey, and flavour powder until well-blended, and heat in a frying pan. Add the strips of pork and turn in the sauce until they take on a thick, glossy, brown coating. Preheat the oven to 400°F (205°C or Gas Mark 6). Place the strips of pork on a rack, and roast for 10 minutes then turn meat once more in marinade. Lower the heat to 350°F (180°C or Gas Mark 4) and roast for a further 10 minutes.
Serving Slice the pork across the grain (that is, across the strips) into ¼–⅓ inch (½ cm) thick slices and arrange tile-piece fashion in four rows on a serving dish.

Although often called Barbecued Pork, it is in fact the Cantonese version of Roast Pork, and is more popular in Canton than anywhere else. In Chinese restaurants abroad, it is often served with a sauce which rather spoils the effect of the tender roast pork inside a rich brown savoury crust.

Tip Out Steamed Pork

Serves 10–12, with other dishes

4 lb (1¾ kg) streaky pork (belly)
1 teaspoon salt
4 tablespoons soya sauce
oil for semi deep-fry
1 large onion
3 oz (75 g) red-in-snow pickled greens
½ tablespoon sugar
1 tablespoon hoisin sauce
3 tablespoons sherry
½ teaspoon flavour powder
¼ pint (125 ml) superior stock

Tip Out Pork is one of the basic ways in which pork is cooked in China. It is very similar to the way in which many Western puddings are made – prepared and cooked in a greased basin, and then tipped out into a dish, before being covered with custard or syrup. In this case pork is cut with the skin attached, and steamed, skin side down, in a heat-proof basin, with a number of supplementary and flavouring ingredients. When ready, the pork is tipped out like a pudding with the skin side facing up. The jelly-like skin is delicious to eat, and is the major attraction of the dish. The pork is usually boiled and fried shortly before being packed into the basin for steaming. There are many variations of this method. The following recipe is one of the most basic. In Szechuan, the dish is hotted up by some chilli pepper or oil during the steaming.

Preparation Boil the pork in one piece in boiling water for 15 minutes. Drain, and rub with salt and 2 tablespoons of the soya sauce; then heat the oil in a pan, and fry the pork, turning it over, for 6–8 minutes over medium heat. Drain; cool; then cut the pork into 2 × 1 inch (5 × 2½ cm) chunks, making sure that each piece has some skin attached. Slice the onions thinly, and shred the pickled greens.

Cooking Arrange the pork, skin side down, at the bottom of a basin, or heat-proof dish. Add the sugar, hoisin sauce, sherry, pickled greens, onion, flavour powder, and remaining soya sauce to the stock, and heat, stirring until well-blended. Pour the mixture evenly over the pork in the basin, then place the dish in a steamer and steam for 1¼ hours. Turn the basin over into a deep serving dish, so that the meat will stand like a small meat pudding with the skin side on top. It is for this reason the dish came to be called 'tip out meat'.

Note In China, it is often the practice to place potato, turnip, bean curd cakes, transparent noodles, and chopped, salted vegetables on top of the meat during steaming. When the contents are tipped out, these materials become the base of the pork, and help to absorb the gravy.

Pork

Kweichow 'Salt and Sour' Tip Out Pork

Serves 8–10, with other dishes

3½–4 lb (1½–1¾ kg) streaky pork (belly)
2 slices root ginger
2 oz (50 g) hot Szechuan pickled greens
2 oz (50 g) sweet chutney
oil for deep-frying
2 tablespoons soya sauce
2 tablespoons vinegar
1 tablespoon sugar
2 tablespoons sherry
2 teaspoons salt

This dish is a variation of Tip Out Steamed Pork. Kweichow is a western province, where dishes are often hot, salty, and sour – straightforward basic qualities of food for the poor, which nowadays often appeal to jaded and sophisticated palates.

Preparation Shred ginger and chop Szechuan pickled greens and chutney into small pieces.

Cooking Boil the piece of pork in water for 5–6 minutes; drain. Deep-fry for 5–6 minutes; then drain, and cut with a sharp knife into 2 × 1½ × 1 inch (5 × 3½ × 2½ cm) pieces, each with skin attached. Place ginger in a basin with soya sauce, vinegar, half of the sugar, and sherry. Place the Szechuan pickle and chutney in a separate basin. Pack the pieces of pork, skin side down, in a heat-proof dish. Sprinkle with salt, and the remaining sugar, and pour the soya/vinegar/sherry mixture evenly over the pork. Arrange the chutney and pickle on top of the pork. Place the basin in a steamer, cover with tinfoil, and steam for 1½ hours. Tip out, and serve as Tip Out Steamed Pork.

Diced Pork Cubes Quick-Fried with Soya Paste

Serves 6–8, with other dishes

2 lb (1 kg) fillet of pork
2½ tablespoons soya paste
1 egg
1½ tablespoons cornflour
2 slices root ginger
1 small onion
6 tablespoons oil for frying
2 teaspoons sugar
1 tablespoon sherry

The texture and quality of pork meat are not unlike those of chicken. Consequently, it is often cooked in the same way – in this case, with soya paste. The only difference is that the time taken for cooking pork must be longer. This dish, which is very economical both in ingredients and fuel, makes a highly savoury meal.

Preparation Soak the pork in water and refrigerate for 30 minutes; then cut into ½ inch (1 cm) cubes. Beat half of the egg in a basin, add the pork cubes, mix with the egg, then sprinkle with cornflour. Shred the ginger, and chop the onion.

Cooking Heat the oil in a frying pan. When it is very hot, add the pork cubes, stir-fry for 4–5 minutes; then drain. Heat 2 tablespoons oil in a separate frying pan over medium heat. Add the ginger and onion, and stir-fry for 1½ minutes at the centre of the pan. Add the soya paste and stir it with the oil, ginger, and onion for 1 minute, before adding the sugar and sherry. Stir them together with the other ingredients for 8–10 seconds, pour in the pork cubes, turn the heat to high, and scramble the pork with the other ingredients for 1½ minutes before serving in a well-heated dish.

Note If soya paste is unavailable, mix 4 tablespoons soya sauce with 1 tablespoon tomato purée, 1 tablespoon blackcurrant jam, and 1 tablespoon apple sauce. Heat and stir over a gentle heat until the mixture is reduced by about one third.

Sweet and Sour Pork

Serves 6–8, with other dishes

2–2½ lb (1–1¼ kg) streaky pork
1 teaspoon salt
1 egg
1¼ tablespoons cornflour
1 medium-sized onion
1 medium-sized green or red sweet pepper
1½ tablespoons soya paste
½ tablespoon soya sauce
oil for deep-frying

Sauce
1 tablespoon cornflour
6 tablespoons water
1 oz (25 g) sweet chutney
1½ teaspoons sugar
1½ tablespoons vinegar
1½ tablespoons soya sauce
1 tablespoon tomato purée
1½ tablespoons orange juice
1½ tablespoons sherry

Preparation Remove the skin from the pork and dice into ¾ inch (1½ cm) cubes; then sprinkle and rub with salt. Beat the egg lightly and add to the pork. When the meat is thoroughly wet, dredge with flour. Slice the onion very thinly; cut the sweet pepper into thick slices, and then cut these slant-wise into approximately 1 × ½ inch (2½ × 1 cm) pieces. Mix the soya paste with the soya sauce. For the sauce, blend the cornflour with half of the water, then mix in rest of ingredients.

Pork

Cooking Either deep-dry the pork or use 6 tablespoons oil and semi-deep-fry it in a frying pan for 5-6 minutes, by stir-frying it over a high heat. Drain thoroughly and place the meat in a basin. Add the soya sauce/paste mixture; mix and marinate the pork for a few minutes. Drain the excess oil from the frying pan, and use the remaining oil to stir-fry the onion for 1 minute over medium heat; then add the sliced sweet pepper and stir-fry for another minute. Add the pork, and stir and toss for 2 minutes. Pour in the sauce mixture; then turn pork and pepper in the sauce gently until the liquid thickens (this should take 10-15 seconds) and gives a translucent, glistening coating to the pieces of pork.

The contrast between the sweet and sour coating and the salty savouriness of the pork inside gives the dish its special appeal.

Twice-Cooked Pork

Serves 6-8, with other dishes

3 lb (1¼ kg) streaky pork (belly)
3 cloves garlic
2 slices root ginger
1 tablespoon salted black beans
3 spring onion stalks
1½ tablespoons soya sauce
1½ tablespoons soya paste
1½ tablespoons tomato purée
2 teaspoons sugar
2 tablespoons sherry
1 teaspoon chilli oil (*or* 2 teaspoons tabasco chilli sauce)
3 tablespoons vegetable oil

Although this dish comes from the western province of Szechuan, it is popular throughout China.

Preparation Crush and chop the garlic, shred the ginger, and soak the black beans in water for 25 minutes, then drain. Cut the spring onions into 1 inch (2½ cm) segments. Mix the soya sauce, soya paste, tomato purée, sugar, sherry, and chilli oil until well-blended.

Cooking Place the pork in boiling water and simmer for 35 minutes. Drain thoroughly. When cool, cut it across the lean and fat into pieces ¼ inch (½ cm) thick, 2 inches (5 cm) broad, and 2 inches (5 cm) long. Heat the oil in a frying pan for 1 minute. Add the black beans; stir-fry for ½ minute. Add the soya/tomato/sherry/sugar/chilli mixture, and mix well with the oil and other ingredients into a sauce-paste. Finally, add the pieces of pork and spring onions. Turn the pork in the sauce-paste for 2-3 minutes until every piece is covered, and serve on a well-heated dish.

The Complete Chinese Cookbook
Tung-Po Pork

Serves 6–8, with other dishes

3 lb (1¼ kg) pork belly (with at least 3 layers each of lean and fat, and with skin attached)
4 tablespoons soya sauce
1½ tablespoons brown sugar
4 tablespoons sherry
3 medium-sized onions
6 tablespoons superior stock

This recipe is attributed to the Chinese classical romantic poet, Soo Tung-Po. Although it is not very different from other red-cooked dishes, it deserves a separate mention because of its fame and universal popularity.

Preparation Boil the pork for 10 minutes, and cut it through the skin into four pieces of equal size. Marinate the meat in a mixture of soya sauce, sugar, and sherry for 2 hours, turning the pieces over four times. Cut the onions into thick slices.

Cooking Arrange the pieces of pork in a casserole, skin side down. Pour any remaining marinade over the meat, place the ginger and onion on top, then add the stock. Cover, and place the casserole in an oven preheated to 400°F (205°C or Gas Mark 6) and cook for 15 minutes; then reduce the temperature to 350°F (180°C or Gas Mark 4) and cook the pork for 2 hours. Open the lid of the casserole, and transfer the pork to a heat-proof dish. Arrange three pieces at the bottom of the dish, skin side down, and the fourth piece on top with the skin side up. Remove the ginger and onion, skim the excess fat from the gravy and pour it over the pork. Cover securely with the lid or tinfoil, and steam the pork vigorously for 10–15 minutes before bringing the dish to the table to serve.

The enjoyment of this dish lies in the appreciation of the jelly-like texture of the skin and fat, and the tenderness of the lean meat. This is perhaps a connoisseur's taste, but essential to the full enjoyment of a Chinese meal with rice.

Chinese Pork Escalope

Serves 6–8, with other dishes

3 lb (1¼ kg) pork belly (with at least 3 layers of lean and fat, and skin)
4 tablespoons soya sauce
3 tablespoons sherry
1½ tablespoons brown sugar
½ tablespoon bay leaves
5 oz (125 g) carrots
5 oz (125 g) radishes
2 teaspoons salt
1 tablespoon sugar
1½ tablespoons vinegar
1 tablespoon sesame oil
2 duck eggs
4 oz (100 g) breadcrumbs
oil for deep-frying

Pork

From Amoy

In the province of Fukien where Amoy is situated, there is a well-known feast called the Whole Pig Banquet, in which a whole pig is used to make 108 dishes. This is one of them.

Preparation Boil the pork for 7–8 minutes; then drain. Cut through the skin into strips of approximately 3 oz (75 g) each, making sure that each has lean, fat, and skin. Marinate strips in a mixture of soya sauce, sherry, brown sugar, and bay leaves for 1½ hours, turning the meat over three times. Shred the carrots and radishes into a colander and rub salt into them. After 10 minutes, rinse them in running water. Drain, then dry on paper towels, and place in a basin. Sprinkle with sugar, vinegar, and sesame oil, and toss them together as a salad.

Cooking Place the bowl of marinated pork in a steamer and steam for 45 minutes. Remove and cool. When the pork is quite cold and solid, break the eggs into a basin, beat lightly, and then wet each piece of pork with the beaten egg. Dredge the pieces of meat in breadcrumbs until completely covered. Heat the oil in a deep-fryer and deep-fry the pork – three or four pieces at a time – for about 3½ minutes each, until golden brown. Cut each piece of pork vertically down through the skin into three slices (each piece a little bigger than a mahjong piece).

Serving Pile the shredded vegetables in the middle of a round dish, and surround them with the breadcrumb-encrusted pieces of pork.

Red-Simmered Pork with Bean Curd Cheese

Serves 6–8, with other dishes

- 1½ lb (¾ kg) lean leg of pork
- 1½ lb (¾ kg) belly of pork
- 1½ tablespoons red bean curd cheese
- 2 cloves garlic
- 3 tablespoons sherry
- 1 tablespoon soya sauce
- 1 tablespoon sugar
- 4 tablespoons vegetable oil
- ½ pint (250 ml) superior *or* secondary stock
- 2 teaspoons sesame oil
- ¼ teaspoon flavour powder

Preparation Cut the pork into 1½ inch (3½ cm) cubes. Crush the garlic; mash the cheese and blend with the sherry, soya sauce, and sugar.

Cooking Heat the oil in a heavy saucepan or casserole. Add the garlic, and stir-fry for 15 seconds. Add the pork, turn the heat to maximum, and stir-fry the meat for 4–5 minutes until it starts to brown. Pour out any excess fat, and pour in the cheese/sherry/soya/sugar mixture. Stir the pieces of pork in this for 1½ minutes, and pour in the stock. When it comes to the boil, cover, place an asbestos sheet under the pan, and simmer very gently for 1½ hours. Stir sesame oil and flavour powder into the gravy; then serve.

This is another dish suitable for serving with rice. It derives its distinction from the special flavour of the bean curd cheese.

Red-Braised Pork Chops

Serves 6–8

6 pork chops
2 medium-sized onions
3 spring onion stalks
2 cloves garlic
3 slices ginger
4 tablespoons soya sauce
3 tablespoons sherry
3 teaspoons sugar
pepper to taste
6 tablespoons vegetable oil
6 tablespoons superior *or* secondary stock
1½ tablespoons hoisin sauce

Preparation Slice the onions thinly and cut the spring onions into 2 inch (5 cm) segments. Crush the garlic and shred the ginger. Cut the bones out of the chops, and cut the meat into pieces 1½ inches (3½ cm) square. Sprinkle with garlic, ginger, onion, soya sauce, sherry, sugar, and pepper. Rub them into the pork, and leave to marinate for 1 hour, turning the meat over twice. Pour the remaining marinade into a bowl.
Cooking Heat the oil in a frying pan with a lid over a high heat. Fry the pieces of pork for approximately 3½–4 minutes on either side, until they begin to brown. Pour away any excess oil. Add all the marinating ingredients, the remaining marinade, and 6 tablespoons of stock; place the lid securely on the pan, and simmer for 15 minutes, turning the meat pieces over a few times – the liquid should be reduced to less than half. Scatter the spring onion segments over the pork, pour in the hoisin sauce, turn the heat to high, and stir-fry quickly for 1 minute more.

This dish should be served very hot on a bed of rice.

Crispy Skin Roast Pork

Serves 6–8

3 lb (1¼ kg) shoulder of pork (with skin attached)
2 teaspoons salt
¼ teaspoon five spice powder
1 tablespoon soya sauce
1 tablespoon honey

Crispy Skin Roast Pork and Cantonese Barbecued Roast Pork (or Cha Shao Roast Pork) are the two most popular roast pork dishes sometimes available

Pork

in Chinese restaurants abroad. The most distinctive quality of Crispy Skin Roast Pork is the unusually crispy skin. With an oven in almost every modern cooker, it is more convenient to roast meat in Western kitchens than in China, where ovens are found in only the largest restaurants, and much technique has to go into the building and control of the fire, which is usually fuelled with firewood or charcoal. Pork with crackling skin is particularly appealing to rice eaters who are sensitive to the blending in the mouth of the soft blandness of the rice with the rich, crackling, aromatic qualities of the pork and its skin. These characteristics should be equally attractive to Westerners.

Preparation Score the skin crosswise at 1 inch (2½ cm) intervals with a sharp knife. Pierce the meat side (as opposed to the skin side) with a fork, also at 1 inch (2½ cm) intervals. Mix the salt with the five spice powder and rub evenly into the meat and skin. Allow the pork to stand for 2 hours. Mix the soya sauce, honey, and 1 tablespoon warm water until well-blended.

Cooking Preheat the oven to 400°F (205°C or Gas Mark 6). Place pork in a roasting pan, meat side up, with skin side sitting in about ¾ inch (1½ cm) water. Roast for 30 minutes, then remove from oven and dry the skin of the pork thoroughly with paper towelling. Allow to stand and dry for 30 minutes, then rub the skin with the soya/honey mixture. Lower the oven temperature to 375°F (190°C or Gas Mark 5) and roast for 1 hour, starting with the skin side up, and turning the meat over twice.

Note Skin may be rubbed or brushed with 2 teaspoons sesame oil after first 30 minutes roasting.

Spare Ribs

It may be that Western people are just beginning to appreciate their own saying – 'the nearer the bone, the sweeter the meat' – and are coming to appreciate spare ribs. In China, spare ribs have always been cooked since time immemorial. But there is a difference between the spare ribs cooked and served in China and those which have become so popular in the West. In China, spare ribs are normally chopped into 1 inch (2½ cm) lengths, so that the cooked pieces can be put into the mouth, and the meat stripped from the bone by a skilled manipulation of the tongue and teeth in an almost unconscious action – an involuntary movement which all Chinese acquire from infancy even before they have lost their milk teeth. Since this skill is lacking in the West, we often find the so-called spare ribs are full length bones which are not chopped at all and have to be eaten with the aid of fingers.

What we Chinese call 'spare ribs' are the rib bones from the rib back of the flank (i.e. the backing to the belly of the pork), and not the loin cutlet which British butchers often call spare ribs. They are usually an inexpensive cut, and are generally marinated before or during cooking (stewing with marinades). The methods of cooking used for spare ribs are roasting and grilling, but a period of simmering or stewing will help make the meat tender.

In preparing the ribs for cooking, the fat and gristle are trimmed from the rib rack. This is usually left whole, or just cut into two or three pieces. It is cut into individual bone strips only after cooking.

In China, however, ribs are more generally fried or steamed, and so they are chopped through the bone into 1 inch (2½ cm) long pieces, with as much meat left on them as possible. Because the individual pieces are much smaller than the spare ribs in the West, they can be quite easily stir-fried and steamed (or simply stir-fried or steamed).

Basic Spare Ribs (Simplest Version)

Serves 8–10, with other dishes

3–3½ lb (1¼–1½ kg) pork spare ribs (ask the butcher to cut them into individual strips)
2 medium-sized onions
2 cloves garlic
2 slices root ginger
2 tablespoons vegetable oil
5 tablespoons soya sauce
1 chicken stock cube
1 tablespoon sugar
salt and pepper to taste

Preparation Cut the onions into thin slices, crush the garlic, and shred the ginger.

Cooking Place the ribs in a large saucepan; cover with 1½ pints (750 ml) water. Bring to the boil over a high heat, and boil briskly for 5 minutes. Skim away all impurities, and drain off three quarters of the water. Reduce heat to low, and simmer for 15 minutes, turning the ribs over two or three times. Add the oil and all other ingredients, and raise the heat temporarily to maximum. Stir and turn briskly for 5–6 minutes until the ribs are brown. Reduce the heat to low, cover, and simmer for 30 minutes or until the liquid is reduced to one fifth, and serve on an attractive dish.

If drier ribs are required, after the final stirring and turning, the ribs can be placed in a roasting pan and put into an oven preheated to 400°F (205° C or Gas Mark 6) for 8–10 minutes.

Braised Spare Ribs with Pimento

Preparation Use the recipe for Basic Spare Ribs (see above), adding one red or green sweet pepper, cut into strips, when the ribs are cooked. Toss and

Pork

turn ribs and pepper strips for an additional 3-4 minutes just before serving. (The presence of the pepper makes this dish more colourful, and adds to the flavour, particularly for those who appreciate the taste of pepper.)

Spare Ribs with Black Beans (Chinese Style)

Serves 8-10, with other dishes

3½ lb (1½ kg) spare ribs
1½ tablespoons salted black beans
1 teaspoon salt
pepper to taste
3 slices root ginger
3 cloves garlic

1 large onion
3 tablespoons soya sauce
6 tablespoons vegetable oil
¼ pint (125 ml) secondary stock
1 chicken stock cube
3 teaspoons sugar
3 tablespoons sherry

Preparation Mix salt and pepper, and rub both sides of the rib cage with the mixture. Shred the ginger, crush the garlic, and chop the onion. Soak the black beans in water for 30 minutes, drain and mash; then mix with the ginger, garlic, onion, and soya sauce. Cut the ribs into individual slices.
Cooking Heat the oil in a heavy saucepan over high heat. Turn the ribs in the hot oil for 7-8 minutes until they begin to brown. Drain away excess oil, and add the black bean mixture to the pan, then reduce the heat to medium and turn the contents over for 4-5 minutes. Pour in the stock, sprinkle with the crushed stock cube, the sugar, and sherry. Stir around and turn a few more times. Cover the saucepan and cook gently for 30 minutes. By this time, the liquid should have been reduced to less than half. Lift the spare ribs out on to a roasting pan, and place in an oven preheated to 400°F (205°C or Gas Mark 6) for 10 minutes.

Spare Ribs with Black Beans (Overseas Chinese Style)

Serves 6-8

2½ lb (1¼ kg) pork spare ribs
1½ tablespoons salted black beans
3 cloves garlic
3 slices root ginger
3 spring onion stalks
3 tablespoons sherry

2 tablespoons soya sauce
¾ tablespoon cornflour
3 teaspoons sugar
¾ teaspoon flavour powder
6 tablespoons vegetable oil
6 tablespoons secondary stock
pepper to taste

Preparation Cut spare ribs into individual bones, and chop each into 1-1½ inch (2½-3½ cm) long pieces. Crush the garlic, shred the ginger, and chop the onion. Soak the blackbeans in water for 30 minutes; then drain and

The Complete Chinese Cookbook

mix with the garlic, ginger, onion, sherry, soya sauce, and 3 tablespoons of water. Mix cornflour with sugar, flavour powder, and 3 tablespoons water.
Cooking Heat oil in a saucepan over high heat. Add the spare ribs and stir-fry for 4–5 minutes until they begin to brown. Drain away excess oil, and add black bean/soya sauce mixture. Continue to stir-fry for ½ minute; then cover and cook over low heat for 8–10 minutes. Remove lid, and add cornflour mixture. Turn heat up to maximum, stir-fry for 1 minute; then serve.

Note The spare ribs can be served dry by arranging them on a well-heated serving dish. However, if some sauce or garnish is desired, blend 3 teaspoons cornflour with 3 tablespoons water, and mix with the sauce at the bottom of the saucepan. Add 2 tablespoons sherry, heat and stir for 1 minute, and pour the sauce over the spare ribs on the serving dish. Garnish with 2 tablespoons of chopped spring onion or parsley if desired.

Salt and Pepper Deep-Fried Spare Ribs

Serves 8–10, with other dishes

3 lb (1¼ kg) spare ribs
1 tablespoon salt
1 teaspoon freshly milled black pepper
2 tablespoons cornflour
1 egg
oil for deep-frying

Preparation Mix salt with pepper and stir-fry together in a small dry frying pan over medium heat for 2–3 minutes, until a distinct bouquet arises. Cut the spare ribs into individual bones and rub them lightly with this mixture. Leave to season for 1–2 hours. Blend the cornflour and egg into a batter.
Cooking Place the spare ribs in a steamer and steam vigorously for 25 minutes. Batter them with the egg/cornflour mixture. Heat the oil in a deep-fryer; place the ribs in a wire basket and deep-fry for 3–4 minutes. When slightly cool, chop them into 2 inch (5 cm) long pieces, place the pieces in the wire basket, and deep-fry again for 3–4 minutes.

Stir-Fried Sliced Pork Dishes

When pork is stir-fried it is always cut into thin slices or matchstick strips, or else shredded, and it is usually stir-fried with other materials – mostly vegetables – which have been cut or shredded into similar sizes or shapes.

Stir-frying has three advantages over other forms of cooking – firstly, it is economical of time (cooking seldom exceeds a few minutes); secondly, by cross-cooking with other, usually cheaper materials, a large quantity of savoury and appealing food can be produced from only a limited quantity

Pork

of meat (for example, 1 lb (400 g) meat can serve 6–7 people); thirdly, by combining pork with other materials which differ in texture, colour, and flavour, a large number of dishes can be easily created. As stir-frying invariably involves quick cooking at a high temperature, finger-tip timing and fire control are crucial. Hence quick stir-frying requires more experience to achieve perfection than other methods of cooking.

Sliced Pork Stir-Fried with Cabbage

Serves 6–8, with other dishes

1 lb (400 g) lean pork
½ medium-sized Chinese cabbage
   or Savoy cabbage
1 teaspoon salt
pepper to taste
1 clove garlic

5 tablespoons vegetable oil
2 tablespoons soya sauce
4 tablespoons stock
   (chicken *or* superior stock)
2 teaspoons sugar
½ teaspoon flavour powder *or*
   ½ chicken stock cube

This dish goes particularly well with rice.

Preparation Cut the pork against the grain into very thin 1 × 2 inch (2½ × 5 cm) slices; rub well with salt and pepper. Cut the cabbage into 1 inch (2½ cm) pieces; crush the garlic.
Cooking Heat 3 tablespoons of the oil in a large frying pan over a high heat. Add the garlic and stir once or twice. Spread the pork slices over the pan and stir-fry them vigorously for 3 minutes; then lift out with a perforated spoon, drain, and keep hot. Pour the remaining oil into the pan and add the cabbage – turn in the oil until all the pieces are well-coated. Stir-fry for 2–3 minutes until they begin to heat through; then pour in the soya sauce, stock, and sugar, and sprinkle with the flavour powder or crushed stock cube. Turn the cabbage in the sauce for 2–2½ minutes, then replace the pork in the pan and stir-fry for a further 2–2½ minutes.

Note It is optional in stir-frying of this sort whether or not to dredge and rub the meat with flour or cornflour. By doing so, the surface of the meat is given a feeling of smoothness, and there is no detraction from the flavour so long as only a small quantity of flour or cornflour is used.

Sliced Pork Stir-Fried with Mushrooms

Serves 6–8, with other dishes

In China we use dried mushrooms much more frequently than fresh ones – they seem to have more 'bite', as well as more flavour. Dried mushrooms

The Complete Chinese Cookbook

must be soaked for 30 minutes before use, and the tough stems discarded. Always retain some mushroom water – 3–4 tablespoons – to add to the frying with some sherry, sesame oil, and flavour powder, during the final stages of cooking. This will add to the flavour of the dish.

Repeat the recipe for Sliced Pork Stir-Fried with Cabbage, using 4oz (100 g) fresh mushrooms and 2oz (50 g) dried mushrooms, which have been previously soaked. As mushrooms are very absorbent, it is best to add them directly to the pork in the frying pan, after the latter has first been stir-fried with garlic and ginger, and then with soya sauce, sugar, stock, and mushroom water. The mushrooms will absorb this tasty sauce. If added earlier, they will only absorb the oil of the stir-frying. An ounce or two of butter mixed with the sauce mixture just before the mushrooms are added should appeal to Western taste.

In such a dish both dried and fresh mushrooms can be used. Add them at the same time. The fresh provide the main bulk, and the soaked, dried mushrooms provide the flavour.

In the final stages, the sherry, sesame oil, and flavour powder mixture, mixed with ½ tablespoon cornflour blended with 2 tablespoons water, can be added to advantage – if cornflour has not previously been rubbed into the pork.

Sliced Pork Stir-Fried with Bamboo Shoots

Serves 6–8, with other dishes

In the West, bamboo shoots are most easily available in cans. Since they are eaten for their crunchy texture, rather than their over-subtle flavour which is appreciated only by the well-cultivated connoisseur, the timing of their cooking need not be precise, since a few minutes more or less cooking will neither increase nor reduce the crunchiness. Repeat the recipe for Sliced Pork Stir-Fried with Cabbage (page 123), substituting Bamboo Shoots for Cabbage. Sliced thinly, they can be fried for 1, 2, or 3 minutes and then added to the sliced pork which has had its 2-stage stir-frying – 2 minutes in oil, garlic, and ginger, followed by 2 minutes with soya sauce, sugar, and stock.

Fresh bamboo shoots have to be treated more carefully as they can be quite tough. They are best cooked in the same way as cauliflower – 2–3 minutes of lubricating and frying in hot oil impregnated with garlic, ginger, and meat, followed by 4 minutes cooking in stock and soya sauce, before the final stir-frying with the pork.

Pork

Sliced Pork Stir-Fried with Young Leeks

Serves 6–8, with other dishes

Young leeks can be treated in the same way as cabbage. Repeat the recipe for Sliced Pork Stir-Fried with Cabbage (page 123). The leeks should be sliced into pieces about the same size as the pork (use all the green part), and added to the pan immediately the pork has been stir-fried. Use an extra $\frac{3}{4}$ teaspoon salt instead of 1 tablespoon soya sauce – i.e. reduce the soya sauce by 1 tablespoon in the later stage of flavouring. The salts will make the leeks greener than ever. To balance the comparatively strong taste of leeks, 1 tablespoon hoisin sauce may be used to advantage during the initial frying of the pork. It will give an extra brownness and piquancy to the meat, combining well with the glistening greenness of the leeks, and thus making the dish an extremely attractive one, both in flavour and appearance.

Sliced Pork Stir-Fried with Pea Pods (Mange-Tout)

Serves 6–8, with other dishes

Pea pods or mange-tout appear to have become popular in the UK only during very recent years. They are, however, very useful in Chinese cooking, especially in stir-frying. They are extremely attractive visually and need little cooking – a couple of minutes stir-frying in oil and flavourers, followed by the final cross-frying with the previously stir-fried sliced pork, should be enough to produce a dish made extremely attractive and appealing by the crispness of the quick-fried pea pods and their jade-like colour.

Sliced Pork Stir-Fried with Golden Needles and Transparent Noodles

Serves 4–8, with other dishes

12 oz (300 g) lean pork
2 oz (50 g) golden needles
4 oz (100 g) transparent noodles
6 large Chinese dried mushrooms
3 spring onion stalks
2 slices root ginger

2 tablespoons vegetable oil
$\frac{1}{2}$ teaspoon salt
3 tablespoons soya sauce
1 teaspoon sugar
$\frac{1}{4}$ pint (125 ml) superior stock
3 tablespoons sherry
$\frac{1}{2}$ teaspoon flavour powder
2 teaspoons sesame oil

The Complete Chinese Cookbook

Transparent noodles and golden needles (lily bud stems) are typical Chinese cooking materials. Although transparent pea-starch noodles (vermicelli) are in themselves tasteless, they are great absorbers and conveyors of other tastes and flavours. Golden needles have an earthy, woody taste, which might have emanated from autumn leaves – appreciation of its taste is very much acquired. To Chinese people living abroad, both these ingredients are extremely evocative of the Good Earth of China: however, to make any dish using these materials interesting, it is essential to use both Chinese dried mushrooms (during the middle stage of cooking) and spring onions and sesame oil during the concluding stage.

Preparation Soak the mushrooms, golden needles, and transparent noodles separately in warm water for 30 minutes. Retain 5–6 tablespoons mushroom water, remove the stems of the mushrooms and discard, and cut the caps into four. Cut the golden needles into 2–3 inch (5–7½ cm) long segments, and leave soaking until required. Cut the spring onions into 2 inch (5 cm) segments, and slice the pork against the grain into 1½ inch (3½ cm) long and ½ inch (1 cm) wide pieces. Shred the ginger.

Cooking Heat the oil in a large frying pan or saucepan. Add the ginger, salt, and pork, and stir-fry over high heat for 3 minutes; then add 1 tablespoon of the soya sauce and the sugar, and continue to stir-fry for 1 minute. Pour in the stock, mushrooms, mushroom water, and golden needles, bring to the boil and boil for 2 minutes. Add the noodles, remainder of the soya sauce, the sherry, and flavour powder; stir several times and simmer gently for 5–6 minutes. Sprinkle with the spring onions and sesame oil, and cook for a further minute. Serve in a deep dish.

Sliced Pork Stir-Fried with Szechuan Pickle

Serves 8–10, with other dishes

1½ lb (600 g) lean pork
3–4 oz (75–100 g) Szechuan pickle
3 tablespoons vegetable oil
1 tablespoon soya sauce
1½ teaspoons sugar
3 tablespoons superior stock

Szechuan Pickle (often called cabbage) is usually available in cans from Chinese provision shops. Its hot pungent saltiness has the effect of doubling the strength of the principal food with which it is cooked. It should be used sparingly by those who have never tried it before, as the dish may easily become too hot or salty for the average liking. Half of an 8 oz (200 g) can should be quite sufficient for 1½–2 lb (¾–1 kg) pork.

Preparation Slice pork against grain into 1 × ¾ inch (2½ × 1½ cm) thin pieces. Slice the pickles similarly.

Cooking Heat oil in a frying pan over a high heat. Stir-fry the pork for 6–7 minutes; add the soya sauce, sugar, and stock, and continue to stir-fry for 1 minute more. Add the sliced pickles, stir-fry for a further 2 minutes, and serve.

Quick-Fried Shredded Pork Dishes

Almost all sliced pork dishes can be cooked as shredded pork dishes simply by cutting the pork, and any other ingredients, into thread-like shreds. However, there are some materials which are more suitable than others for shredding into threads; others already exist in threads or shredded form, so the pork is shredded to cross-cook and stir-fry with them. The cooking method for quick-fried shredded pork is very similar to that used for sliced pork – the participating ingredients are stir-fried separately, and finally combined in a quick crescendo of a last hot sizzling assembly. The choice of meat for shredding is very much the same as that used for slicing – pork chop, tenderloin, leg, lean parts of shoulder and belly, and the meatier parts of spare ribs. As the cooking time for shredded meat can be even shorter than that for sliced meat, and as there is greater surface area exposed to the heat of the pan and oil, it is often seasoned or marinated before the actual cooking.

Shredded Pork Stir-Fried with Bean Sprouts

Serves 4–6, with other dishes

12 oz (300 g) lean pork
1 lb (400 g) bean sprouts
1 medium-sized onion
2 cloves garlic
2 slices root ginger
2 spring onion stalks

1½ teaspoons salt
1 tablespoon cornflour
5 tablespoons vegetable oil
2 tablespoons soya sauce
1½ teaspoons sugar
½ teaspoon flavour powder
2 tablespoons sherry

Preparation Slice the onion thinly. Crush the garlic, shred the ginger, and cut the spring onions into 2 inch (5 cm) segments. Shred the pork into matchstick shreds, sprinkle with salt and cornflour, and rub these into the meat.

Cooking Heat 3 tablespoons of the oil in a large frying pan or saucepan. Add the onion, garlic, and ginger, and stir-fry together over a high heat for 1 minute. Add the pork, spread it out over the pan, and stir-fry together with the other ingredients for 4 minutes. Remove with a perforated spoon and put aside to keep hot. Add the remaining oil, and after a moment, the bean sprouts. Turn them in the oil, and stir-fry over a high heat for 2 minutes. Sprinkle the bean sprouts with soya sauce, sugar, flavour powder, and sherry, and continue to stir-fry for 2 minutes. Replace the pork in the pan, and stir together with the bean sprouts. Add the spring onions, stir-fry for 2 minutes; then serve.

Shredded Pork Stir-Fried with Onion and Spring Onion

Serves 4–6, with other dishes

Repeat the recipe for Shredded Pork Stir-Fried with Bean Sprouts, using 2 large onions, and 3 spring onion stalks. The idea is to use onion as a basic ingredient with the pork; the spring onions, which are almost a garnish, are added only during the last minute of stir-frying together. Onion requires longer cooking than bean sprouts, and should be stir-fried first of all in oil for 2–3 minutes before adding the pork. Stir-fry them together for a further 3–4 minutes before the spring onion segments are added. As onion is a strong-tasting vegetable, it will not be overpowered by the extra tablespoon of soya sauce and the teaspoon of sugar which should be added. If a slightly hotter dish is required, 1 tablespoon hoisin sauce may be added with the soya sauce, sugar, and sherry. The dish can be served after the spring onions have been stir-fried with the pork and onion for 1 minute.

Shredded Pork Stir-Fried with Celery

Serves 4–6, with other dishes

Repeat the recipe for Shredded Pork Stir-Fried with Bean Sprouts, using celery instead of bean sprouts. The celery should be shredded into matchstick strips, and given an extra minute of stir-frying with the pork, after the meat has been replaced in the pan.

Shredded Pork with Asparagus Tips

Serves 6–8

Use 1 lb (400 g) asparagus. Remove the tough parts, and slice the stalks lengthwise into double matchstick size strips. Blanch the asparagus by simmering it in boiling water for 2 minutes, then drain thoroughly. Repeat the recipe for Shredded Pork Stir-Fried with Celery.

Shredded Pork with Bean Curd Skin and Broccoli

Serves 4–6, with other dishes

1 lb (400 g) lean pork
4 oz (100 g) bean curd skin
8 oz (200 g) broccoli
1 teaspoon salt
1 tablespoon cornflour

2 large Chinese dried mushrooms
4 tablespoons vegetable oil
3 tablespoons soya sauce
8 tablespoons superior stock
2 tablespoons sherry
½ teaspoon flavour powder
2 teaspoons sesame oil

Preparation Shred the pork and sprinkle with salt and cornflour. Soak the bean curd skin and mushrooms separately for 30 minutes; then drain. Discard mushroom stems and cut skin and caps into thin strips. Cut the broccoli into thin branches.

Cooking Heat 3 tablespoons oil in a large frying pan. Stir-fry the pork over high heat for 3 minutes; then add the skin, mushrooms, half of the soya sauce, and half of the stock, and continue to stir and turn for further 3 minutes. Cover and simmer gently over low heat for 5 minutes. Heat the remaining oil in a saucepan and stir-fry the broccoli for 2 minutes. Pour in 4 tablespoons stock, the remaining soya sauce, and the sherry; stir several times, then cover, and leave to cook for 5 minutes over a low heat. Combine the broccoli and its sauce with the pork and other ingredients in the frying pan. Sprinkle with flavour powder and sesame oil, and stir-fry over a medium heat for 2 minutes.

Minced Pork Dishes

In China meat is not minced by putting it through a mincer but by the drumbeat action of a pair of choppers held in both hands, with the meat placed on a chopping board 6 inches (30 cm) thick. The connoisseurs say that this way prevents the loss of much valuable meat juice, which is squeezed out by a mincer. In the West, it is much easier to obtain minced meat by using a mincer or by asking the butcher to mince it – ask for medium mince.

Steamed Minced Pork with Cauliflower

Serves 6–8

8 oz (200 g) belly of pork
8 oz (200 g) lean pork
1 medium-sized cauliflower
2 teaspoons salt

2 tablespoons soya sauce
1 tablespoon cornflour
1 egg
2 cloves garlic
2 slices root ginger
pepper to taste

Preparation Mince the pork, mixing the fat through the lean. Add half of the salt, half of the soya sauce, and the cornflour. Lightly beat the egg, crush and chop the garlic and ginger, and add to the pork, mixing well. Clean the cauliflower and break into individual branches discarding the coarse stem. Arrange the branches in the bottom of a large bowl, sprinkle with the remaining salt and soya sauce, add the pepper, then spread the pork mixture in a thick layer over the top, until the cauliflower is completely covered.
Cooking Place the bowl in a steamer and steam for 1 hour. Serve in the bowl

This is very much a home-cooked dish, popular with both young and old.

Steamed Minced Pork Cake

Serves 4–6

1 lb (400 g) minced pork
1 large onion
2 water chestnuts
1 slice root ginger
1 clove garlic

1 egg, lightly beaten
1½ teaspoons salt
1 teaspoon sugar
1½ tablespoons soya sauce
pepper to taste
2 Chinese sausages

Preparation Chop onion and water chestnuts finely, shred and chop ginger, crush and chop garlic. Add them all to the minced pork, together with the egg, salt, sugar, soya sauce, and pepper. Mix well. Spread the mixture out like a thick pancake on a large, round, greased, heat-proof dish. Slice the sausage slantwise into ¼ inch (½ cm) thick slices, and stud them into the pork at regular intervals.
Cooking Place the heat-proof dish in a steamer and steam for 40 minutes. Serve from this dish.

Chinese sausages are similar to Italian salami, and are generally available from Chinese provision stores.

Deep-Fried Meat Balls

Makes approximately 24

1 lb (400 g) minced pork
2 water chestnuts
1 onion
1 clove garlic

1 slice root ginger
1 egg
2 tablespoons cornflour
2 teaspoons salt
1 tablespoon soya sauce
oil for deep-frying

Pork

Preparation Chop the water chestnuts coarsely. Chop and mince the onion, garlic, and ginger; and beat the egg lightly. Mix them with the minced pork, cornflour, salt, and soya sauce until well-blended, and form into balls about the size of walnuts.

Cooking Heat oil in deep-fryer. Fry the meat balls six at a time by lowering them into the oil in a wire basket. Deep-fry each lot for about 3 minutes at a time, and put aside in a well-heated dish to keep hot. Finally, put all the meat balls together in the wire basket and give them a final deep-fry for 1½ minutes. Drain thoroughly, and serve.

These meat balls can be served plain to be eaten dipped in Salt and Pepper Mix, or they can be covered in Sweet and Sour Sauce (see Index).

Lions' Heads

Serves 8–12

A 1½ lb (600 g) lean pork
4 oz (100 g) fat pork
4 water chestnuts
2 medium-sized onions
4 Chinese dried mushrooms
2 tablespoons cornflour
1 teaspoon salt
2 tablespoons soya sauce
1 teaspoon sugar
pepper to taste

B 6 tablespoons superior stock
1 tablespoon soya sauce
2 tablespoons sherry
½ teaspoon flavour powder
⅛ tablespoon cornflour

8 oz (200 g) spinach
1 clove garlic
4 oz (100 g) pea-starch transparent noodles
2 tablespoons oil for deep-frying
2 tablespoons vegetable oil
1½ tablespoons soya sauce

Preparation Mince the pork, the water chestnuts, and the onion coarsely. Soak the mushrooms for 30 minutes, drain and discard the stems, and mince the caps. Combine these ingredients with all the others in list A, and make four large meat balls. Heat the oil for deep-frying. Mix all the ingredients in list B until a well-blended sauce mixture. Clean the spinach thoroughly, removing all the coarse tough parts. Crush the garlic; soak the noodles for 20 minutes, and then drain.

Cooking Place two meat balls at a time in a wire basket and deep-fry for 5–6 minutes until golden brown. Drain on paper towelling. Cook the other two similarly. Stir-fry the garlic and spinach in a large frying pan. After 1 minute, when the spinach is well-coated, add the soya sauce. Stir-fry for a further 2 minutes, then pour in the noodles, and toss gently with the spinach

The Complete Chinese Cookbook

for 3 minutes. Transfer the spinach and noodles to a large earthenware pot or casserole. Place the meat balls on top of the spinach and noodles, and cover with a lid or tinfoil. Steam for 30 minutes, or bake in an oven preheated to 375°F (190°C or Gas Mark 5) for 25 minutes. Meanwhile, heat the sauce mixture B in a small saucepan for 2–3 minutes until it thickens.
Serving Pour the sauce over the 'Lions' Heads' in the casserole, and serve.

This is a dish which is usually served at parties.

Pork Specialities

Pork Trotters with Gravied Eggs

Serves 8–10

3 lb (1¼ kg) pork trotters
4 eggs
2 medium-sized onions
2 cloves garlic
6 tablespoons soya sauce
1 tablespoon sugar
6 tablespoons sherry
8 tablespoons superior stock

Preparation Clean the trotters thoroughly, boil them in water for 25 minutes, and drain. Slice the onions thinly, crush and chop the garlic, and hard-boil the eggs.
Cooking Place the trotters in a casserole, with the onion and garlic, and sprinkle with 4 tablespoons of the soya sauce, ½ tablespoon of the sugar, 3 tablespoons of the sherry, and the superior stock. Place the casserole in an oven preheated to 350°F (180°C or Gas Mark 4) and cook for 1½ hours, turning the trotters over every 30 minutes. Add the hard-boiled eggs to the casserole, sprinkle with the remaining soya sauce and sherry, and cook for a further 40 minutes at the same temperature, turning the eggs and trotters every 20 minutes.
Serving Just before serving, cut each egg into quarters and arrange the pieces around the trotters in a deep dish. Pour over the gravy from the casserole. If there is insufficient gravy, add a small quantity of superior stock, together with ½ tablespoon soya sauce and ¼ tablespoon sherry, and heat until sizzling. Stir, and pour over the trotters. The meat and skin of the trotters should be glistening brown and jelly like, set off by the yellow yolks of the eggs surrounding them.

Quick-Fried Pork Kidney with Celery and Wood Ears

Serves 4–6, with other dishes

12 oz (300 g) pork kidneys
6 oz (150 g) celery
1 oz (25 g) wood ears
2 cloves garlic
3 spring onion stalks
4 tablespoons vegetable oil
2 slices root ginger
1 teaspoon salt

Marinade
2 tablespoons soya sauce
2 tablespoons sherry
pepper to taste

Sauce
2 teaspoons cornflour
½ teaspoon flavour powder
2 teaspoons sugar
2 teaspoons vinegar
1 tablespoon soya sauce
3 tablespoons chicken stock

This kidney dish is considered a speciality mainly because it is cooked in a very short time.

Preparation Remove membrane from kidneys, cut each into halves, and score or slice each piece crosswise halfway through at ¼ inch (½ cm) intervals, until each piece is covered with a network of cuts. Cut each piece into 1 inch (2½ cm) wide strips. Place in a basin, add the well-blended marinade ingredients and marinate for 30 minutes. Crush the garlic, cut the spring onions into 1 inch (2½ cm) segments, and slice the celery into ½ inch (1 cm) pieces. Soak the wood ears in warm water for 30 minutes, rinse under running water, and drain. Blend the sauce ingredients well.

Cooking Heat 2 tablespoons of the oil in a frying pan, add the garlic and ginger, and stir-fry over high heat for 1 minute; then remove. Add celery, wood ears, and salt; stir-fry for 3 minutes, then remove and put aside. Pour the remaining oil into the centre of the pan; when it is hot, add the kidneys and stir-fry quickly for 1 minute. Add the spring onion, the celery, and wood ears to the kidney. Pour in the sauce mixture, and any left-over marinade. Stir-fry for a further minute; serve in a well-heated dish and eat immediately.

The Chinese regard this as a delicacy mainly for the crunchiness of the kidneys.

Whole Happy Family

Serves 4–6, with other dishes

- 3 oz (75 g) bêche de mer
- 4 Chinese dried mushrooms
- 2 oz (50 g) Chinese roast pork
- 1 chicken breast
- 2 oz (50 g) smoked ham
- 4 oz (100 g) bamboo shoots
- 4 oz (100 g) broccoli (*or* heart of spring greens)
- 1 tablespoon dried shrimps
- 1 tablespoon cornflour
- 3 tablespoons soya sauce
- 3 tablespoons sherry
- 1 teaspoon flavour powder
- 2 teaspoons sugar
- ½ pint (250 ml) chicken stock
- 3 tablespoons vegetable oil
- 6 small meat balls (see page 130)
- 1 teaspoon salt
- 3 tablespoons fresh peeled shrimps
- 4 tablespoons green peas

This is a grand assembly of animal and vegetable items from both land and sea, all gathered together as if in one 'whole happy family'.

Preparation Soak and simmer bêche de mer in water overnight, and cut into 1 inch (2½ cm) segments. Soak mushrooms in water for 30 minutes, remove the stems, and dice the caps into ¼ inch (½ cm) pieces. Cut the roast pork into ½ inch (1 cm) cubes. Heat the chicken breast in boiling water, dice into ¼ inch (½ cm) pieces, and cut the ham similarly. Chop the bamboo shoots and broccoli into ½ inch (1 cm) cubes. Soak the dried shrimps in water for 1 hour, and drain. Blend the cornflour with 3 tablespoons water, and add the soya sauce, sherry, flavour powder, sugar, and half of the cold chicken stock.

Cooking Heat the oil in a saucepan and add the meat balls. Stir-fry for 4 minutes; then push to the sides. Add the bêche de mer, roast pork, and salt; stir-fry for 3 minutes; then pour in the remaining stock, and add the chicken, ham, bamboo shoots, broccoli, dried shrimps, shrimps, and peas. Simmer for 30 minutes over low heat; then add the cornflour/sherry mixture, and heat gently for a further 10 minutes.

Quick-Fried Pig's Liver

Serves 4–6, with other dishes

- 1 lb (400 g) pig's liver
- 1 medium-sized onion
- 4 oz (100 g) bamboo shoots
- 6 large Chinese dried mushrooms
- ¾ tablespoon cornflour
- 2 tablespoons soya sauce
- ½ teaspoon salt
- 1 teaspoon sugar
- 1 tablespoon sherry
- 2 tablespoons vegetable oil
- 6 tablespoons lard

Pork

Preparation Slice onion and bamboo shoots thinly; soak the mushrooms for 30 minutes, remove the stems, and cut the caps into quarters. Slice the liver into thin 2 × 1 inch (5 × 2½ cm) wide pieces. Place these pieces in a large bowl, and pour in half a kettle of boiling water, stir two or three times, and drain away the water. Sprinkle the liver with cornflour, and marinate in the soya sauce, salt, sugar, and sherry.
Cooking Heat the oil in a frying pan. Add the onion, bamboo shoots, and mushrooms; then stir-fry over a medium heat for 2 minutes, and set aside. Add the lard, heat, and when it is very hot, pour in the liver. Spread out over the pan and stir-fry over high heat for 2 minutes. Pour away excess fat, put the onion, bamboo shoots, and mushrooms back into the pan, and stir-fry with the liver for 1 minute. Serve from a well-heated dish.

Red-Cooked Pork Tripe

Serves 4–6, with other dishes

2 lb (1 kg) tripe
1 tablespoon salt
2 slices root ginger
2 large onions
4 large Chinese dried mushrooms
1 oz (25 g) parsley
3 tablespoons lard
4 tablespoons soya sauce
3 tablespoons sherry
1 tablespoon vinegar
2 teaspoons sugar
¼ pint (125 ml) superior stock

Tripe appears to be more extensively used in Chinese than in Western cooking, although in some parts of Western Europe it is extremely popular. In China, some pigs are specially bred for their tripes, which are exceptionally thick (about 1 inch, or 2½ cm) and meaty. This is one of the many ways in which tripe can be prepared.

Preparation Wash tripe thoroughly. Dissolve salt in 2 pints (generous litre) boiling water, add tripe, and boil for 20 minutes; then drain, discarding water. Cut tripe into 2 inch (5 cm) triangles. Shred ginger, and slice onions thinly. Soak mushrooms in warm water for 30 minutes, remove stems and cut caps into thin strips. Chop the parsley.
Cooking Heat lard in flame-proof casserole, and stir-fry onions and ginger for 2 minutes. Push to sides, and stir-fry tripe for 3 minutes over medium heat. Add mushrooms, and all other ingredients. As soon as the contents of the casserole come to the boil, remove from the heat, and place in oven preheated to 350°F (180°C or Gas Mark 4) for 1½ hours.
Serving Sprinkle with parsley, bring to table, and serve.

Ham Dishes

Ham is not used as often as pork in China, although shredded smoked ham is frequently used as a garnish for egg dishes, and quick- or stir-fried dishes. Here is a selection of the most popular ham dishes.

Steamed Ham

Serves 6–10, with other dishes

2–3 lb (1–1¼ kg) fresh ham

2 tablespoons sugar
4 tablespoons sherry

Sugar and sherry are added to give even ordinary ham a sweetened flavour.

Preparation and Cooking Place ham in a heat-proof dish and steam for 1 hour; then brush with a mixture of sherry and sugar, and steam for 30 minutes. Turn over, and brush again with the sherry-sugar mixture, and steam for a further 30 minutes. Pour the remaining sherry-sugar mixture over the ham, and steam for a final 30 minutes.
Serving Cut the ham into fairly thick slices, and then cut these into double mahjong-size pieces.

Toasted Gold Coin Ham

Serves 6–8, with other dishes

1½ lb (600 g) round piece fresh ham
8 oz (200 g) ham fat

1½ tablespoons sugar
3 tablespoons sherry
8 Chinese steamed buns (*or* Man Tou buns, *or* use crumpets)
2 tablespoons lard

Preparation and Cooking Mix the sugar with the sherry into a consistent blend. Brush ham with the mixture. Steam for 30 minutes, turn meat over, brush and steam again for 30 minutes, and then repeat. Steam the buns or crumpets for 10 minutes. Cut each piece into slices as thick as a very thin slice of bread; slice the ham similarly, and cut the fat into slices about quarter as thick. Place a piece of fat on each piece of ham, brush with the sugar-sherry mixture, then with melted lard, and then skewer them through the centre like a kebab. Put five or six ham/fat combinations on each skewer, and either toast under the grill, or roast on a rack in an oven preheated to 400°F (205°C or Gas Mark 6) for 10–12 minutes. Grill the sliced buns or crumpets until well-toasted.

Pork

Serving As soon as they are ready, pull the ham and fat combinations off the skewers, and arrange them, one on top of each other, with ham and fat alternating, until they rise like a tower of gold coins. The toasted buns should be arranged in four smaller piles around the Gold Coins. Eat in sandwich fashion, by placing a piece of ham and fat between two pieces of toasted bun. Plum Sauce, Sweet and Sour Sauce, hoisin sauce, and mustard can all be brushed on the ham to enhance piquancy and flavour if desired.

Honey Pear Ham

Serves 4, with other dishes

4 large pears
8 oz (200 g) Yunnan ham (use Smithfield if Yunnan not available)
3 oz (75 g) rock sugar

oil for deep-frying

Sauce
2½ tablespoons cornflour
1½ tablespoons sugar
1½ tablespoons honey
¼ pint (125 ml) water

This is a very well-known south-west China dish, which has a high reputation throughout the country. It developed in Kunming, where the Yunnan ham originated. Unlike Sweet and Sour, Sweet and Savoury is a flavour much more frequently found in China than in the West.

Preparation Slice the ham into thin slices, 2 inches (5 cm) long, 1 inch (2½ cm) wide. Use it to line the bottom of a flat heat-proof dish. Peel the pears, cut each into six slices, and deep-fry them for 30 seconds in hot oil. Place them on top of the ham. Mix the sauce ingredients into a consistent blend.

Cooking Sprinkle the pears and ham with rock sugar, place them in a steamer, and steam for 25 minutes. Heat the sauce mixture until it starts to boil and thicken. Pour over the ham and pears, after first tipping the latter from the heat-proof dish into a large serving dish.

Sliced Ham Stir-Fried with Celery

Serves 4–6, with other dishes

8 oz (200 g) cooked ham (steamed *or* baked)
12 oz (300 g) celery
1 clove garlic
1 slice root ginger

½ teaspoon flavour powder
½ tablespoon cornflour
4 tablespoons secondary stock
3 tablespoons vegetable oil
1½ teaspoons sugar
1½ tablespoons light-coloured soya sauce

The Complete Chinese Cookbook

Like pork, ham can be stir-fried with a wide variety of vegetables. However, as ham is stronger tasting and saltier than pork, a smaller amount is used with the same quantity of other ingredients.

Preparation Slice ham into $1\frac{1}{2} \times 1$ inch ($3\frac{1}{2} \times 2\frac{1}{2}$ cm) thin pieces. Clean celery and cut into 1 inch ($2\frac{1}{2}$ cm) segments. Crush and chop garlic, and shred ginger. Parboil celery for 2 minutes and drain. Blend flavour powder, cornflour, and stock until smooth.

Cooking Heat oil in frying pan, and stir-fry garlic and ginger over medium heat for 30 seconds. Add ham, turn in oil for 1 minute, remove and keep hot. Pour in celery, turn heat to high, and stir in oil for 3 minutes. Add sugar and soya sauce, replace ham in pan, and stir-fry with celery for 2 minutes. Stir in flavour powder/cornflour mixture, and turn the contents of the frying pan over a few times.

Chinese Sausages

To Western eyes, Chinese sausages are not sausages but miniature salamis. They are often used in flavouring, or cooked in steamed rice, but they can be cross-cooked with other materials, in the same way as ham.

The Chinese sausage is usually about the same length as a Western sausage, but only half as thick in diameter. When used alone, it is generally sliced diagonally into $\frac{1}{4}$ inch ($\frac{1}{2}$ cm) thick pieces, fried in a little oil for 2–3 minutes over gentle heat, and served in a small dish or saucer as a side-dish.

The sausages are often used to garnish vegetables, having been lightly fried first, then arranged on top of the vegetables, and the whole steamed for a few minutes. Being red or reddish-brown in colour with patches of transparent fat, they lend colour, as well as flavour, to vegetable dishes. Chinese sausages are often seen strung together in pairs in the windows of Chinese provision shops or restaurants where Chinese congregate. Because of their similarity to salamis, they are easily acceptable to Westerners; and like their Western counterpart, they are usually bought in shops, rather than produced at home.

Beef

牛 肉

Beef is not so widely used in Chinese as in Western cooking, being less popular than pork. Nevertheless, it is an important item of meat, and should be available from all good butchers and in restaurants of any standard.

There are beef dishes from every region of China, but they are mainly eaten by Chinese Moslems, who have a somewhat kosher outlook, and think that pork is unclean. There is also a good range of beef dishes from the western province of Szechuan, where a great many oxen are employed for haulage in the salt-mines. A proportion of them, as would be expected, eventually end up on the table. In the other parts of China there is probably only one beef dish for every ten pork dishes. Taken in the main, the majority of Chinese regard the ox and cow more as the source of muscular power than as a source of flesh. Unlike the pig, which we Chinese regard as existing primarily for its total edibility (besides, hog's hair is valuable for exporting for the production of good brushes and tooth-brushes), we Chinese keep cows and oxen more or less as people in the West nowadays keep cars – in ones, twos, or threes. They are there to work – pulling the plough, doing some haulage, or grinding the maize. It is only in the great grassland regions of western Manchuria, and Inner Mongolia, stretching westwards to distant Sinkiang (Chinese Turkestan) that great herds of cattle exist. This is the region where the Chinese Moslems roam. It is of little wonder that they are the originators of many of the Chinese beef dishes.

In the rest of China, not only are there no herds of cattle, but there are no dairies as such. The Chinese as a rule do not drink milk, and there is no butter or cheese made from milk. These items are, however, becoming better known in China, as a result of Western influence during the past half century. The Western impact has, perhaps imperceptibly, increased the Chinese interest in beef, and in fact some of the best beefsteaks I have ever eaten I had in Tientsin and Shanghai.

Practically all Chinese pork dishes can be made with beef, by substituting beef for pork in the recipes. To achieve this change successfully, one has to remember that beef, unlike pork, is not suitable for medium-length cooking (5 to 25 minutes): to be tender, it has either to be cooked very quickly, in under 2–3 minutes (it is therefore suitable for quick stir-frying), or for a much longer time than 25 minutes, preferably 1 hour and upwards.

Another difference between pork and beef is in the stronger and more definite taste of the latter. Because of this, beef is generally cross-cooked with the stronger-tasting vegetables, such as onion, leek, garlic, and turnip. It is usually stewed with turnips, and stir-fried with onions and leeks. Ginger is often added to eliminate its 'rawness'.

Unlike pork and chicken, beef is never diced into small cubes and cooked – rather it is cut in thin slices, or in shreds and strips.

As with the other meat chapters, we start with Red-Cooking, which can also be called the Chinese version of the 'Eternal Stew'. However, if well-cooked, it can be excellent and most delectable – one of the best dishes ever created.

Red-Cooked Beef

Serves 6–8, with other dishes

3 lb (1¼ kg) shin beef
2 large onions
2 slices root ginger
2 cloves garlic
1 piece Chinese dried tangerine peel
3 tablespoons vegetable oil
1 teaspoon salt
4 tablespoons soya sauce
1 tablespoon sugar
6 tablespoons sherry

Preparation Slice the onions thinly. Shred the ginger and crush the garlic. Soak the tangerine peel in water for 20 minutes; then drain.
Cooking Boil the beef for 10 minutes, then cut it into 1–1½ inch (2½–3½ cm) cubes. Heat the oil in a heavy pan, add the meat cubes, and stir-fry over a high heat for 5–6 minutes. Remove the beef and put aside. Add the onions, ginger, and garlic to the remaining oil in the pan, and stir-fry over a medium heat for 3–4 minutes. Add 1½ pints (750 ml) water, salt, and 2 tablespoons of the soya sauce. Bring to the boil, add the beef and tangerine peel, and return to the boil. Reduce the heat to minimum, cover, and simmer very

Beef

gently for 1 hour. Add the remaining soya sauce, sugar, and sherry. Insert an asbestos mat under the pan and continue cooking over a very low heat for another 2 hours, turning the beef every 30 minutes. Alternatively, if the beef is cooked in a casserole, it can be cooked in the oven at 300°F (150°C or Gas Mark 2) for 2½ hours.

Serving This is a very tasty dish to eat with rice. It is best cooked in an iron pot or casserole so that the container can be brought to the table for serving.

Because of the long cooking, all the tendons in the muscles of the shin beef turn into delicious jelly. This makes the texture more interesting than if it were simply lean beef. Shin is a fairly inexpensive cut of meat.

Red-Cooked Beef with Tomato

Serves 6–8

In north China, beef is often cooked with tomatoes which are readily available.

Preparation The dish can be prepared simply by adding 1 lb (400 g) skinned tomatoes to the recipe for Red-Cooked Beef during the last hour of cooking. An extra teaspoon of salt or 1½ tablespoons of soya sauce must also be added. If ordinary stewing beef is used, the total cooking time can be reduced by 1½ hours. 1 lb (400 g) skinned tomatoes, each sliced into four, can be added during the last 45 minutes of cooking, with some salt or soya sauce, plus ½ tablespoon of hoisin sauce. A tablespoon of chopped chives or spring onions is sometimes sprinkled over the meat before serving.

Red-Cooked Beef with Yellow Turnip

Serves 6–8

Use the recipe for Red-Cooked Beef with Tomato, substituting 1 medium-sized turnip for the tomatoes. Cut the turnip into 1½ inch (3¾ cm) triangular axe-head shape pieces and add to the pan at least 1 hour before serving. They appear golden and transparent when cooked. A tablespoon of chopped chives or spring onions is sometimes sprinkled over the meat before serving.

The taste of beef with turnips is a very traditional Chinese one.

The Complete Chinese Cookbook

Braised Marinated Beef with Star Anise

Serves 8–10, with other dishes

4 lb (1¾ kg) braising beef *or* topside
4 tablespoons soya sauce
1½ tablespoons hoisin sauce
6 tablespoons sherry
1 tablespoon sugar
1 teaspoon salt
1 tablespoon vinegar
pepper
2 tablespoons flour
2 cloves garlic
2 slices root ginger
4 tablespoons vegetable oil
2 cloves star anise

Preparation Pound the beef evenly with a wooden hammer or the back of a heavy Chinese chopper. Prick it in about a dozen places with a fork; then place it in a deep dish to marinate for 2 hours in a mixture of soya sauce, hoisin sauce, sherry, sugar, salt, vinegar, and pepper. Turn it over every 30 minutes. Drain, and keep the remainder of the marinade for later use. Dredge the beef with flour, crush the garlic, and shred the ginger.

Cooking Heat the oil in a heavy frying pan. Add the garlic, ginger, and star anise. Stir-fry gently over a medium heat for 1 minute, then add the beef, and brown it on both sides by frying it over a medium heat for 6–7 minutes. Lower the heat to minimum and insert an asbestos sheet beneath the pan. Add 4 tablespoons water to the remaining marinade, blend well, and pour over the beef. Cover and cook very gently for 45 minutes, turning the meat twice, and basting it every 15 minutes with the liquid at the bottom of the pan. Check to make sure that the liquid has not run dry: if it has, mix together 1 tablespoon soya sauce, 1 tablespoon sherry, and 2 tablespoons stock, and continue to baste the beef with this mixture, cooking the meat for a further 45 minutes, keeping only a small amount of liquid in the pan, but never allowing it to run dry.

Serving When cooked, allow the beef to stand for 1 minute, then slice it into thin slices, about 1½ × 2 inches (3½ × 5 cm). Beef prepared in this manner can be eaten hot or cold, dipped in Soya-Mustard Dip (see Index).

Moslem Long-Simmered Beef

Serves 6–10, with other dishes

4 lb (1¾ kg) shin beef
1 piece Chinese dried tangerine peel
2 large onions
6 tablespoons vegetable oil
6 tablespoons soya sauce
4 tablespoons sherry
1½ tablespoons sugar
2 slices root ginger

Beef

The following recipe, which comes from the Yu I-Sung Moslem restaurant in Peking, shows that there is no absolute rule in Chinese cooking. For the beef is long-simmered, after first being stir-fried and then cooked quickly in water before the cooking proper commences. This is an unusual procedure.

Preparation Soak the tangerine peel in water for 20 minutes; then drain. Slice the onions and cut the beef into 1½ inch (3½ cm) cubes.
Cooking Heat the oil in a large pan over a high heat. Stir-fry the beef cubes for 6–7 minutes, then drain and discard the excess oil. Pour the beef into a large pan of boiling water, and boil vigorously for 3 minutes. Drain the beef, and place it in a heavy pot or casserole. Just cover the meat with fresh water and add all the other ingredients. Bring to the boil, cover, and turn the heat down to minimum. Insert an asbestos sheet under the pan. Keep tightly closed and cook for 4 hours, turning the beef over once every hour. The beef may be cooked in a casserole in the oven – the temperature should then be kept at 280°F (140°C or Gas Mark 1) after the initial boil. If the liquid in the pan or casserole runs short after 3–3½ hours cooking, add a small cup of water and turn the beef over.

The tendons in shin beef have a jelly-like quality which adds variation and interest to the texture of the meat, and a special succulence to the dish.

Steamed Beef Balls with Oyster Sauce

Serves 4–8, with other dishes

1½ lb (600 g) lean beef
3 water chestnuts
2 medium-sized onions
1 egg
1 teaspoon salt
2 tablespoons flour
2 tablespoons cornflour

oil for deep-frying
2 tablespoons oyster sauce
2 teaspoons shrimp sauce
1 tablespoon soya sauce
½ tablespoon sherry
3 tablespoons water
½ teaspoon chilli sauce
2 teaspoons cornflour
1 tablespoon chopped parsley

Preparation Mince the beef and chop the water chestnuts and onions finely. Mix with the egg, salt, and flour, and shape into balls the size of walnuts. Dredge with the cornflour.
Cooking Place the beef balls in a wire basket and fry them in very hot oil in 3–4 lots for 3 minutes each. Place the balls in a bowl in a steamer, and steam vigorously for 10 minutes. Meanwhile prepare the sauce by mixing the remaining ingredients together (except for the parsley) until they have blended into a consistent mixture; then heat until it thickens. Pour this over the meat balls after removing them from the steamer. Sprinkle them with chopped parsley and serve.

When oysters are in season, there is no reason why four large oysters should not be chopped up and added to the sauce. In this case, double the sherry used, and increase the heating time by 30 seconds. Sauce made with fresh oysters is invariably more interesting than sauce made with oyster sauce. In fact, sauce made with fresh oysters is one of the most exciting sauces used in Chinese noodle cooking in the coastal areas of China.

Steamed Beef Balls with Szechuan Cabbage

Serves 4–8, with other dishes

Preparation Repeat the recipe for Steamed Beef Balls with Oyster Sauce, but omit the ingredients for the sauce. Instead, use 1 medium-sized cauliflower, and 3–4 oz (75–100 g) pickled Szechuan cabbage.

The cauliflower should be broken up into individual branches – about 1½ × 2 inch (3½ × 5 cm) pieces – and used to pack the bottom of a heat-proof dish or basin. Cover this with a layer of all the pre-fried meat balls, and then a layer of sliced Szechuan pickled cabbage. Leave the dish uncovered, and steam at full strength for 20 minutes. The moisture which seeps through the hot-spiced pickles down to the meat balls and cauliflower below will enrich and give extra spice to them.

Quick Stir-Fried Shredded Beef and Beef Slices

Except in a few instances, shredded beef and beef slices are always cooked with one or two other ingredients cut or sliced into similar shapes and sizes as the beef itself. These materials are generally vegetables – occasionally dried vegetables are used with fresh vegetables.

Most vegetables which are cooked with shredded beef can usually also be stir-fried with beef slices. The only adjustment which needs to be made is in the cutting of the meat. To avoid repetition, I have included both types of beef in the same section.

Quick Dry-Fried Beef Ribbons

Serves 4–8, with other dishes

1 lb (400 g) lean beef
3 tablespoons soya sauce
1 teaspoon sugar
1 tablespoon sherry
2 chilli peppers
4 tablespoons vegetable oil

Beef

This is one of the few instances where beef is fried almost entirely on its own, with the addition of seasonings and two pieces of chilli pepper, to make it extremely hot and spicy.

Preparation Slice the beef with a sharp knife into matchstick strips. Add the soya sauce, sugar, and sherry; mix well and marinate for 1 hour. Cut the peppers into similar size strips, discarding the pips.
Cooking Heat the oil in a frying pan until it is very hot. Add the peppers and stir-fry quickly for 20 seconds. Add the beef and stir-fry over a high heat for 3 minutes. Reduce heat to medium and continue to stir-fry until nearly all the liquid has evaporated or appears to have been absorbed into the meat; about 3–4 minutes. Reduce heat to very low and continue to stir-fry for 2 more minutes so that the beef becomes completely dried. Quick stir-frying has to be maintained throughout these last stages to prevent burning.
Serving When this dish is successful there is a feeling that all the tasty-savouriness has gone into the beef. It should be served in a flat, very well-heated serving dish. The beef should by then be in brown crispy shreds and is highly savoury and an excellent accompaniment to drinks.

In Western kitchens, the last stage of cooking can be done under a grill.

Quick-Fried Spiced Steak in Oyster Sauce

Serves 4–8, with other dishes

1¼ lb (500 g) beef (rump *or* fillet)
3 tablespoons oyster sauce
1 tablespoon soya sauce
1 tablespoon hoisin sauce

2 tablespoons sherry
1½ tablespoons cornflour
5 tablespoons vegetable oil
3 tablespoons superior stock
2 spring onion stalks
2 slices root ginger

This is a favourite dish in Canton, where cooking meat and seafoods together is widely practised.

Preparation Cut the beef (against the grain) into 1½ × 2 inch (3½ × 5 cm) very thin slices. Marinate in a basin for 30 minutes with soya sauce, hoisin sauce, and half of the sherry. Dust with half of the cornflour. Finally add 1 tablespoon of the oil and work it into the beef with the fingers. In another bowl, mix the oyster sauce, the stock, and the remaining cornflour. Cut the spring onions into 1 inch (2½ cm) segments.
Cooking Heat the oil in a large frying pan over a high heat. When it is very hot, pour in the marinated beef, spread it out in the pan and stir-fry quickly for 1 minute. Pour away any excess oil and drain the beef. Place the pan over the heat again, and use the oil left in it to stir-fry the ginger and spring onions together for 30 seconds. Return the beef to the pan and pour in the

remainder of the sherry. Stir and turn the beef round a few times, and spread it out in the pan. Pour the oyster/stock mixture evenly over the beef. Stir and scramble for 20 seconds over a high heat, and dish out immediately on to a well-heated serving plate.

Ideally, the steak should be eaten the moment it is served. It is a great dish, and being comparatively quick and easy to prepare, it is often seen and used in domestic cooking as well as at parties.

Quick-Fried Sliced Steak with Tomatoes

Serves 4–8, with other dishes

1¼ lb (500 g) lean beef (rump *or* fillet)
4–5 firm medium-sized tomatoes
1 teaspoon salt
1½ tablespoons soya sauce
1 tablespoon sherry
pepper
2 spring onion stalks
1 clove garlic
½ tablespoon cornflour
6 tablespoons stock
3 tablespoons vegetable oil

Preparation Slice the beef very thinly against the grain into 1½ × 2 inch (3½ × 5 cm) slices. Marinate with half of the salt, the soya sauce, and the sherry for 15 minutes. Peel the tomatoes, cut each one into quarters, and sprinkle with the remaining salt, and pepper to taste. Cut the spring onions into 2 inch (5 cm) segments. Crush the garlic. Blend the cornflour with 3 parts stock.

Cooking Heat the oil in a large frying pan. Add half of the onions and garlic and stir-fry for 15 seconds. Add the beef and stir-fry over a high heat for 1 minute. Stir in the remainder of the stock and continue to stir-fry and scramble for 15 seconds. Add the cornflour mixture. Stir until the liquid in the pan thickens, then add the tomato wedges, spreading them evenly over the pan. Allow these to heat through for 30 seconds. Sprinkle with the remainder of the spring onions, and serve.

Quick-Fried Beef Ribbons with Onion

Serves 4–8, with other dishes

1¼ lb (500 g) lean beef
4 medium-sized onions
2½ tablespoons soya sauce
1 tablespoon hoisin sauce
2 tablespoons sherry
1 teaspoon sugar
salt
pepper to taste
½ tablespoon cornflour
4 tablespoons vegetable oil

This is one of the most commonly seen beef dishes, and one of the most easily successful.

Beef

Preparation Slice the beef against the grain into matchstick strips. Cut the onions into similar strips. Mix the soya sauce, hoisin sauce, half of the sherry, the sugar, ½ teaspoon salt, and the pepper; add to the beef, and marinate together for 15 minutes. Dust with cornflour.
Cooking Heat 2 tablespoons of the oil in a frying pan. Add the onion and some salt, and stir-fry over a high heat for 3 minutes. Push the onion to the sides of the pan. Pour the remaining oil into the pan, and when it is hot, add the beef and any remaining marinade. Stir-fry quickly for 1 minute, then bring in the onions from the side of the pan and stir-fry together with the beef for 1 minute. Add the remaining sherry, stir-fry for a further 30 seconds, and serve.

This dish is a good accompaniment to rice, and should be served piping hot.

Quick-Fried Beef Ribbons with Young Leeks

Serves 4–8, with other dishes

Preparation Repeat the recipe for Quick-Fried Beef Ribbons with Onion, using 8 oz (200 g) young leeks instead of the onions.

This is a particularly attractive dish – there is a striking contrast in colour between the rich brown of the beef and the glistening green of the well-oiled leeks. The strong flavours of both ingredients appear to blend well together over high heat.

Quick-Fried Beef Ribbons with Spring Onions and Shredded Carrots

Serves 4–8, with other dishes

Carrots and spring onions combine to give this dish colour appeal.

Repeat the recipe for Quick-Fried Beef Ribbons with Onion using 3–4 oz (75–100 g) spring onions and 2 small, young carrots instead of the onions. Clean the spring onions and chop them into 2 inch (5 cm) segments (include the green parts), and slice the carrots into matchstick strips. Stir-fry the carrots for 1 minute before adding the beef, and add the spring onions to the pan only during the last minute's stir-frying over a high heat, together with the beef and other ingredients. An additional tablespoon of oil will probably be required during the stir-frying.

The Complete Chinese Cookbook

Hot Spiced Beef Ribbons Quick-Fried with Shredded Sweet Peppers and Chilli Peppers

Serves 4–8, with other dishes

Preparation Repeat the recipe for Quick-Fried Beef Ribbons with Onion using 1 large green pepper, 1 large red pepper, 2 chilli peppers, and ½ teaspoon of five spice powder instead of the onions. Remove the seeds from both peppers and slice them into matchstick shreds. Remove the pips from the chilli peppers and chop each into four pieces.

Cooking Heat half of the oil in a frying pan, and stir-fry the chilli pepper over a high heat for 40 seconds. Use a perforated spoon to remove most of the nearly-burnt chilli pepper. Stir-fry the red and green peppers for 1 minute, then push them to the sides of the pan. Add the remaining oil and beef to the centre of the pan and stir-fry for 30 seconds. Sprinkle the beef with the five spice powder and stir-fry for another 30 seconds. Bring in the peppers from the sides of the pan and stir-fry them with the beef for 1 minute. Sprinkle the remaining sherry over the beef and peppers. Turn and toss several times; then serve.

This is a dish from Szechuan in west China and is therefore very hot – a boon to those who like hot spicy foods.

Beef Barbecue

Serves 6, with other dishes

2½ lb (1 kg) lean beef (rump *or* fillet)
4 tablespoons soya sauce
2 tablespoons sherry
1 tablespoon vinegar
1 teaspoon sugar
dash of pepper
2 cloves garlic
2 slices root ginger
6 spring onion stalks
6 eggs

Beef Barbecue is one of the Chinese modern dishes (originating probably from the great grasslands of the north west) which is a great favourite in Peking. Thinly-sliced beef, either marinated or unmarinated, is grilled over wire-mesh grates fitted over the top of an earthenware pot charcoal brazier with a diameter across the top of about 18–24 inches (45–60 cm).

If unmarinated, diners should dip the slices of beef into one or several of the following dips on the table: Salt and Pepper Mix, Hot Mustard Sauce, Soya-Oil-Garlic Dip, Soya-Mustard Dip, Soya-Sherry Dip, Soya-Chilli-Oil Dip, and hoisin sauce (see Index). The barbecued beef should then be eaten

Beef

with ordinary Man Tou (steamed buns), Flower Roll Steamed Buns, or Silver Thread Steamed Buns, or it can be eaten with British toasted buns.

If the beef is to be marinated before being barbecued, the following recipe can be used.

Preparation Cut the beef against the grain into 1 × 2 inch (2½ × 5 cm) very thin pieces. Add the soya sauce, sherry, vinegar, sugar, and pepper. Crush the garlic, shred the ginger, and add them to the beef with the other seasoning ingredients. Leave the meat to marinate for 30 minutes. Slice each onion stalk into two. Give each a bash with the side of a chopper, and cut into 2½ inch (6 cm) segments. Tie each segment into a love-knot. Arrange them in three or four small saucer-size plates, and place them strategically around the table for the use of diners. Beat an egg in each of six bowls, one for each diner.

Cooking and Serving When the charcoal in the brazier is fully ablaze, and most or all of the smokiness has dissipated, bring it to the dinner table. (It should be of the heavy wooden type used by Elizabethans or in Old English kitchens.) Place it on a large metal tray. When the meal commences, each diner will pick up a piece of beef and a segment of spring onion with a pair of extra long wooden or bamboo chopsticks, and place them on top of the wire-netted grate to barbecue for 1–1¼ minutes. He should then pick them up again quickly, and dip them into the beaten egg (both to cool and take a coating) and then into the dips and mixes, before eating them with his steamed or toasted buns.

To repair to the East Market in Peking to eat this dish after a freezing day out in the open, was one of the relieving features of the great student demonstrations of the 1930s.

Red-Cooked Oxtail

Serves 6–8, with other dishes

5–6 lb (2–2½ kg) oxtail, chopped into its natural segments
2 cloves garlic
3 slices root ginger

1 teaspoon salt
6 tablespoons soya sauce
1½ tablespoons hoisin sauce
4 tablespoons sherry
¼ pint (125 ml) superior stock
2 teaspoons sugar

Like all meats, oxtail can be red-cooked, and there seems to be no better way of preparing it.

Preparation Crush the garlic. Clean the oxtail and boil the segments for 3–4 minutes in boiling water. Place them in a heavy pot or casserole with the garlic, ginger, salt, soya sauce, and hoisin sauce. Add 1½ pints (750 ml) water.

Cooking Bring contents of pan to the boil. Put an asbestos sheet under the pan and leave to simmer over the lowest heat for 1½ hours. Turn the contents over once every 30 minutes. Add the sherry, stock, and sugar, and continue to simmer over the lowest heat for another hour, turning the contents over after 30 minutes. If cooked in a casserole in the oven, cook at 300°F (150°C or Gas Mark 2) for 3 hours.

Serving Oxtail so cooked should be served in a bowl or deep dish. Eat it with plain boiled rice, and ample gravy.

Hot Spiced Chinese Peppered Steak

Serves 6–10, with other dishes

3 lb (1¼ kg) beef
2 slices root ginger
4 tablespoons soya sauce
4 tablespoons sherry
2 teaspoons sugar
½ teaspoon salt
1 tablespoon hoisin sauce
¼ teaspoon freshly milled black pepper
¼ teaspoon red chilli pepper
5 tablespoons vegetable oil

Preparation Shred the ginger. Cut the beef along the grain into pieces 3–4 inches (7½–10 cm) long, 1 inch (2½ cm) thick, and 2 inches (5 cm) wide. Sprinkle them with soya sauce, sherry, sugar, salt, hoisin sauce, shredded ginger, pepper, and chilli pepper; rub in well. Allow the beef to marinate for 1 hour. Rub with 1½ tablespoons of the oil, and continue to marinate for another 30 minutes.

Cooking and Serving Heat the remaining oil in a large frying pan. Add the beef strips and marinade, and gently stir-fry over a medium heat for 9–10 minutes, turning the strips over as they fry. Remove the strips of beef from the pan, place them on a chopping board, and slice them against the grain into ¼ inch (⅓ cm) slices. Arrange them on a serving dish in fish scale fashion, and serve.

Lamb & Mutton

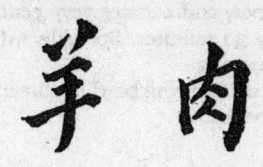

羊肉

We Chinese do not make a distinction between lamb and mutton: sheep's meat is sheep's meat, regardless of the age of the animal. In fact, we even call goats mountain sheep (San Yang); and, indeed, in many hilly and mountainous southern provinces, goat meat is eaten more often than lamb or mutton. It is in the north, in the provinces which border Mongolia, in Inner Mongolia, and Sinkiang, that lamb and mutton come into their own. They form the principal meat diet of the Chinese Moslems. Owing to the proximity of Peking to Inner Mongolia, and the large number of Chinese Moslem restaurants which have been established in the capital, mutton and lamb have become the favourite meats eaten in Peking. Yet there are not a great many lamb dishes. The best known are probably Mongolian Hot-Pot, Mongolian Brazier-Grilled Lamb, and Thrice-Cooked Lamb of Lung Fu Ssi (from the 'East End' of Peking), which have all become special features and attractions of that city.

However, we shall start from the easier and more practical lamb dishes and graduate towards those which are practised on a larger national scale.

Red-Cooked Lamb

Serves 10–12

5–6 lb (2–2¼ kg) leg of lamb *or* mutton
6 spring onion stalks
½ teaspoon salt
6 tablespoons soya sauce
1 tablespoon hoisin sauce
2 slices root ginger

Preparation Chop the lamb or mutton into 2 × 1 inch (5 × 2½ cm) pieces. Wash in fresh water, and drain. Cut the spring onions into 1½ inch (3¾ cm) segments.

Cooking Place the pieces of lamb or mutton in a large casserole or heavy cooking pan. Add salt, soya sauce, hoisin sauce, ginger, half of the spring onions, and 2 pints (generous litre) water. Bring to the boil; then insert an asbestos sheet under the pot, and simmer very gently for 2½ hours, turning the meat over once every 30 minutes. Sprinkle with the remaining spring onions 5 minutes before serving.

Serving Serve either in a large serving bowl or tureen, or else in the casserole in which the meat was cooked.

Tung-Po Red-Cooked Lamb

Serves 6

2¼ lb (1¼ kg) saddle of lamb
4 oz (100 g) potato
4 oz (100 g) carrots
2 medium-sized onions
1 clove garlic
1 dried chilli pepper
8 tablespoons vegetable oil
1 teaspoon salt
4 tablespoons soya sauce
1 slice root ginger
2 teaspoons brown sugar
4 tablespoons sherry

Tung-Po, the great Chinese poet of the Sung Dynasty, is said to have created a great many Chinese dishes during his banishment from Court. However, it is doubtful whether he created this dish, as he was banished not to the north or west, but to the south, where people mostly ate goat. Nevertheless the dish is called by his name. It is taken from the Yu I-Sung, which is a well-known Moslem restaurant in Peking.

Preparation Slice the lamb into large thin pieces, about ¼ inch (½ cm) thick, and then cut again crosswise into triangular 1½ inch (3½ cm) pieces. Peel the potato and carrots, and cut them into similar triangular pieces. Slice the onions thinly, crush the garlic, and chop the pepper into four pieces, removing the seeds.

Cooking Pour the oil into a large frying pan over a high heat. When very hot, add the pieces of lamb, and stir-fry for 4–5 minutes. Drain and set aside. Place the potato and carrot in the remaining oil. Stir-fry together for 5–6 minutes; then drain and put to one side. Place the lamb at the bottom of a heavy pan or cooking pot over a low heat, and add sufficient water to cover. Add the salt, soya sauce, garlic, ginger, pepper, and brown sugar. When the contents start to boil, cover the pan and insert an asbestos sheet underneath it. Leave to cook gently for 2 hours, turning the meat every 30 minutes; then add the fried carrots, potato, and sherry, and cook for a further 15 minutes.

Serving When serving, lift the contents of the cooking pot into a large serving bowl or deep dish, so that the carrots and potato will be arranged at the bottom of the dish, and the lamb on top.

Lamb and Mutton

Note The same dish can, of course, also be cooked in the oven by simmering it at 300°F (150°C or Gas Mark 2) for 2½ hours, and adding the carrots, potato, and sherry during the last 30 minutes.

Sliced Lamb Quick-Fried with Spring Onions

Serves 6, with other dishes

1½ lb (600 g) leg of lamb
6 spring onion stalks
2 cloves garlic
2 slices root ginger
2 tablespoons soya sauce
½ teaspoon salt
1 tablespoon sherry
4 tablespoons vegetable oil

Preparation Slice the lamb thinly into 2 × 1 inch (5 × 2½ cm) slices. Crush the garlic and shred the ginger. Add the garlic, ginger, soya sauce, salt, and sherry to the lamb and marinate for 30 minutes. Cut the spring onions into 2 inch (5 cm) segments (include all the green parts).
Cooking Heat the oil in a large frying pan. When very hot, pour in the marinated lamb, and stir-fry quickly over a high heat for 1½ minutes. Add the onion segments and continue to stir-fry for 1½ minutes. Dish out on to a well-heated serving plate; serve and eat immediately.

This is a highly savoury and aromatic dish, which is both quick to prepare and universally appealing.

Shredded Lamb Quick-Fried with Ginger and Young Leeks

Serves 6, with other dishes

1½ lb (600 g) leg of lamb
8 oz (200 g) young leeks
4 slices root ginger
1 chilli pepper
2⅓ tablespoons soya sauce
2 tablespoons sherry
4 tablespoons vegetable oil
1 teaspoon salt

Preparation Slice the lamb against the grain into matchstick strips. Cut the leeks, ginger, and pepper into similar shreds. Combine soya sauce and sherry, and marinate the lamb in the mixture for 20 minutes.
Cooking Heat 2¼ tablespoons of the oil in a frying pan. Add the pepper and ginger, and stir-fry them together for 30 seconds. Pour in the marinated lamb, spread the shredded meat out evenly over the pan, and stir-fry quickly for 1½ minutes over a high heat. Remove with a perforated spoon and put aside. Add the remainder of the oil to the pan; then add the leeks and salt, and stir-fry for 1 minute. Return the lamb to the pan. Toss and mix well; then stir-fry together for 1½ minutes. Dish out on to a well-heated serving plate, and serve.

The Complete Chinese Cookbook

Long-Simmered Lamb of Lung Fu Ssi

Serves 6–8

3 lb (1½ kg) leg of lamb
2 medium-sized onions
5 cloves garlic
2 teaspoons salt
5 slices root ginger
1 chilli pepper
6 tablespoons soya sauce
¼ teaspoon freshly milled pepper
1 tablespoon chopped coriander leaves *or* parsley
1 tablespoon chopped chives
3 tablespoons sherry
1 tablespoon vinegar

This recipe comes from the well-known Pai Kwei Chinese Moslem restaurant of Lung Fu Ssi, in Peking. The lamb is cooked very simply. The important thing is that the pieces of meat must be dipped in a specially mixed dip served at the table.

Preparation Chop the lamb into 1½ × 1 × ½ inch (3½ × 2½ × 1 cm) pieces. Rinse in fresh water, and drain. Heat 2 pints (generous litre) of water in a saucepan. When it boils, add the lamb pieces. Boil for 30 seconds, then pour away all the water and scum. Cut the onions into slices and crush the garlic.
Cooking Place the pieces of lamb in a heavy cooking pot or saucepan, or in a heat-proof casserole. Just cover them with water. Add the salt, onion, 2 slices of the ginger, and 2 cloves of garlic. Bring to the boil, then lower the heat to a minimum. Insert an asbestos sheet underneath the pan, and leave to simmer gently for 2½ hours, turning the lamb over every 45 minutes. The pot should be kept securely covered all the time.
Serving Shred the remaining ginger, crush and chop the 3 remaining garlic cloves and chop the chilli pepper finely. Mix these three ingredients with all the other unused ingredients and then divide the mixture among three or four bowls. Place these strategically around the table.

If the lamb is cooked in either an earthenware or iron pot, or in a casserole, it should be brought to the table in its container. Each diner may then dip the plain-cooked lamb in the dip sauce before eating it.

Quick-Fried Triple Lamb

Serves 6

12 oz (300 g) leg of lamb
8 oz (200 g) lamb's liver
2 lamb's kidneys
2 spring onion stalks
2 slices root ginger
2 cloves garlic
4½ tablespoons soya sauce
3 tablespoons sherry
5 tablespoons vegetable oil
2 tablespoons sesame oil

Lamb and Mutton

Preparation Cut the lamb into thin 2 × 1 inch (5 × 2½ cm) slices; clean and remove any gristle from the liver and kidneys. Cut the liver into slices similar to the lamb meat. Cut each kidney into three flat slices, give each several crosswise cuts halfway through, and then cut each slice into three pieces. Chop the spring onions into ¼ inch (½ cm) segments, shred the ginger, and crush and chop the garlic. Marinate the lamb slices in 1½ tablespoons of the soya sauce, 1 tablespoon of the sherry, and the spring onions. Marinate the liver in 1½ tablespoons of the soya sauce, 1 tablespoon of the sherry, and the shredded ginger; and marinate the kidneys in 1½ tablespoons of the soya sauce, 1 tablespoon of the sherry, and the garlic. All three items should be marinated for 30 minutes.

Cooking Heat 2 tablespoons of the vegetable oil in a large frying pan. When the oil is very hot, pour in the marinated lamb meat, and stir-fry for 1½ minutes over a high heat. Remove, and set aside to keep hot. Add 1 tablespoon of vegetable oil to the pan. Pour in the marinated liver. Stir-fry quickly for 1 minute, then put aside and keep hot. Add the remaining vegetable oil to the pan, then add the kidneys, and stir-fry quickly for 30 seconds. Add the sesame oil. Return the lamb and liver to the pan. Stir-fry the contents over high heat for 45 seconds, then remove to a well-heated dish, and serve.

The three different types of lamb, with their three quite different textures, tastes, and marinades, give the dish quite a distinctive character. Eat with freshly cooked boiled or steamed rice.

Peking Mongolian Sliced Lamb Hot-Pot

Serves 6–8

5 lb (2 kg) leg *or* shoulder of lamb
1 pint (500 ml) secondary stock
1½ pints (750 ml) superior stock *or* chicken stock
1 lb (400 g) Chinese cabbage *or* a mixture of Savoy cabbage and celery
8 oz (200 g) spinach
4 oz (100 g) pea-starch transparent noodles, soaked and drained
1 teaspoon salt

This dish is called Peking Mongolian, as it originated in Mongolia and later achieved fame and recognition in Peking. Thinly-sliced lamb, cooked at the table by the diners themselves, in a funnelled charcoal-burning hot-pot, was first introduced to Peking in 1855, in the reign of Emperor Shanfeng of the Manchu Dynasty. It has been gaining in popularity ever since, and is now recognized as one of the gastronomic features of Peking. The best-known establishment for this do-it-yourself hot-pot is the Tung Lai Sung Restaurant in the East Market, where over twenty meat-slicing specialist chefs work full-time. A half-pound chunk of meat would usually be cut into 30 thin slices, and the average slicing speed of a specialist is from 12-16 slices per minute. In the West, the slicing can be done with a mechanical cutter, or you can slice or shave as well as is necessary with a sharp knife. To achieve reasonable results is probably easier than one would at first imagine, since it is not essential that the slices of meat are of an absolutely regular shape or thickness, just so long as they are not too thick.

Table Dips Provide a selection of the following ingredients for the diners to use when mixing table dips: soya sauce, hoisin sauce, chilli sauce, mustard, tomato sauce, vinegar, sesame paste, chopped ginger, chopped garlic, chopped spring onions, and chopped coriander leaves. These items can be placed in individual sauce dishes, or in some cases, two or more items, such as ginger and vinegar, or chilli sauce and soya sauce can be combined. Usually the mixing is done by the diners themselves according to their individual taste.

Cooking Utensil The traditional Peking hot-pot is different from many southern hot-pots in that it has a large squat funnel which rises from the centre of the cooking pot, and the foods are cooked in the 'moat' surrounding the funnel. The moat is approximately 5 inches ($12\frac{1}{2}$ cm) deep and 3-4 inches ($7\frac{1}{2}$-10 cm) wide at the top, as it should be able to hold at least 4-5 pints (3 litres) food and liquid. The base must be firm so that there will be little chance of the pot tipping over.

At the Tung Lai Sung in Peking the funnel is exceptionally squat, measuring about 5-6 inches ($12\frac{1}{2}$-15 cm) in diameter at the base, and tapering to 3-4 inches ($7\frac{1}{2}$-10 cm) at the top. As it is nearly 12 inches (30 cm) high, it holds a good stack of charcoal inside, insuring the steady heat which is essential to this type of cooking and eating. The usual way of starting such a burner is to place a few pieces of burning charcoal at the bottom of the funnel, then stack more charcoal on top of this. After a short period of fanning through the side-opening at the base of the funnel, the smouldering will soon develop into burning, and within a few minutes there will be a beautiful blaze. The moat outside the funnel should be filled with stock before the first charcoal is introduced.

Because the average Western home lacks such equipment, any heavy cooking pot or large casserole placed on top of a methylated spirit stove, calor-gas burner, or electric stove will do. However, Peking hot-pots are becoming more easily available from Chinese food-stores and supermarkets.

Cooking and Eating As soon as the stock starts to boil furiously, about a quarter of the vegetables and noodles should be put into the pot, along with the salt. Within 1-2 minutes, the contents will be boiling again. At this point, the diners begin to put their own slices of meat into the cauldron. These should be pushed underneath and submerged in the boiling stock with the aid of bamboo chopsticks. Plastic ones should not be used.

Lamb and Mutton

Meanwhile, the diners can start to mix their own dips from any of the ingredients provided on the table. They can mix one or two types of dip ingredient together or experiment with several.

The slices of meat should cook in the stock within 1½ minutes. They should then be lifted out with a pair of chopsticks and dipped into one or more of the dips before eating.

As the meal progresses, the stock becomes tastier and tastier – until finally all the remaining meat, vegetables, and noodles on the table are added to the moat for a final boil-up. This is done by placing a lid over the moat, thus allowing the contents to boil or simmer for 3–4 minutes. These are then divided among the individual bowls of the diners for a grand 'wash-down'.

The point about this type of cooking-while-you-eat is the simplicity in the choice of materials, the freshness due to instant cooking, and the variety and livening effect of the quick dip in the various piquant sauces before consumption.

Peking Mongolian Barbecued or Brazier-Grilled Sliced Lamb

When winter comes around in Peking, another favourite feature of cook-at-the-table eating is the Mongolian Barbecue of Sliced Lamb. The lamb is cut into slices similar in size to those in the previous recipe, but the cooking method is different in that the lamb is brazier-grilled on the table. The brazier consists of an earthen pot with fine-mesh wire grills over the top, on which the slices of lamb are cooked. The fire is fanned to a full blaze outside in the open, and then brought in and placed on the dining table on a metal tray, although as often as not the cooking and eating are done in the courtyard.

This dish was first introduced to Peking by visiting Mongolian dignitaries in 1644 in the reign of Emperor Tun Chi. It is now one of the features of the Tung Lai Sung Restaurant in the East Market, but the two best-known places for this dish are the Barbecue Wan of the South City, which has been operating for one hundred years, and the Barbecue Chi of the North City which has been operating for nearly two hundred years.

The only vegetable used with this type of lamb dish is sliced onion or spring onions. The wire grills are first of all rubbed with fat or oil, and tested with a drop of water. If the water sizzles, the grill is hot enough to commence the barbecue.

Each diner can mix his own selection of dips in his dip bowl (empty bowls are given to each diner for this purpose). Provide the same dip ingredients as in the previous recipe, but the diners may beat an egg in another bowl and use that as an additional dip. Usually when a slice of lamb and a slice of onion have been grilled for about 1 minute, the diner plunges them into the beaten egg to cool and coat them before dipping them into one or more of the dips before eating. The lamb can be eaten on its own or with Chinese steamed buns, either the plain ones called Man Tou, or with the fancier ones called Lotus Leaf Buns (Ho Yeh Pao). It can also be accompanied by Toasted Cake (Shao Pin). The joy of eating lamb which is hot, tender, and aromatic is soul-consuming!

Such a meal is best staged outdoors in the West, as most ceilings are low in modern buildings.

A modern barbecue is suitable, but it is better to use a small brazier of the type normally used by road-menders and building-site workers in the winter – a strong perforated tin loaded with charcoal for cooking. A fine-meshed grill should be fitted over the top of the brazier. The arrangement need not be placed on top of a table, but on some brickwork to raise it to table level. Small plain wooden tables or boxes can then be placed all around the brazier from which the diners can operate (with chopsticks 24 inches (60 cm) long), and on which the dip bowls can be placed.

The Japanese 'Hibachi' stove, which is a derivation of the Peking-Mongolian brazier, is, of course, excellent for the job, so long as it is a large one.

The approximate calculation for meat is 12–16 oz (300–400 g) of lamb per diner (although some student colleagues of my younger days have been known to consume 25 dishes, or about 5 lb (2½ kg)!). When eaten in small thin slices one at a time, the total quantity eaten is often not realized

Chicken

鶏

Chicken is one of the most versatile items of food in China; it is also one of the most convenient because of its widespread availability. Every village in China is roused by the crowing cock, and every farmyard or peasant holding in the land is alive with the sound of clucking chickens. A chicken dish on the table is associated with a feeling of occasion or festivity, and it is invariably augmented by a wide selection of side-dishes and condiments. When extra food is needed on the unexpected arrival of guests or relatives, or when there is a celebration in the family, a chicken can always be killed to provide a special meal.

In many dishes produced in China, chicken and pork are often interchangeable because of their many similarities. They are both white, and unlike beef, they do not become so tough after being cooked for a short period as to need very prolonged cooking before they are tenderized again. Chickens come in convenient unit sizes, and the meat is always ready for cooking, unlike the larger animals which cannot be killed and prepared for a meal with the same speed. Hence, although chicken is rather more of a delicacy than pork on the Chinese dinner table, it is nearly as extensively used.

As with the majority of other foods in Chinese cooking, chicken can be cooked either whole or chopped through the bone into square or oblong pieces. To enjoy chicken served in this way we Chinese have learnt to become experts in disengaging and stripping the meat from the bone; this is done with dexterity within the mouth. The breast meat can be cut into thin slices and stir-fried with other ingredients; or the meat can be minced, mixed with other ingredients and formed into balls or cakes, or else served as velveteen chicken. Sometimes chicken meat is shredded into matchstick strips for quick-frying with other ingredients, such as pimento or mushrooms, which

The Complete Chinese Cookbook

are also cut or shredded into similar strips. In this form, chicken is used very extensively with noodles, which are similar in shape to chicken strips, and prepared by frying or cold-tossing or even used with ham as a garnish.

The total number of dishes which can be produced from chicken, including all the possible combinations and regional variations, certainly runs into many hundreds. The recipes included in this chapter are only a selection.

Red-Cooked Chicken

Serves 4-6, with other dishes

1 4-5 lb (1¾-2 kg) chicken *or* capon
2 medium-sized onions
3 spring onion stalks

5-6 tablespoons soya sauce
3 slices root ginger
2 teaspoons sugar
¼ teaspoon salt
3 tablespoons sherry

This is really a form of Chinese stewing and it is one of the most popular and common ways of cooking chicken in China because of its simplicity. Red-cooking mainly differs from Western stews in that ginger, soya sauce, and sugar are used. These three ingredients have a marked contribution to the end-product; the ginger eliminates any rankness and untoward taste in the bird, the soya sauce enhances its savouriness, and sugar helps to enrich it. Most meats can be red-cooked, and Red-Cooked Chicken is one of the favourite dishes on a Chinese dinner table at home.

Preparation Wash the chicken thoroughly, inside and out; then place it in a heavy pot with 1¼ pints (750 ml) of water. Bring to the boil and continue boiling for 5 minutes, turning the bird over a few times. Pour away all the water and impurities. Meanwhile, slice the onions thinly and cut the spring onions into 2 inch (5 cm) pieces.

Cooking Put the chicken into a heat-proof casserole, pour over ¼ pint (125 ml) of fresh water, then add the soya sauce, ginger, onions, sugar, and salt. Bring the liquid to the boil, then put the casserole in an oven preheated to 375°F (190°C or Gas Mark 5). Cook in the oven for 1¼ hours, turning the bird over two or three times. Remove the casserole from the oven and sprinkle the spring onions and sherry over the chicken. Return the casserole to the oven for a further 30 minutes.

Serving Serve the chicken from the casserole or in a large bowl or tureen. It should be sufficiently tender to take apart with a pair of chopsticks but fingers may be used discreetly. Although the cooking here is simple, the chicken should be delicious.

Chicken

Note Instead of cooking the chicken in a casserole, it could also be cooked in a pot over a very low heat, with an asbestos sheet inserted under the pot, if necessary.

Chinese Roast Chicken

Serves 4–6, with other dishes

1 3–4 lb (1¼–1¾ kg) roasting chicken
1 clove garlic
2 slices root ginger
1½ tablespoons soya sauce
1 teaspoon salt
1 tablespoon vegetable oil

For the best flavour, use a free-range chicken.

Preparation Wash and dry the chicken, inside and out. Leave it in an airy place for 1 hour to dry out. Crush the garlic, shred the ginger, and chop both very finely. Combine the garlic and ginger with the soya sauce, salt, and vegetable oil, and blend thoroughly. Rub the chicken all over with this mixture and allow the seasoning to sink in for 30 minutes before cooking.
Cooking Roast the chicken for 1 hour in an oven preheated to 400°F (205°C or Gas Mark 6).
Serving The chicken can either be served carved in the Western style or else chopped into fricassée or Chinese double-mahjong pieces. It should have a better flavour than the average roast chicken, without the rankness and sometimes unpleasant taste often present in a battery-produced chicken.

Crispy-Skin Pepper Chicken

Serves 4–6, with other dishes

1 3–4 lb (1¼–1¾ kg) chicken
1½ tablespoons salt
1 teaspoon freshly-milled black pepper
3 slices root ginger
2 tablespoons soya sauce
2 tablespoons vegetable oil

This is a good way of cooking battery-produced chicken. The unpleasant rankness is eliminated and the meat becomes richer in flavour.

Preparation Wash and dry the chicken thoroughly; then leave it in an airy spot for 1 hour to dry further. Mix the salt and pepper in a very dry saucepan and heat over a low heat for 2 minutes until a distinct peppery 'bouquet' arises from the mixture. Shred the ginger and chop it very finely. Rub the bird with the ginger and then with the salt and pepper mixture, inside and out. Repeat. Retain the remainder of the salt and pepper mixture for further rubbing. Leave the chicken in a refrigerator overnight. Repeat the rubbing process the next day and again refrigerate the chicken overnight. The rubbing process may be repeated once more, if desired. Before roasting the chicken, mix the soya sauce and oil in a bowl by beating them together for 15 seconds, then rub bird with this mixture.

Cooking Place the chicken in an oven preheated to 300°F (150°C or Gas Mark 2) for 2 hours. Increase the heat to 400°F (205°C or Gas Mark 6) for 10 minutes. The skin of the chicken should be evenly browned and crispy and the meat should have a delicious flavour by this time.

Serving The chicken can be served either carved in the normal Western style or chopped into fricassée or Chinese double-mahjong pieces.

Note The chicken is left in the refrigerator to season for two nights.

White-Cut Chicken

Serves 4–6, with other dishes

1 2–3 lb (1–1¼ kg) young chicken
3 slices root ginger
1 tablespoon salt
2 tablespoons soya sauce
2 teaspoons sesame oil

This is a basic chicken dish. Its interest is greatly increased by the variety of dips and mixes into which the pieces of chicken can be dipped when served at the table (see the chapter on Table Condiments, page 47). The quality of the chicken meat is also of prime importance here; it must be juicy and rich in flavour. Hence free-range chickens are preferable to battery-produced birds for this dish.

Preparation Clean the chicken thoroughly.

Cooking Bring 3–4 pints (1½–2 litres) of water to the boil in a heavy saucepan. Add the ginger and salt, and immerse the chicken in the boiling water. Reduce the heat to a simmer and insert an asbestos sheet under the pan. Simmer for 30 minutes; then leave the chicken to cool in the stock (which can be used for other purposes).

Serving When the chicken is cool, place it on a heavy chopping-board and chop it into 2 × 1 inch (5 × 2½ cm) double-mahjong pieces. Reassemble these pieces in a serving dish, roughly in the shape of a chicken. Pour over the soya sauce and sesame oil, mixed together. Serve with a variety of table condiments, dips, and mixes.

Wind-Cured Chicken

Serves 4–6, with other dishes

1 4–5 lb (1¾–2 kg) chicken
2 tablespoons salt
1 teaspoon freshly-milled black pepper
1 tablespoon lard

Chicken

A freshly-killed chicken is normally used for this dish in China, together with Szechuan pepper. Since such chicken and the Szechuan pepper berry are hard to obtain, we have to compromise in the ingredients, as well as in the length of hanging time. In China, the bird is usually hung for 10 days: here in the West, I doubt if it would be advisable to hang it longer than about five days.

Preparation Clean and rub the chicken dry, inside and out. Mix the salt and pepper and heat the mixture in a dry pan over a low heat for about 2 minutes, until a distinct peppery 'bouquet' arises. Rub the chicken twice with this salt and pepper mixture; then hang it up in a cool, airy place overnight, away from the sun and other vagaries of climate. Mix the remainder of the salt and pepper mixture with lard, blending well. On the next day, rub the chicken with this impregnated lard and hang it up in an airy spot. After 4–5 days of hanging the chicken should be cured and ready for cooking.

Cooking The chicken is normally cooked either by boiling vigorously for 25 minutes or by 35 minutes vigorous steaming. In the West, it can best be cooked by steaming for 10 minutes, followed by 40 minutes roasting at 400°F (205°C or Gas Mark 6).

Serving Chop the bird into fricassée or mahjong-size pieces and pile them up on a serving dish. If the chicken has been boiled, the stock is a useful by-product. Wind-Cured Chicken has a taste and quality of its own; the stock, too, is extremely rich in flavour.

Note It is best not to try Wind-Cured Chicken in the summer as it might turn out into something quite different!

Salt-Buried Chicken

Serves 4–6, with other dishes

1 2–3 lb (1–1¼ kg) chicken
6–7 lb (3–3½ kg) coarse sea-salt

Preparation Clean the chicken thoroughly and hang it up to dry overnight. Heat the salt in a heat-proof casserole.

Cooking When the salt is quite hot, make a hole in it and bury the chicken completely. Put the lid on the casserole and place it over a low heat for 10 minutes. Put the casserole in an oven preheated to 375°F (190°C or Gas Mark 5) for 1 hour.

Serving Excavate the chicken. Chop it into fricassée or double-mahjong pieces, and pile them on a well-heated serving dish.

Note The salt may be used again.

The Complete Chinese Cookbook
Tramp's Chicken

Serves 4–6, with other dishes

1 3–4 lb (1¼–1¾ kg) chicken
1 large onion
1 3 oz (75 g) leek
2 slices root ginger

2 cloves garlic
1½ teaspoons salt
pepper to taste
1½ tablespoons lard
1 tablespoon soya sauce
2 teaspoons sesame oil

From the province of Kiangsi

This dish is said to have been derived from Chu Yuan Chang, First Emperor of the Ming Dynasty, who went to the south, and while travelling incognito through the province of Kiangsi, learned this recipe.

Preparation Slice the onion thinly, chop the leek into 1 inch (2½ cm) segments, shred the root ginger, and crush and chop the garlic.
Cooking Heat a large pan of water and boil the chicken in it for 40 minutes. Clean the chicken giblets thoroughly; then cut the intestines into ½ inch (2½ cm) segments and slice the kidney, liver, and heart thinly. Dip them into boiling water, boil for 1 minute; then drain. Chop the chicken, through the bone, into large fricassée or double-mahjong pieces. Arrange them in a serving dish or bowl and sprinkle with salt and pepper. Heat the lard in a frying pan. Add the onion, leek, ginger, and garlic. Stir-fry over a high heat for 1½ minutes. Add the giblets and stir-fry them with the vegetables for 3 minutes. Add the soya sauce and sesame oil and continue to stir-fry for a further 3 minutes.
Serving Pour the contents of the frying pan over the pieces of chicken, and serve.

Aromatic Crispy Chicken (1)

Serves 4–6, with other dishes

1 3–4 lb (1¼–1¾ kg) chicken
2½ teaspoons salt
3 slices root ginger
2 tablespoons chopped coriander leaves

2 tablespoons soya sauce
dash of five spice powder
2 tablespoons sherry
oil for deep-frying
spring greens
tomatoes

Preparation Clean the chicken. Rub it thoroughly with the salt, inside and out, and leave to dry overnight. Shred the ginger and mix it with the chopped coriander leaves, soya sauce, five spice powder, and sherry. Rub

Chicken

the chicken with this mixture twice during a period of 2 hours, and leave to dry in an airy place.

Cooking Roast the chicken in an oven preheated to 300°F (150°C or Gas Mark 2) for 1½ hours. Drain the bird and place it in a wire basket; then deep-fry in hot oil for 6–7 minutes, by which time the skin should have become quite crispy.

Serving Chop the chicken into 24 pieces through the bone. Assemble these pieces on a well-heated serving dish in the shape of a chicken. Garnish with spring greens and tomatoes.

Aromatic Crispy Chicken (2)

Serves 4–6, with other dishes

1 3–4 lb (1¼–1¾ kg) chicken
5–6 pints (2½–3 litres) Herbal Master Stock
oil for deep-frying
spring greens
tomatoes

The end result of this recipe is much the same as the previous recipe, but the preparation is somewhat different. Instead of rubbing seasonings on the bird to marinate it, in this recipe the chicken is hot-marinated in herbal master stock before it is deep-fried.

Preparation Clean the chicken thoroughly. Submerge it in a pan of boiling water, boil for 5–6 minutes, then drain.

Cooking Bring the herbal master stock to the boil in a large heavy saucepan, then lower the chicken into the stock and simmer for 35 minutes, until it turns brownish-red. Remove the chicken from the stock and drain for 20 minutes. When well-drained, deep-fry the chicken for 10 minutes until the skin is crispy and aromatic.

Serving Chop the chicken into 24 pieces through the bone. Reassemble these pieces in the shape of a chicken on a well-heated serving dish. Garnish with spring greens and tomatoes.

Cold Crystal Chicken

Serves 4–6, with other dishes

1 3–4 lb (1¼–1¾ kg) young chicken
5–6 oz (125–150 g) smoked ham
1 tablespoon gelatine *or* gelatine powder
¾ pint (375 ml) superior stock
1 tablespoon cornflour
½ teaspoon flavour powder
2 teaspoons salt
4 tablespoons sherry *or* white wine

From Canton

The Complete Chinese Cookbook

Preparation Clean the chicken thoroughly and boil it in 3 pints (1½ litres) of water for 35 minutes. Remove the chicken from this stock and drain well. Skim the fat from the stock and retain ½ pint (250 ml) of stock for later use. Chop the chicken into 20–24 pieces and cut the ham into thin slices. Arrange the pieces of chicken and ham alternately in a deep dish, placing the chicken pieces skin-side down.

Cooking Blend the gelatine with the superior stock, cornflour, flavour powder, salt, and sherry or wine. Add the reserved chicken stock and heat until the liquid begins to thicken. Pour this mixture over the chicken and ham pieces, and place the dish in a refrigerator for 3–4 hours.

Serving When the sauce has turned to jelly, turn the Cold Crystal Chicken on to a large serving plate. This is a summer dish, and the jellied meat is often garnished with colourful vegetables and fruits. Cherries, lychees, strawberries, lettuce, spinach, and even flowers may be used.

Royal Concubine Chicken

Serves 4–6, with other dishes

1 3–4 lb (1¼–1¾ kg) chicken
oil for deep-frying
2 tablespoons soya sauce
8 oz (200 g) streaky pork
2 medium-sized onions
2 slices root ginger
2 cloves garlic
1½ tablespoons lard
2 teaspoons salt
½ pint (250 ml) superior stock
½ pint (250 ml) Chinese yellow wine *or* red wine *or* dry sherry

Preparation Clean and dry the chicken thoroughly. Deep-fry it in hot oil for 7–8 minutes, until evenly browned. Remove the bird from the oil and dip it into a pan of boiling water to remove excess oil. Rub it thoroughly with soya sauce. Chop the pork, cut the onions into thin slices, shred the ginger, and crush the cloves of garlic.

Cooking Place the chicken in a heat-proof casserole. Heat the lard in a frying pan. Add the pork, onions, ginger, and garlic. Stir-fry for 6–7 minutes; then add the mixture to the casserole containing the chicken. Add the salt, and pour in the superior stock and wine or sherry. Bring the sauce to the boil, then cook in the oven for approximately 1 hour at 375°F (190°C or Gas Mark 5).

Note It is best to use a free-range bird in this recipe.

Chicken

Distilled Chicken

Serves 4–6, with other dishes

1 3–4 lb (1½–1¾ kg) chicken
4 Chinese dried mushrooms
4 oz (100 g) bamboo shoots

3 oz (75 g) ham
2 slices root ginger
2 teaspoons salt
4 tablespoons dry sherry
½ teaspoon flavour powder

From the province of Yunnan

The traditional Chinese method of preparing Distilled Chicken involves the use of a special casserole with a funnel running through the centre. Steam passes through this funnel, and on coming into contact with the lid of the casserole it condenses and drops on to the ingredients in the casserole. When the cooking process is completed, the pieces of meat and other ingredients are immersed in a crystal-clear stock. Since the specialized type of casserole used by the Chinese is not available in this country, a little ingenuity is necessary to cook this dish successfully. Put the meat and other ingredients in a heat-proof casserole. Place a pair of chopsticks across the dish and cover it with a lid, preferably one which is rather larger than the casserole. The rising steam will be caught by this lid, and as it condenses, it will drop into the casserole. The casserole should be placed inside a large boiler on a trivet and steamed for 3–4 hours.

Preparation Soak the mushrooms for 30 minutes. Clean the chicken thoroughly and chop it into about 20 pieces. Place the pieces of chicken in the casserole, then add the ginger, salt, and sherry. Cut the bamboo shoots into slices, approximately 1½ × 1 inch (3½ × 2½ cm), and mix with the chicken pieces. Cut the ham into pieces in the same way as the bamboo shoots and place on top of the other ingredients. Remove the stalks from the mushrooms and mix the mushroom caps with the ham.

Cooking Place the casserole on a trivet in a boiler containing 1–2 inches (2½–5 cm) of water. Keep the water boiling gently for 3–4 hours, adding more when necessary.

Serving At the end of the cooking time, sprinkle the flavour powder into the casserole and serve immediately.

The aim of the dish is to achieve pristine purity, which all the polite diners will pretend to marvel at and appreciate. In the end they will convince themselves that the dish is extraordinarily nourishing and good for their delicate health.

The Complete Chinese Cookbook

Drunken Chicken

Serves 4–6, with other dishes

1 3 lb (1¼ kg) young chicken
1½ tablespoons salt

2 medium-sized onions
4 slices root ginger
½–1 pint (250–500 ml) dry sherry
   or Chinese yellow wine

This is an unfailingly successful dish for use as an *hors d'œuvre* or as a canapé at a cocktail party.

Preparation and Cooking Clean and truss the chicken. Bring 2½ pints (1¼ litres) of water to the boil in a pan and add the salt, onions, and ginger. Boil for 5 minutes; then add the chicken and simmer for 15 minutes. Turn off the heat. Let the bird cool in the liquid for 3 hours; then drain it and put it into a large jar. Pour the sherry or wine over the chicken and turn it several times to ensure that it is completely immersed. Let the chicken soak in the sherry for at least 48 hours, turning it every 12 hours.
Serving Drain and untruss the chicken. Chop it through the bone into fricassée or double-mahjong pieces. Arrange the pieces in the centre of a large dish of *hors d'œuvres*, or divide them among several saucer-sized dishes to pass around during a cocktail party. Eat with the fingers, or speared with cocktail sticks.

Beggar's Chicken

Serves 4–6, with other dishes

1 3–4 lb (1¼–1¾ kg) chicken
3 teaspoons salt
2 medium-sized onions
8 oz (200 g) streaky pork

2 tablespoons lard
1 large piece of pork suet, about
   8–12 oz (200–300 g)
1 large lotus leaf *or* 2 large
   water lily leaves
7–8 lb (3–3¼ kg) sticky mud

From the province of Chekiang

Preparation Dig a hole in the ground 1 foot (30 cm) deep and 2 feet (60 cm) in diameter. Clean the chicken and rub it inside and out with salt. Soak the lotus leaf or water lily leaves in water for 20 minutes. Cut the onions into thin slices and chop the pork coarsely. Stir-fry the onion and pork together in lard for 7–8 minutes and stuff the chicken with the mixture. Wrap the chicken first in the pork suet, securing it with skewers or by sewing; then wrap it in the lotus leaf, securing it with string. Place this parcel on some newspaper, and cover it with mud. When it is completely covered wrap it up with a double sheet of newspaper and secure with string.

Chicken

Cooking Build a bonfire of wood and charcoal in the hole previously dug in the ground. When the flames have subsided, make a hollow in the hot cinders and bury the chicken parcel in it. Cover it completely with smouldering charcoal and cinders. Leave the chicken buried for 3 hours.
Serving When ready, the chicken is dug out and unwrapped from the parcel. It can be eaten whichever way you like – it is meant to be a meal for the beggars.

Melon Chicken

Serves 4–6, with other dishes

1 2–3 lb (1–1¼ kg) young chicken
1 melon
2 large Chinese dried mushrooms
3 oz (75 g) bamboo shoots
3 oz (75 g) best ham
2 tablespoons oil
1 slice root ginger
4 tablespoons button mushrooms
   or Chinese grass mushrooms
salt and pepper

This makes an attractive party dish.

Preparation Soak the dried mushrooms for 30 minutes, remove the stalks, and cut each mushroom cap into six pieces. Chop the bamboo shoots and ham into pieces about the size of small sugar lumps.
Cooking Steam the chicken for 1 hour. Remove all the bones; then chop the chicken meat into pieces about the same size as the cubes of ham. Heat the oil in a frying pan; then add the ginger, bamboo shoots, and both sorts of mushrooms. Fry for 3 minutes. Add the ham and chicken; stir-fry gently for 3 minutes. Season to taste with salt and pepper. Slice off the top quarter of the melon, and keep it aside to use as a lid. Scoop out all the soft flesh from the inside, and mix it with the fried chicken and other ingredients. Pack the cavity in the melon with this mixture, secure the lid with toothpicks; then put it into a heat-proof bowl with a close-fitting lid, and steam for 25 minutes.
Serving Bring the melon to the table in the bowl and serve by opening the lid and leaving it against the melon, as if the contents were a natural part of the fruit.

A large honeydew melon is the best type to use with this dish.

Beaten Chicken

Serves 4-6, with other dishes

- 1 3-4 lb (1¼-1¾ kg) chicken
- 1 tablespoon sesame oil
- 2 tablespoons sesame jam *or* peanut butter
- 2 tablespoons soya sauce
- 1 tablespoon roasted sesame seeds

From the province of Szechuan

This is a cold chicken dish and each piece is beaten with a rolling pin before serving. It is fairly unusual and is seldom seen in other parts of China.

Preparation and Cooking Clean the chicken and place it in a saucepan with 4 pints (generous 2 litres) of water. Bring the water to the boil. After it has boiled for 2 minutes, add 1 medium-sized cup of cold water and bring to the boil once more. Let it boil for 2 minutes, then add another cup of water. Continue this process for about 30 minutes; then leave the chicken in the water to cool for 3 hours.

Serving Remove the chicken from the water and drain well. Chop it through the bone into about 12 pieces. Place these pieces on a chopping board and give each a heavy bash with a rolling pin. Mix the sesame oil, sesame jam or peanut butter, and soya sauce into a paste. Brush each piece of chicken with this paste, sprinkle with the roasted sesame seeds, and serve on a large platter, garnished with parsley springs or fresh coriander leaves if desired.

Wine-Sediment Paste Chicken

Serves 4-6, with other dishes

- 1 3-4 lb (1¼-1¾ kg) young chicken
- 2 teaspoons salt
- ½ teaspoon freshly-milled black pepper
- 1½ tablespoons Kaoliang (Chinese liqueur) *or* brandy
- 3 tablespoons wine-sediment paste
- 2 teaspoons sugar
- 1 teaspoon flavour powder
- ⅛ teaspoon five spice powder
- 2 tablespoons soya sauce
- 1 tablespoon sherry

From Foochow

This chicken is redder in colour than any other Chinese chicken dish, as it is prepared not with ordinary soya sauce, but with a bright, deep red wine-sediment paste, which is processed from fermented ground rice and wine lees or sediment. It is available from many well-stocked Chinese provision shops, especially if the proprietor is from the province of Fukien.

Chicken

Preparation and Cooking Clean the chicken thoroughly and boil it for 25 minutes in a large pan of water. Let the chicken cool in the water for 2 hours; then drain it and hang it up in an airy spot to dry out.
Marinading Blend the salt, black pepper, and Kaoliang or brandy together and rub the bird with this mixture, inside and out. When marinade has dried on the chicken rub it with the remaining mixture and leave it to dry. Blend the remaining ingredients together and rub the chicken with the mixture until it is completely covered. Place in a jar and leave it in a cool place overnight, or for several days.
Serving Chop the chicken through the bone into 15-20 pieces. Pile the pieces in the centre of a serving dish and surround them with radishes.

Serve as part of an elaborate *hors d'œuvre* or as a main course.

Eight-Precious Steamed Chicken

Serves 4-6, with other dishes

1 4-5 lb (1¾-2 kg) chicken *or* capon
2 oz (50 g) chestnuts
4 large Chinese dried mushrooms
3 oz (75 g) glutinous rice
2 oz (50 g) bamboo shoots
2 oz (50 g) smoked ham
1 oz (25 g) lotus seeds

2 golden needles (lily bud stems)
2 oz (50 g) peeled shrimps
1 teaspoon salt
2 teaspoons sugar
2 tablespoons sherry
1 tablespoon soya sauce
½ tablespoon cornflour
½ teaspoon flavour powder
½ pint (250 ml) superior stock
½ tablespoon lard

Shanghai style

Duck is more frequently used in this recipe than chicken, but if it is not available, chicken makes just as appealing and succulent a dish.

Preparation Dip the chicken in boiling water for 3 minutes; then drain. Discard the heart, but retain the kidney and liver and slice them thinly. Slash the chestnut shells and cook them in boiling water for 25 minutes. Remove the shell and skin and chop each chestnut into four pieces. Soak the mushrooms for 20 minutes, remove the stalks, and cut the caps into six pieces. Steam the glutinous rice for 20 minutes. Chop the bamboo shoots and ham into ⅛ inch (¼ cm) cubes. Simmer the lotus seeds and golden needles in water for 5 minutes; then drain. Chop the golden needles into 1 inch (2½ cm) pieces. Mix all these ingredients in a bowl with the peeled shrimps, salt, sugar, and 1 tablespoon of the sherry. Stuff the chicken with the mixture and secure with skewers or by sewing with thick thread.
Cooking Place the chicken in a heat-proof bowl and steam for 3-3½ hours.

The Complete Chinese Cookbook

At the end of the cooking time, pour the liquid that has collected in the steaming bowl into a small saucepan. Add all the remaining ingredients, blend well, and cook over a medium heat, stirring constantly, until the gravy thickens and has a glossy appearance.

Serving Cut the chicken into six to eight pieces and carefully remove the main bones. Spread the stuffing on a well-heated serving dish; then place the chicken pieces on top and pour over the gravy. Steam for 5 minutes, and serve.

Diced Chicken

Chicken meat diced into cubes about half the size of sugar lumps is a very popular and traditional form of cooking chicken in China. When cooked and served in this manner, the chicken is usually stir-fried with additional sauces and seasonings, but without the use of the supplementary ingredients which are usually added to dishes where the chicken is chopped and cooked in larger pieces. Breast meat is usually used for diced chicken dishes. As chicken prepared in this manner is boneless, it is very acceptable and appealing to Westerners.

Vinegar-Tossed Chicken Cubes

Serves 4–6, with other dishes

10 oz (250 g) chicken breast meat
2 tablespoons vinegar
2 oz (50 g) bamboo shoots
½ teaspoon salt
¾ tablespoon cornflour
1 dried chilli pepper
1 medium-sized onion
1 slice root ginger
1 clove garlic
2 teaspoons cornflour
3 tablespoons superior stock
1 tablespoon sherry
2 tablespoons lard
1 tablespoon vegetable oil

A favourite dish in Peking

Preparation Cut the chicken and bamboo shoots into small cubes. Rub them with salt and ¾ tablespoon cornflour. Chop the chilli pepper as finely as possible, discarding the seeds. Chop the onion, ginger, and garlic as finely as possible and mix together well. Blend the 2 teaspoons of cornflour with the stock, sherry, and vinegar.

Cooking Melt the lard in a frying pan over a high heat. Add the chicken and bamboo shoot cubes and the chilli pepper. Stir-fry for 2 minutes; then remove from the pan, and keep hot. Stir-fry the onion, ginger, and garlic mixture with the oil over a high heat for 2 minutes. Pour in the cornflour, stock, sherry, and vinegar mixture and stir until the mixture thickens. Return the chicken and bamboo shoots to the pan, stir-fry them with the sauce for 1½ minutes, and serve immediately.

This is a fairly spicy dish. Serve with boiled rice.

Kung-Po Chicken Cubes

Serves 4-6, with other dishes

- 10 oz (250 g) chicken breast meat
- 1 teaspoon salt
- 4 teaspoons cornflour
- 2 dried red chilli peppers
- 3 tablespoons superior stock
- 2 teaspoons vinegar
- 2 teaspoons tomato purée
- 1 teaspoon sugar
- 1 small onion
- 2 tablespoons lard
- 1½ tablespoons vegetable oil
- 1 teaspoon red chilli oil

From the province of Szechuan

Preparation Dice the chicken into small cubes and rub them with salt and 2 teaspoons of the cornflour. Chop the peppers and discard the seeds. Mix the remaining cornflour with the stock, vinegar, tomato purée, 2 tablespoons water, and the sugar. Chop the onion as finely as possible.
Cooking Melt the lard in a frying pan over a high heat. Add the chicken cubes and stir-fry for 2 minutes; then remove them from the pan and keep hot. Pour the vegetable oil into the centre of the pan. Add the onion and chilli peppers and stir-fry for 2 minutes. Add the chilli oil and the cornflour mixture, and stir until the mixture thickens. Return the chicken cubes to the pan, stir-fry for 1½ minutes, and serve on a well-heated dish.

Note This is a very hot dish and is particularly appealing to those who like really spicy food. However, it is a good idea to serve a large dish of rice with the Kung-Po Chicken Cubes to dampen the fire – should it be necessary!

Diced Chicken in Soya Jam

Serves 4-6, with other dishes

- 8-10 oz (200-250 g) chicken breast meat
- 2 tablespoons soya jam *or* paste
- 1 egg white
- 3 teaspoons cornflour
- 1 tablespoon ginger water
- 1 tablespoon sherry
- 1 teaspoon sugar
- 2 tablespoons lard

The Complete Chinese Cookbook

Preparation Dice the chicken meat into ⅓ inch (¾ cm) cubes. Blend the egg whites, cornflour, and 2 teaspoons water into a batter, and use it to coat the chicken cubes. Mix the soya jam, 2 teaspoons ginger water, sherry, and sugar into a smooth paste.

Cooking Melt 1½ tablespoons of the lard in the centre of a small frying pan, add the chicken cubes, and stir-fry over a high heat for 1 minute. Remove the chicken and keep it hot. Add the remaining lard to the pan and beat in the soya jam with a spoon for about 30 seconds, until most of the moisture has evaporated. Return the chicken cubes to the pan and stir-fry for 1 minute with the soya paste until they turn brown and glistening. Serve immediately on a well-heated dish.

Chopped Chicken

Apart from cooking it whole or diced into cubes, another way of cooking chicken is to chop it into eight to twenty pieces through the bone. Chopped chicken is sometimes cooked along with other ingredients, but frequently it is cooked on its own.

Deep-Fried Eight Piece Chicken

Serves 4–6, with other dishes

1 3–4 lb (1¼–1¾ kg) roasting chicken
2 slices root ginger
2 teaspoons salt
1 egg
2 tablespoons flour
½ pint (250 ml) oil

In China, what we call deep-frying is often not actually deep-frying in the Western sense. Usually no more than ¼–½ pint (125–250 ml) of oil is used. The food to be fried – such as meat balls, chopped pieces of chicken, or meat – is turned in the oil with a pair of bamboo chopsticks, a metal spoon, or else a spatula.

Preparation Clean the chicken and chop it through the bone into eight pieces (or more if you like). Shred the ginger and chop it very finely. Mix it with the salt. Rub the chicken pieces with this mixture. Beat the egg lightly, blend it with the flour to a smooth batter; then coat the chicken.

Cooking Heat the oil in a frying pan. When it is very hot, drop in three or four pieces of chicken and stir them round with bamboo chopsticks or metal spoons. Cook in this way for 3–4 minutes until each piece is evenly fried. Remove the chicken pieces and keep them hot in the oven. Continue deep-frying until all the pieces have been cooked.

Chicken

Serving Chicken cooked in this manner is best eaten with dips and mixes (see section on Table Condiments). The best accompaniment of all is Salt and Pepper Mix.

Hot Pepper Chicken

Serves 4-6, with other dishes

1 3-4 lb (1¼-1¾ kg) chicken
2 teaspoons salt
2 dried chilli peppers
3 fresh chilli peppers

2 tablespoons lard
1½ tablespoons soya sauce
1 tablespoon vinegar
6 tablespoons superior stock
½ teaspoon flavour powder
1½ teaspoons cornflour

From the province of Kiangsi

Preparation Clean the chicken and chop it into about 20 pieces. Boil in water for 5 minutes and drain thoroughly. Rub the chicken pieces with salt and place them in a heat-proof bowl, skin side down. Chop both the dried and fresh chilli pepper, discarding the seeds.

Cooking Heat the lard in a small pan. Add the peppers and stir-fry over a medium heat for 2 minutes. Pour the lard and pepper mixture evenly over the chicken pieces. Blend the remaining ingredients in a bowl; then cook the sauce in a small pan over a low heat for 4-5 minutes until it thickens slightly. Pour the sauce evenly over the pieces of chicken. Place the bowl of chicken in a steamer and steam for 45 minutes. Turn out the contents of the bowl on to a dish, and serve. By this time, the chicken will have absorbed all the flavours of the combined ingredients, and should possess many of the local flavours of Kiangsi.

Crackling Aromatic Chicken Legs

Serves 4-6, with other dishes

2 lb (1 kg) chicken legs
   (drumsticks and upper legs)
2 teaspoons salt
2 medium-sized onions
4 slices root ginger

2 cloves garlic
3 tablespoons soya sauce
1 tablespoon sugar
¼ teaspoon five spice powder
2 tablespoons sherry
1½ tablespoons cornflour
oil for deep-frying

This is a favourite dish in Peking.

Preparation Clean the chicken legs, rub them with salt, and leave them to season overnight. Chop the onions. Shred the ginger, crush the garlic, and chop them both. Put the chicken legs in a bowl with the onion, ginger,

garlic, soya sauce, sugar, five spice powder, and sherry. Rub the mixture into the chicken legs thoroughly and leave them to marinate for 2 hours.
Cooking Place the marinated chicken legs in a heat-proof bowl. Steam vigorously for 25 minutes. When the chicken legs have cooled slightly, rub them with cornflour and place them in a wire basket, four at a time. Deep-fry for 4–5 minutes. Drain well and continue deep-frying until all the legs have been fried.
Serving Place the crispy fried chicken legs on a chopping board and chop them in two. Arrange the pieces on a flat serving dish and decorate by banking them with green vegetables (e.g. lettuce, quick-fried spring greens, spinach, or broccoli). The brownness of the chicken legs and the greenness of the vegetables should make an attractive and happy combination.

Steamed Chicken in Ground Rice

Serves 4–6, with other dishes

1 3–4 lb (1½–1¾ kg) chicken
2 teaspoons salt
pepper to taste
2 egg whites
5 oz (125 g) roasted ground rice (coarse grain)

2 teaspoons chicken fat
2 tablespoons light-coloured soya sauce
2 tablespoons chicken stock
½ teaspoon flavour powder
⅓ tablespoon vinegar
1½ tablespoons sherry

Ground rice is often used in China in the same manner as breadcrumbs are used in the West; it is frequently used to coat pieces of meat for further cooking. When using ground rice (usually in coarse grains), it is often fried or roasted first until it is slightly brown and aromatic. When applied as a coating, ground rice definitely produces an aromatic effect on the final product.

Preparation Chop the chicken into 14–16 pieces, rub them with salt and sprinkle them with pepper. Beat the egg whites with a fork for 15 seconds. Dip the chicken pieces in egg white and roll them in roasted ground rice until evenly coated.
Cooking Place the pieces of chicken in a heat-proof bowl and steam for 2 hours. Pour off the chicken juice which has collected in the bowl. Heat the chicken fat in a small pan. Add the remaining ingredients including the liquid formed during steaming, and bring to the boil. Pour the mixture into two small sauce boats and use as a dip when the chicken is served.

Chicken

Cantonese Crystal Chicken

Serves 4–6, with other dishes

1 3 lb (1¼ kg) young chicken
2 teaspoons salt
2 tablespoons sherry
½ teaspoon flavour powder
1 teaspoon sugar
1 tablespoon gelatine
1 pint (500 ml) superior stock
5–6 oz (125–150 g) ham

This is a dish which can be made a day before it is used.

Preparation Clean and dry the chicken thoroughly. Mix the salt, sherry, flavour powder, sugar, and gelatine into the stock until well-blended.
Cooking Boil the chicken for 30 minutes; then leave it to cool. Chop it into 20–24 pieces. Cut the ham into thin slices. Interleave the pieces of chicken and ham like roof tiles in a deep oblong or oval dish. Heat the stock mixture, stirring all the time until all solids are well dissolved. Cool for 15 minutes; then pour over the chicken and ham. Place the dish in a refrigerator to cool for at least 3 hours, or overnight.
Serving Turn the jellied chicken and ham on to a large flat dish and serve. In presenting this dish in China the jellied chicken is often surrounded by a bank of fresh vegetables and flowers. There is a version in which the chicken is banked all around with chrysanthemums and other flowers, and it is called 'South of the River 100 Flower Chicken'.

Braised Chicken with Chestnuts

Serves 4–6, with other dishes

1 3–4 lb (1¼–1¾ kg) chicken
20 chestnuts
giblets from 2 chickens
6 medium-sized Chinese dried
   mushrooms
1 large onion
3 tablespoons vegetable oil
2 slices root ginger
4 tablespoons soya sauce
1 tablespoon sugar
¼ pint (125 ml) chicken stock
3 tablespoons sherry
1 teaspoon salt

Preparation Clean the chicken and chop it into 16–20 pieces. Boil the giblets in water for 5 minutes; then slice each of them into four. Soak the mushrooms in warm water for 30 minutes and retain the water at the end of this time. Cut off the mushroom stalks. Slice the onion thinly. Boil the chestnuts for 25 minutes; then remove the shells and skins.
Cooking Heat the oil in a large saucepan. Add the ginger and onion, and

stir-fry for 2 minutes. Add the chicken pieces and giblets and continue to stir-fry for a further 5–6 minutes. Pour in the soya sauce, mushroom water, sugar, stock, sherry, and salt. Bring to the boil and simmer for 10 minutes. Add the chestnuts and mix them with the other ingredients. Simmer, covered, for 30 minutes, stirring every 10 minutes; then serve.

Sliced Chicken

Diced chicken cubes, as we have seen, are usually used in pure chicken dishes, with only flavouring and seasoning ingredients added. Chicken cooked whole or chopped into large chunky pieces is usually served in dishes in which the supplementary ingredients seldom constitute more than 15% to 30% of the total ingredients. But in the case of sliced chicken dishes, the chicken meat may consist of up to 50% of the total ingredients. Because of the high regard we Chinese have for chicken (since it is always free range and tasty, never mass-produced), dishes in which sliced chicken is combined with cheap and readily available vegetables are regarded as chicken dishes. Since chicken is one of the most versatile of meats and can be used in conjunction with many other ingredients, the number of dishes which can be created with chicken meat is practically inexhaustible. The following recipes are some of the best-known, most popular, or easiest to produce sliced chicken dishes.

Sliced Chicken with Mushrooms

Serves 4–6, with other dishes

6 oz (150 g) chicken breast meat
1 teaspoon salt
1 tablespoon cornflour
10 large Chinese dried mushrooms
1 small onion
2 tablespoons lard
1 slice root ginger
2–3 tablespoons mushroom water
1½ tablespoons soya sauce
1½ tablespoons sherry
2 tablespoons superior stock *or* chicken stock
¼ teaspoon flavour powder
1 teaspoon sugar

Although this is quite a common and easy to produce dish, for those who like the distinctive flavour of mushrooms – especially the flavour of Chinese dried mushrooms – it is a dish one seldom gets tired of.

Preparation Cut the chicken meat thinly into 1½ × 1 inch (3½ × 2½ cm) slices. Rub them with salt and dredge with cornflour. Soak the mushrooms in ¼ pint (125 ml) warm water for 30 minutes. Retain 2–3 tablespoons of the mushroom water at the end of this time. Chop the onion finely.

Cooking Melt the lard in a frying pan, add the ginger and onion, and stir-fry for 2 minutes over a medium heat. Add the chicken slices, spreading them over the surface of the pan. Cook for 1½ minutes, turning twice. Remove the chicken slices and keep them hot. Add the mushrooms to the pan and stir-fry for 1 minute. Add the mushroom water and all the remaining ingredients, and turn the mushrooms in this mixture. Return the chicken to the pan and increase the heat to high. Stir-fry the chicken and mushrooms together for 1½ minutes; then serve.

If Chinese dried mushrooms are unavailable, substitute a larger quantity of well-rinsed fresh mushrooms and two tablespoons of ordinary dried mushrooms. Add an extra tablespoon of lard to the pan before stir-frying the mixed fresh and dried mushrooms, and cook them for 3 minutes before adding the other ingredients. When cooked in this way the dish can be almost as good as if Chinese dried mushrooms had been used. But it is important to give the fresh mushrooms a good rinsing before use so that all their blackness is washed away; otherwise black will become the dominant colour of the dish.

Sliced Chicken with Cucumber

Serves 4–6, with other dishes

Preparation This is a variation of the recipe for Sliced Chicken with Bamboo Shoots (see below). Here the cucumber is cut into slices similar in size to the chicken slices; it should not be cut just across the vegetable, but along the skin, so that some slices will be wholly green. As cucumber requires very little cooking it does not require any separate frying; in other words, after the chicken slices have been stir-fried for the first time in the lard and impregnated with ginger and garlic, they do not need to be removed from the pan as the cucumber can then be added and stir-fried with the other ingredients. It is important not to use just any quantity of coloured flavouring ingredients. All the best sliced chicken dishes leave the chicken extremely white to contrast sharply with the colours of the supplementary ingredients.

The Complete Chinese Cookbook
Tangerine Peel Chicken

Serves 4–6, with other dishes

10 oz (250 g) chicken breast meat
2 pieces dried tangerine peel
2 teaspoons salt
1¾ tablespoons cornflour
2 cloves garlic
2 slices root ginger
2 dried chilli peppers
1 medium onion
2 tablespoons vegetable oil
3 tablespoons chicken stock
1 tablespoon sugar
1 tablespoon vinegar
1 tablespoon soya sauce
3 tablespoons water
1 tablespoon sherry

From the province of Szechuan

The use of tangerine peel to flavour meat is typical of the south and west of China. It is used in much the same way as orange is used with duck in France – generally with a fairly strong tasting meat, such as beef, mutton, or duck. However, in this case it is used with chicken.

Preparation Cut the chicken thinly into 1½ × 1 inch (3½ × 2½ cm) slices. Rub them with salt and dredge with 1 tablespoon of the cornflour. Crush the garlic. Shred the ginger and chilli peppers. Slice the onion thinly. Soak the tangerine peel in water for 20 minutes; then drain.

Cooking Heat the oil in a frying pan, add the ginger, chilli pepper, tangerine peel, and garlic, and stir-fry for 1 minute. Spread the chicken slices over the pan. Stir and turn them in the impregnated oil for 2 minutes. Add the stock and stir for 1 minute. Mix the remaining cornflour and all the other ingredients together until well-blended. Pour the mixture over the chicken and stir until the sauce thickens. Remove the tangerine peel, and serve. This dish from the west of China is not only sweet and sour but also very hot.

Sliced Chicken with Bamboo Shoots

Serves 4–6, with other dishes

6 oz (150 g) chicken breast meat
2–3 oz (50–75 g) dried bamboo shoots
6 oz (150 g) fresh *or* canned bamboo shoots
½ teaspoon salt
1 tablespoon cornflour
1 clove garlic
2 tablespoons lard
1 slice root ginger
2 tablespoons light-coloured soya sauce
1 tablespoon sherry
4 tablespoons good chicken stock
½ teaspoon flavour powder
1 tablespoon hoisin sauce

Chicken

For this dish to have a really good flavour, it is necessary to use a percentage of dried bamboo shoots as well as the fresh or canned bamboo shoots.

Preparation Cut the chicken meat thinly into 1½ × 1 inch (3½ × 2½ cm) slices. Rub them with salt and dredge with cornflour. Soak the dried bamboo shoots for 30 minutes in 6 tablespoons of boiling water; then slice them thinly. Cut the fresh or canned bamboo shoots into similar slices. Crush and chop the garlic.
Cooking Heat the lard in a frying pan; then add the ginger and garlic. Stir-fry over a medium heat for 1 minute, then add the chicken slices. Stir-fry for 1½ minutes. Remove the chicken slices and keep them hot. Stir-fry the dried bamboo shoots in the remaining oil for 2 minutes. Add the fresh bamboo shoots and stir-fry for 2 minutes. Pour in the soya sauce, sherry, chicken stock, flavour powder, and hoisin sauce. Turn the bamboo shoots in this mixture for 1 minute. Return the chicken slices to the pan and increase the heat to high. Stir-fry all the ingredients together for 1½ minutes.
Serving Serve on a well-heated platter.

Bamboo shoots have, in fact, only a faint and subtle flavour which does not amount to very much to the majority of people. Many people just eat them for their crunchy texture. Even in China, bamboo shoots are interesting only when very well prepared and cooked. In this dish, the flavour of bamboo shoots is enhanced by using dried bamboo shoots, and made more interesting by the addition of hoisin sauce, flavour powder, sherry, and chicken stock. Like bean curds, bamboo shoots can only be made tasty by the flavouring ingredients which are cooked with them, yet their own subtle flavour must be allowed just to suggest itself in the total orchestration.

Sliced Chicken with Smoked and Salted Fish

Serves 4–6, with other dishes

8 oz (200 g) chicken breast meat
4 oz (100 g) smoked fish (salmon *or* haddock)
2 oz (50 g) anchovy
2 slices root ginger

2 tablespoons sherry
½ tablespoon chicken fat
¼ pint (125 ml) chicken stock
1 teaspoon salt
2 spring onion stalks
½ teaspoon flavour powder

From the south-east coast of China

Preparation Cut the chicken into about 12 thin slices, and arrange them on the base of a heat-proof dish, skin side down. Slice the smoked fish in the same way and interleave these pieces with the chicken slices in roof-tile fashion. Chop the ginger and sprinkle it over the chicken and fish with the

sherry, chicken fat, 4-5 tablespoons of the stock, and half of the salt. Cut the anchovy into six pieces and arrange them on top of the chicken and salmon. Chop the spring onion stalks.
Cooking Place the dish in a steamer and steam for 20 minutes. Heat the remainder of the stock in a small saucepan; then add the spring onions, flavour powder, and remaining salt. When the mixture comes to the boil, pour it over the chicken and salmon. Turn on to a serving dish, and serve immediately.

This is an unusual dish which possesses the unique flavour of chicken impregnated with the flavour of smoky and salted fish.

Cantonese Sliced Chicken in Fruit Sauce

Serves 4-6, with other dishes

10 oz (250 g) chicken breast meat
1 teaspoon salt
1 tablespoon cornflour
2 tablespoons orange juice
2 tablespoons lychee juice
2 teaspoons sugar
1 tablespoon tomato purée
2 teaspoons light-coloured soya sauce
3 teaspoons cornflour
3 tablespoons water
2 tablespoons vegetable oil

It is more often the practice and tradition of the south to use fruits and fruit juices for cooking savoury dishes. This dish is an example.

Preparation Cut chicken thinly into 1½ × 1 inch (3½ × 2½ cm) slices. Rub them with salt and dredge with 1 tablespoon cornflour. Mix all the remaining ingredients except the vegetable oil, and blend them to a smooth sauce.
Cooking Heat the oil in a frying pan and spread the chicken slices evenly over the pan; then turn them over. Stir-fry and scramble for 2 minutes. Pour the sauce into the pan and turn the chicken gently until the sauce thickens. Serve immediately.

This is a very fruity dish, combining the tender savouriness of chicken with the refreshing quality of the fruit juice. It should be a sensation to those who have never tried it before.

Sliced Chicken with Pea Pods or Mange-Tout

Serves 4–6, with other dishes

8 oz (200 g) chicken breast meat
6 oz (150 g) pea pods
1 teaspoon salt
1 tablespoon cornflour
4 tablespoons chicken stock
1 tablespoon light-coloured soya sauce
2 tablespoons white wine
½ teaspoon flavour powder
2 teaspoons cornflour
2 tablespoons vegetable oil
1 slice root ginger
1 tablespoon lard

Preparation Cut chicken thinly into 1½ × 1 inch (3½ × 2½ cm) slices. Rub them with salt and dredge with 1 tablespoon cornflour. Blend together the chicken stock, soya sauce, wine, flavour powder, and 2 teaspoons cornflour.
Cooking Heat the oil in a frying pan and add the ginger. Stir-fry for 30 seconds, then discard the ginger. Put the chicken slices in the pan and stir-fry for 2 minutes over a high heat. Remove the chicken from the pan and keep it warm. Add the lard to the pan, then the pea pods. Stir-fry for 2 minutes. Return the chicken to the pan and mix with the pea pods. Pour in the sauce mixture and cook, turning and scrambling for 1¼ minutes. Serve immediately.

Gold Coin Chicken

Serves 4–6, with other dishes

1 3 lb (1¼ kg) young chicken
4 pints (2 litres) master stock (*or* soya-herbal stock)

Preparation Clean the chicken thoroughly inside and out. Dip it in boiling water for 1 minute; then drain.
Cooking Bring the master stock to the boil in a large saucepan. Immerse the chicken completely and simmer in the stock for 20 minutes; then turn off the heat and let the chicken stand in the stock and hot-marinate for 40 minutes. It will have turned a rich brown at the end of this time.
Serving Remove the chicken from the stock and place it on a chopping board. Cut the chicken thinly into 2 inch (5 cm) rounds or 'coins', with a Chinese chopper or a very sharp cleaver. Use the breast meat and the drumsticks – if using the latter, remove the leg bone first, and slice through the cross section. Place these 'coins' on an oval serving dish, arranged in three rows. The middle row should be the longest.

The Complete Chinese Cookbook

Shredded Chicken

As a rule in Chinese cooking, the foods are cut and reduced to harmonize with the natural size and shape of the bulk material of the dish. If the bulk food in the dish is noodles or spaghetti, the chicken has to be shredded into strips or threads. In the case of chicken itself, since much of its meat exists in strip form, we find it only natural to shape and trim it into more perfect strips or shreds, about the size of matchsticks or slightly larger. These strips can be used to fry and cook with such materials as bean sprouts, shredded bamboo shoots, asparagus, celery, ham, french beans, noodles, pea-starch transparent noodles, and numerous other things which exist naturally in strip or shred form, or which can be easily rendered into strips or shreds.

Chinese shredded chicken is not simply chicken meat torn from the bone into shreds. Breast meat, neatly cut into shreds, is often used. Smaller shreds are called 'chicken threads', and the larger strips are called 'willow leaf strips'. Chicken threads are about the length and thickness of matchsticks, perhaps a little thinner. Willow leaf strips can perhaps be termed chicken slivers. They are about 2–3½ inches (5–8¼ cm) long. The following section contains dishes where chicken meat is used in these shapes and sizes.

Slivered Chicken with French Beans

Serves 4–6, with other dishes

8 oz (200 g) chicken breast meat
6 oz (150 g) french beans
½ teaspoon salt
1 egg white
1 tablespoon cornflour
3 tablespoons vegetable oil
2 slices root ginger
2 tablespoons chicken stock
1 tablespoon sherry
1 teaspoon sugar
1½ tablespoons light-coloured soya sauce
½ teaspoon flavour powder

Preparation Cut the chicken into willow leaf strips. Rub them with salt, dampen with egg white, and dredge with cornflour. Top and tail the french beans and slice them diagonally into strips the same length as the chicken slivers. Simmer in boiling water for 2 minutes; then drain.

Cooking Heat 2 tablespoons of the oil in a frying pan. Add the ginger and chicken, spreading the chicken strips evenly over the pan. Stir-fry over a medium heat for 2 minutes, then remove the chicken from the pan. Add the remaining oil and pour in the french beans. Stir-fry for 1 minute over a high heat. Pour in the chicken stock, sherry, sugar, soya sauce, and flavour powder. Cook, stirring, for 2 minutes. Return the chicken to the pan, stir-fry for 1 minute; then serve.

Chicken

Although quite simple, this is a satisfying dish, which can be served either at a party dinner or for a home meal. The whiteness of the chicken and the greenness of the beans make an attractive contrast.

Slivered Chicken with Cucumber

Serves 4–6, with other dishes

Preparation Repeat the instructions given in the recipe for Slivered Chicken with French Beans (see page 184), substituting cucumber for the french beans. Slice the cucumber lengthwise into strips about the same length and thickness as the chicken slivers. There is no need to simmer the cucumber before stir-frying it, as it requires very little cooking. Cucumber used in this way should not be peeled. Indeed, it should only be lightly scraped so that all its green coolness can be retained.

Slivered Chicken with Asparagus

Serves 4–6, with other dishes

Preparation This recipe is a variation of Slivered Chicken with French Beans (see page 184). Use asparagus instead of french beans. Remove the hard coarse parts of the asparagus, split each spear into four, and cut into slivers the same size as the pieces of chicken. Parboil the asparagus strips for 5 minutes, and drain, before proceeding with the cooking instructions.

Chicken Threads with Bean Sprouts

Serves 4–6, with other dishes

6 oz (150 g) chicken breast meat
12 oz (300 g) bean sprouts
½ teaspoon salt
pepper to taste
1 tablespoon cornflour
2 cloves garlic
2 tablespoons vegetable oil
2 slices root ginger

2 tablespoons chicken fat
2 tablespoons light-coloured soya sauce
¼ teaspoon chilli sauce
2 teaspoons vinegar
2 tablespoons chicken stock
1 tablespoon sherry
¼ teaspoon flavour powder
2 tablespoons chopped chives

Preparation Use a razor-sharp knife to cut the chicken into threads or matchstick strips about 1½ inches (3½ cm) long. Sprinkle them with salt, pepper, and cornflour, discarding any excess cornflour. Crush and chop the garlic.

Cooking Heat the oil in a large frying pan and add the ginger. Stir-fry for 30 seconds, then discard the ginger. Add the chicken threads and turn them in the oil for 1½ minutes over a medium heat. Remove them from the pan and keep them hot. Put the chicken fat and garlic in the pan and stir-fry for 30 seconds. Add the bean sprouts and turn them in the oil for 1 minute over a high heat, until they are all evenly coated. Add the soya sauce, chilli sauce, and vinegar, and stir-fry for 1 minute. Return the chicken threads to the pan and sprinkle them with chicken stock, sherry, flavour powder, and chives. Stir-fry for 1 minute, mixing all the ingredients together; then serve.

Chicken Threads with Sliced Pepper

Serves 4–6, with other dishes

6 oz (150 g) chicken breast meat
2 large green sweet peppers
2 dried red chilli peppers
½ teaspoon salt
1 tablespoon cornflour
2 tablespoons vegetable oil
2 slices root ginger
2 tablespoons chicken fat
2 tablespoons soya sauce
2 teaspoons sugar
3 teaspoons vinegar
2 tablespoons chicken stock
1 tablespoon sherry

Preparation Using a razor-sharp knife, slice the chicken into very thin threads 1½ inches (3½ cm) in length. Sprinkle with salt and rub them with cornflour, discarding any excess cornflour. Slice the sweet peppers in the same way as the chicken, and shred the chilli peppers.

Cooking Heat the oil in a large frying pan, and add the ginger. Stir-fry for 1 minute, then remove it from the pan. Add the chicken threads and stir-fry for 2 minutes; then remove from the pan and keep warm. Put the chicken fat and chilli peppers into the frying pan, stir-fry for 1 minute; then add the green pepper threads and turn them in the fat for 2 minutes. Pour in the soya sauce, sugar, vinegar, and stock, and cook, stirring, for 1 minute. Return the chicken threads to the pan, and pour in the sherry. Mix and assembly-fry all the ingredients together for 1 minute; then serve.

Chinese Chicken-Celery Salad

Serves 4–6, with other dishes

8 oz (200 g) roast chicken meat
8 oz (200 g) celery
1 slice root ginger
1½ teaspoons salt
pepper to taste
1½ tablespoons soya sauce
1 teaspoon sugar
2 teaspoons vinegar
¼ teaspoon chilli oil
1 tablespoon salad oil
½ teaspoon flavour powder
1½ tablespoons sherry
2 teaspoons sesame oil

Chicken

Preparation Using a razor-sharp knife, cut the chicken into matchstick threads. Shred the ginger finely and scatter it over the chicken. Sprinkle with salt and pepper, and mix with the seasonings. Slice the celery into pieces about twice the size of matchsticks, sprinkle with soya sauce, sugar, vinegar, and chilli oil, and toss the celery and seasonings together. Mix the chicken and celery in a salad bowl and sprinkle with salad oil, flavour powder, sherry, and sesame oil. Toss these ingredients together; then serve. This salad makes an interesting starter to a Western meal.

Minced Chicken Dishes

In Chinese cookery, the term 'Fu-Yung' indicates dishes prepared with beaten egg or egg white. The Chinese often blend minced chicken with beaten egg or egg white, resulting in quite a large range of well-known Fu-Yung dishes which can be cooked very quickly. This section contains a selection.

Tri-Colour Scrambled Chicken Fu-Yung

Serves 4–6, with other dishes

9 oz (225 g) chicken breast meat (use only white meat)
7 eggs
6 tablespoons superior stock
1 teaspoon salt
1½ tablespoons white wine
2 tablespoons cornflour
¾ teaspoon flavour powder
pepper to taste
5 oz (125 g) lard
1½ tablespoons tomato purée

The three colours make this an interesting dish. It originated in the former East Market in Peking. Serve with plain boiled rice.

Preparation Mince the chicken very finely. Separate the egg whites and yolks and put them into different bowls. Mix 6 oz (150 g) of the chicken with the egg whites and 4 tablespoons of the stock. Add two thirds of the salt, 1 tablespoon wine, two thirds of the cornflour, ½ teaspoon of the flavour powder, and pepper to taste. Blend these ingredients together well. Mix the egg yolks with the remaining chicken. Add the remaining stock, salt, wine, cornflour, flavour powder, and pepper to taste.

Cooking Heat 3 oz (75 g) of the lard in a frying pan. When it is almost smoking-hot, remove from the heat for 4–5 seconds. Pour in the chicken and egg white mixture and scramble it quickly. Return the pan to a medium heat and continue to scramble and stir-fry for 30 seconds. Remove the pan from the heat and put half of the mixture along one side of a well-heated dish. Add the tomato purée to the remaining mixture and return the pan to the heat. Stir rapidly with a scrambling motion. After 10–12 seconds, spoon the resulting pink mixture on to the middle of the serving dish. Melt the remaining lard in a clean frying pan. Add the chicken and egg yolk mixture. Stir and scramble for 30–35 seconds, then spoon on to the serving dish.

This white, red, and yellow striped dish is very attractive.

Fu-Yung Chicken Slices

Serves 4–6, with other dishes

3 oz (75 g) chicken breast meat
2 oz (50 g) white fish
3 egg whites
2 teaspoons minced onion
1 teaspoon minced root ginger
1 oz (25 g) water chestnuts, minced

½ teaspoon salt
3½ teaspoons cornflour
1 teaspoon plain flour
6 tablespoons chicken stock
¼ teaspoon flavour powder
2 tablespoons white wine
¼ teaspoon salt
8 oz (200 g) lard

This is a pure white dish, consisting of minced chicken blended with egg white (often with the addition of minced white fish). It is cooked and presented in slices, and smothered in a white sauce.

Preparation Mince the chicken and fish very finely. Beat the egg whites with a fork for 10 seconds. Combine the cornflour and flour. Mix together the chicken, fish, onion, ginger, water chestnut, egg white, and salt; then add 1½ teaspoons of the cornflour and flour mixture, and beat until the ingredients are well-blended and form a runny paste. Mix all the remaining ingredients, except the lard, to form a smooth sauce. Add ¼ teaspoon salt.
Cooking Heat the lard in a large frying pan. Take a tablespoon of the chicken Fu-Yung mixture and slide it on to the surface of the boiling fat. (If it turns brown or curls up at the edges, the fat is too hot.) After 4–5 seconds frying, turn the piece of Fu-Yung with a fish-slice and fry the other side for the same length of time. Remove from the pan and place on a well-heated serving dish. Continue until all the Fu-Yung mixture has been used. Heat the sauce until it boils and thickens, then pour over the Fu-Yung Chicken Slices. This dish is best eaten immediately.

This is a typical dish from Peking, popular throughout the north, but regarded with not quite the same enthusiasm in the south.

Chicken

Sweet Corn and Velveteen of Chicken

Serves 4–6, with other dishes

4–5 oz (100–125 g) chicken breast meat
small can sweet corn
2 egg whites
1½ tablespoons cornflour
½ pint (250 ml) chicken stock
1 teaspoon salt
2 teaspoons sugar
¼ teaspoon flavour powder
1 tablespoon chicken fat
½ tablespoon chopped ham

Some Chinese dishes are for accompanying wine, others lend weight to a meal, and others, like this one, function mainly as an aid to downing rice, which is very important in Chinese food consumption. Hence some dishes which may seem quite uninteresting to foreigners have a curious appeal to the Chinese. This is an example. It is essentially a domestic dish, of southern origin.

Preparation Mince the chicken finely. Beat the egg whites with a fork for 10 seconds, then mix well with the minced chicken. Blend the cornflour in a small bowl with 6 tablespoons of water.

Cooking Bring the chicken stock to the boil in a saucepan. Add the salt, sugar, flavour powder, and cornflour mixed with water. Stir until the liquid is somewhat thickened. Pour the chicken and egg white mixture into the pan in a very thin stream, stirring constantly until the mixture is well-blended. Add the sweet corn and chicken fat and heat for 3–4 minutes. Give the mixture a final stir; then pour it into a large serving bowl and garnish with the chopped ham.

Chicken Specialities

There are a number of miscellaneous chicken dishes which are difficult to classify under any precise category; however, they are distinctive and intriguing, and too interesting to miss or overlook. Indeed, many of them make frequent appearances on the Chinese dinner tables, both at home and during banquets.

Red, White, and Black with Chicken Velveteen

Serves 4-6, with other dishes

8 large Chinese dried mushrooms
12 oz (300 g) chicken breast meat
4 oz (100 g) best ham
3 egg whites

1 teaspoon salt
1½ tablespoons cornflour
¼ pint (160 ml) chicken stock
½ teaspoon flavour powder
4 tablespoons white wine
oil for deep-frying

This is one of those Chinese semi-soup dishes, which are served now and then during the long procession of courses at a Chinese party dinner. They help to break the monotony of quick-fried savoury dishes, and they are particularly useful for eating with rice.

Preparation Soak the mushrooms in warm water for 30 minutes then remove the stalks. Cut the chicken meat into about 20 thin slices. Trim the edges carefully so that each slice is a standard size of about 1 × 2 inches (2½ × 5 cm). Mince the trimmings finely. Add the egg whites, ½ teaspoon of the salt, and ¾ tablespoon of the cornflour, blended with 3 tablespoons of stock. Beat into a batter. Add the remaining salt and cornflour, the flavour powder, and wine to the rest of the stock. Mix until well-blended. Cut the ham into slices about the same size as the chicken slices.

Cooking Dip the chicken slices in the minced chicken and egg white batter. Heat the oil in a deep-fryer and lower the pieces of battered chicken into the pan to fry at a low heat for 10-12 seconds, turning once. Remove, drain, and place in the bottom of a deep casserole or heat-proof dish. Insert the pieces of ham in fish-scale fashion between the chicken slices. Arrange the mushrooms artistically in the dish. Add the remaining batter to the stock mixture and mix until well-blended. Heat the stock until it begins to boil, then pour it over the chicken, ham, and mushrooms. Place the casserole in an oven preheated to 350°F (180°C or Gas Mark 4) for 20 minutes, with the lid on. If you are using a dish, cover it with tinfoil while it is in the oven. Serve from the casserole dish. This is a rather 'way-out' recipe, derived from east China.

Paper-Wrapped Chicken

Serves 4-6, with other dishes

half 2-3 lb (1-1¼ kg) spring chicken
1 slice root ginger
2½ tablespoons soya sauce

1 tablespoon sherry
2 teaspoons sugar
½ teaspoon flavour powder
4 large Chinese dried mushrooms
3 spring onion stalks
large sheet of cellophane paper

Chicken

This was originally a southern Cantonese dish, but it is now popular throughout the country. Usually the chicken is wrapped in transparent cellophane paper, although recently there has been a drift to using rice paper, which is edible. Rice paper does not insulate the contents of the 'envelope' from the deep-frying oil; furthermore, as it is non-transparent, it encloses the wrapped chicken in a parcel exactly the same as an egg roll, and indeed, it tastes like an egg-roll! In this recipe, we adhere to the use of cellophane paper.

Preparation Cut and scrape the chicken meat from the bones. Shred the ginger coarsely. Marinate the meat for 1 hour in a mixture of soya sauce, sherry, sugar, shredded ginger, and flavour powder. Soak the mushrooms in a bowl of water for 30 minutes; then remove the stalks and slice the caps into thin strips. Cut the spring onions into 1½ inch (3½ cm) segments.

Wrapping The orthodox way of wrapping is envelope fashion. Cut the sheet of cellophane into pieces about 6 × 5 inches (15 × 12½ cm). Wrap about ¼–½ oz (10 g) of the marinated chicken meat in each piece of cellophane, with two or three segments of spring onion, and two or three mushroom strips. The cellophane should be made into an envelope, with a long tongue which can be well tucked in.

Cooking When all the chicken has been wrapped, deep-fry the packages, six at a time for 3 minutes. Drain well. (Frying should never exceed 3¼ minutes at once as that would blacken the cellophane paper.) When all the envelopes have been fried, give them a final deep-fry together for 1 minute, then drain thoroughly.

Serving When ready, arrange the packages on a round serving dish, radiating from the centre, or pile them up in tile-piece or fish-scale fashion. They can be surrounded by a bank of green vegetables – lettuce, hearts of greens, or watercress, if desired.

A novel way of wrapping, discovered recently by a British connoisseur who has lived a lifetime in China, and who employs a Chinese butler and chef at his home near Regent's Park, is to make a long pack about 6 inches (15 cm) long, simply by screwing and twisting the paper to close at the ends when the stuffings have been inserted. When it is ready, each pack can be cut in half with a pair of scissors, and the chicken inside eaten without being unwrapped, thus preventing a lot of greasy fingers. In fact, each piece of wrapped chicken can be picked up by the fingers at the screwed up end and the contents can be pushed into the mouth and conveniently eaten like an ice-cream cone! This way of wrapping can be highly recommended, although it is most unorthodox.

Duck, Pigeon, Turkey and Frogs

鴨 鴿 火
雞 田 雞

After chicken, duck is by far the most widely-eaten fowl in China. Apart from the innumerable streams, canals, rivers, lakes, and waterways of China, every village has its pond, which helps in the rearing of this land-based waterfowl. On the dining table, its meat is considered one degree more special than chicken; and as it is a strong tasting meat, many people regard it as more interesting than chicken, which is eaten almost every day by the well-to-do.

The most famous duck dish of China is, of course, Peking Duck. The duck used is, in fact, a battery-reared and manually-fed white-feathered duck, especially raised for the purpose of providing the material for this famous dish. It has a long, broad back, short wings and short legs, and has the appearance of being strong and well-built. Despite the traces of fat in its muscle fibres, when the duck is cooked there is no sense of greasiness in its crimson/white flesh, compared with the dark tough meat of many other ducks. In the latter stages of their rearing, the birds are given little chance for exercise in water (as prolonged exercise might harden the muscles) and their feeding is partly left to nature and is partly artificial and forced. Because of the care taken, particularly in the last stage of fattening, the meat is especially appealing and tender.

This famous table-duck was first exported to England and America in 1875, to Japan in 1888, and to the USSR in 1956, where it came to be known as the 'Moscow white-feathered duck'.

Pigeons are widespread throughout China; they are common both in the north and south. In Peking small pipes are often fitted to their feet, so that they make a piping noise or music as they swirl through the air. Since almost everything in China eventually lands on the dining table, including pigeons, there is quite a range of pigeon dishes. Unlike duck, pigeon is not considered a great dish, but when daintily prepared, many connoisseurs consider it a delicacy.

Duck

There are many famous duck dishes in China. The following are some of the most popular or best-known. Since all fowls and meat can be red-cooked (which is simply cooked with soya sauce), we will start with Red-Cooked Duck.

Red-Cooked Duck

Serves 6–10, with other dishes, or is sufficient for 2–3 meals

4–5 lb (1¾–2 kg) duck
2 medium-sized onions
3 spring onion stalks

2 slices root ginger
1 piece dried tangerine peel
1 teaspoon salt
4 tablespoons soya sauce
2 teaspoons sugar
4 tablespoons sherry

This dish is very similar to Red-Cooked Chicken, but as duck is a stronger-tasting meat, more onion and spring onion are used, and we usually cook the duck for slightly longer.

Preparation Clean the duck thoroughly and remove its tail. (Be sure to remove its oil sacs too.) Slice the onions thinly and cut the spring onions into 2 inch (5 cm) segments. Place the onion, ginger, and tangerine peel inside the cavity of the duck.

Cooking Heat 2 pints (generous litre) of water in a heavy pan or casserole. When it boils, place the duck in it and boil for 4–5 minutes, turning the bird over a few times. Pour away three quarters of the water, and skim off impurities. Sprinkle the salt and half of the soya sauce over the contents of the pan; then insert an asbestos sheet under the pan. Cover, and simmer gently over a low heat for 45 minutes, turning the bird over every 15 minutes. Add the remaining soya sauce, sugar, and half of the sherry, and continue simmering for 20 minutes; then add the remainder of the sherry. Scatter the spring onions over the duck, and simmer for a further 20 minutes.

Serving Serve in the cooking pot or casserole, or in a deep dish or tureen. The duck should have become quite tender, and can be taken to pieces with a pair of chopsticks.

The Complete Chinese Cookbook

Dry-Fried Red-Cooked Duck

Serves 6–10, with other dishes

Preparation and Cooking Repeat the recipe for Red-Cooked Duck, but chop the duck into 2–2½ inch (5–6 cm) square pieces. After the initial pan boiling, which should be prolonged to 6–7 minutes, pour away three quarters of the water. Add all the supplementary ingredients; then cover, and simmer gently for 45 minutes. Remove the lid and increase the heat; then turn the pieces of duck over and over until the liquid is almost gone. Add 2 tablespoons lard, 2 additional tablespoons of sherry, and all the spring onion segments, and stir-fry over a medium heat for 4–5 minutes. Serve in a large flat serving dish or a deep dish.

Eight-Precious Duck

Serves 10–12

5–6 lb (2–2½ kg) duck
6 Chinese dried mushrooms
6 tablespoons glutinous rice
3 tablespoons barley
4 tablespoons chestnut meat
3 tablespoons lotus seeds
3 tablespoons gingko nuts
4 tablespoons bamboo shoots

4 tablespoons roast pork
3 tablespoons smoked ham
6 tablespoons soya sauce
1 teaspoon salt
6 tablespoons sherry
3 spring onion stalks
2 slices root ginger
1 pint (500 ml) superior stock
½ tablespoon sugar

This is a party dish; it is called 'eight-precious' because eight different types of ingredients (or more) are usually used as stuffing for the duck. It is cooked by long-simmering.

Preparation Soak the mushrooms for 20 minutes, and remove the stalks. Boil the glutinous rice and barley for 5–6 minutes, then drain and rinse under running water. Blanch the chestnuts, lotus seeds, and gingko nuts; dice the bamboo shoots and chestnut meat, and shell the lotus seeds. Combine the mushrooms, rice, barley, chestnut meat, lotus seeds, nuts, pork, ham, and bamboo shoots in a basin. Add 3 tablespoons of the soya sauce, ¼ teaspoon of the salt, and 3 tablespoons of the sherry; mix well. Wipe the duck clean with a damp cloth, and stuff it with the mixture. Sew and skewer it firmly closed. Cut the spring onions into 2 inch (5 cm) segments.

Cooking Place the duck in a heavy pot or casserole, with the spring onion segments and ginger. Add the stock, the remainder of the soya sauce, the salt, and the sherry. Bring to the boil, insert an asbestos sheet under the pot; then cover, and simmer very gently for 1 hour, turning the bird over several times. Add the sugar, and some water if necessary in case the duck becomes too dry, and simmer gently for a further hour. Alternatively, the container can be placed in a steamer and steamed for 2 hours – no extra liquid should be added.

Serving Scoop out the stuffing and spread it on a well-heated serving dish as a bed. Quarter the duck and arrange the pieces neatly on top or else carve it in Western fashion. By this stage, the duck should be tender enough to be taken apart with chopsticks.

Cantonese Roast Duck

Serves 6–10, with other dishes

4–5 lb (1¾–2 kg) duck
3 teaspoons salt
2 spring onion stalks
2 cloves garlic
2 tablespoons vegetable oil
3 tablespoons chopped onion
1 tablespoon chopped parsley
2 teaspoons star anise
1 teaspoon peppercorns
2 tablespoons sherry
2 tablespoons soya sauce
1½ teaspoons sugar
3 tablespoons honey
1 tablespoon vinegar
1½ teaspoons cornflour
½ teaspoon flavour powder

This dish is unique – the duck is filled with liquid or sauce, and then roasted.

Preparation Wipe the duck clean with a warm damp cloth. Tie the neck tightly with string, so that no liquid will drip out. Hang it up to dry for 2 hours; then rub it generously with salt, inside and out. Cut the spring onions into 1 inch (2½ cm) segments. Crush the garlic. Heat the oil in a small saucepan; then add the chopped onion, spring onion segments, parsley, garlic, star anise, and peppercorns; stir-fry over a medium heat for 2 minutes. Pour in ½ pint (250 ml) water, bring to the boil and boil gently for 5–6 minutes. Add the sherry, soya sauce, and sugar; blend well. Pour this mixture into the cavity in the duck, sew up carefully, and make more secure with skewers, so that no liquid will run out. Mix the honey, vinegar, and ¼ pint (125 ml) boiling water.

Cooking Preheat the oven to 400°F (205°C or Gas Mark 6). Roast the duck on a rack (or hang the duck tail side up in the oven) for 10 minutes. Baste thoroughly with the honey/vinegar/water mixture. Reduce the oven temperature to 350°F (180°C or Gas Mark 4) and roast for 1 hour, basting at 30 minute intervals. Reduce the heat again, to 325°F (160°C or Gas Mark 3) and roast for a further 20 minutes. Allow the duck to cool slightly, then carefully remove the strings and skewers and pour the sauce into a bowl. Blend the cornflour with 1 tablespoon water, and add to the sauce, with the flavour powder. Heat the mixture in a small pan and serve as gravy.

Serving The duck may be carved or chopped as desired, and served in a well-heated, deep dish.

Hangchow Soya Duck

Serves 8–12, with other dishes

5–6 lb (2–2½ kg) duck
4 tablespoons salt

2 teaspoons bicarbonate of soda
4 pints (generous 2 litres) soya sauce

Hangchow Soya Duck is a pressed duck which is considered to be a speciality dish of this lake city in east China. In its processing and cooking, it is twice marinated, hung, sunned, and finally steamed. The following recipe is taken from the Restaurant of Heavenly Perfume, Hangchow.

Preparation Clean the duck thoroughly, inside and out. Hang it up to dry in an airy place for 3–4 hours.

First Marinating and Pressing Mix the salt with the bicarbonate of soda. Rub the duck three times with the mixture, both inside and out. Be sure to rub the beak and knife entries of the bird generously. Tuck the head of the bird under its wing, and place it at the bottom of a large, strong jar. Place a wooden lid or frame on top of the bird. The lid must be one size smaller than the mouth of the jar, so that it will sit on top of the bird. Place a weight of 25–30 lbs (12–14 kg) on top of the lid. Leave the lid and duck in that position for 36 hours; then change the position of the bird and leave it for 36 hours (total 72 hours).

Second Marinating and Pressing Remove the weight and the lid. Pour in the soya sauce (just enough to cover the duck). Renew the pressing with the sauce lid and weight for 24 hours. Change the position of the bird twice, each time after 24 hours of pressing and marinating (total: 72 hours).

Hot Dip and Sunning Fix a suitably sized bamboo or wooden cross inside the bird to open and extend the cavity. Heat a panful of soya sauce (enough to cover the bird); dip the duck in it, and simmer for 1 minute; then remove and drain. Pass a string through the bird's beak and hang it up to sun and dry for 2–3 days (2 if sunny, 3 if not).

Steaming By the 8th day, the Soya Duck is ready for cooking. Place it in a heat-proof dish and steam uncovered for 2 hours.

Carving and Serving To carve the bird, first cut off the wings and legs, then cut the body into halves, each of which is then chopped into 2 inch (5 cm) square pieces. Arrange the pieces on the serving dish in the shape of a duck.

This duck is said to be so palatable that it rivals Peking Duck in fame and appeal.

Duck, Pigeon, Turkey and Frogs

Quick-Fried Ribbon of Duck with Shredded Ginger

Serves 4–8, with other dishes

10 oz (250 g) roast duck meat
4 slices root ginger
1 tablespoon black beans
3 oz (75 g) celery
3 oz (75 g) young leeks
1 red sweet pepper
2 cloves garlic
2 red chilli peppers
4 tablespoons lard
1 tablespoon soya sauce
2 teaspoons sugar
1 tablespoon vinegar

Preparation Soak the black beans for 20 minutes; then drain. Slice the duck meat into matchstick strips. Cut the celery, leeks, sweet pepper, and ginger into similar strips. Crush the garlic and cut the chilli peppers into four pieces.
Cooking Heat the lard in a large frying pan. Add the ginger and chilli pepper and stir-fry for 1½ minutes over a medium heat. Add the black beans and garlic, and stir-fry for a further 1½ minutes, before adding all the other vegetables. Turn the heat up to maximum for 2 minutes; then add the duck meat, soya sauce, and sugar, and continue to stir-fry for 2 minutes. Finally, add the vinegar and stir-fry for 1 minute more.
Serving Dish out on to a well-heated plate; serve and eat immediately.

The dish is a great favourite in the western province of Szechuan, where most dishes are extremely hot. The hotness of this dish is derived from the chilli pepper, impregnated oil, and the addition of the vinegar. The heavy use of black salted beans is another typical Szechuan technique.

Wine-Simmered Duck

Serves 8–10

4–5 lb (1¾–2 kg) duck
1½ pints (750 ml) white wine
  (Hock, Graves, Moselle)
2 teaspoons salt
2 tablespoons brown bean paste
3 medium-sized onions
3 slices root ginger

Preparation Clean the duck thoroughly, inside and out; then rub it both inside and out firstly with salt, and then with bean paste. Slice the onions and shred the ginger into strips. Stuff the duck with the onions and ginger and close the cavity securely with skewers. Leave to season for 2 days.
Cooking Bring the wine to the boil in a heavy pan or casserole and lower the duck into it. When it comes to the boil again, turn the heat down to minimum and insert an asbestos sheet under the pan. Simmer gently for 3

hours, turning the bird over every 45 minutes. Serve in the pan or casserole. The meat should be so tender that it is possible to take the bird to pieces with a pair of chopsticks.

Drunken Duck

Serves 10–15 persons for a party meal, with many other dishes

3–4 lb (1¼–1¾ kg) duck
4 cloves garlic
4 slices root ginger
1 chilli pepper
6 spring onion stalks
1 tablespoon salt
¼ teaspoon freshly ground pepper
1 pint (500 ml) sherry *or* Chinese Shao Shing yellow wine

Preparation Crush and chop the garlic, and shred the ginger and chilli pepper. Clean the duck thoroughly, removing the oil sacs. Cut the spring onions into ½ inch (1 cm) segments.
Cooking Heat 2 pints (generous litre) water in a large pan. Add the garlic, ginger, chilli pepper, onions, salt, and pepper. Bring to the boil, and lower the duck into the pan. When the liquid comes to the boil again, reduce the heat to low. Simmer for 30 minutes, turning the bird every 10 minutes; then allow it to cool in the liquid for several hours. Remove and drain the duck (reserve the stock for other uses) and place in the refrigerator overnight.
Marinating in Wine Cut off the legs and wings, and chop the body into four pieces. Place all the pieces of duck in a large jar with a stopper. Pour in the sherry or wine and cover the jar tightly; refrigerate for 1–4 days.
Serving When ready to serve, remove all pieces of duck from the container. Drain and chop them into oblong pieces, about 1½ × 1 inch (3½ × 2½ cm), and serve cold.

This makes an excellent *hors d'œuvre*, and can also be used as a canapé at a cocktail party.

White-Simmered Duck with Ham and Chinese Cabbage

Serves 6–10, with other dishes

3–4 lb (1¼–1¾ kg) duck
8 oz (200 g) smoked ham
1 lb (400 g) Chinese celery cabbage *or* Savoy cabbage *or* celery
8 Chinese dried mushrooms
4 oz (100 g) bamboo shoots
3 slices root ginger
2 teaspoons salt
1 teaspoon flavour powder

Duck, Pigeon, Turkey and Frogs

Preparation Soak the mushrooms in warm water for 20 minutes; then drain, and remove the stalks. Slice the ham and bamboo shoots into thin slices, 2 × 1 inch (5 × 2½ cm). Cut the cabbage or celery into 2 × 3 inch (5 × 7½ cm) pieces. Clean the duck inside and out. Place it in a large pan and cover with water. Bring to the boil and simmer for 15 minutes; then skim off the fat and any impurities, and discard about one third of the liquid.

Cooking Add the ginger, bamboo shoots, ham, and mushrooms to the pan. Bring to the boil, reduce the heat to minimum; then insert an asbestos sheet under the pan, and simmer gently for 45 minutes. Allow the pan to cool; then refrigerate for 2 hours. Skim away the fat which has coagulated. Insert the pieces of cabbage under the duck, bring the contents of the pan to the boil, add salt and flavour powder, and simmer gently for 35 minutes.

Serving The duck can be served in the cooking pot or casserole, or in a large soup tureen. When well-cooked, the dish is extremely rich, and at the same time sweet and refreshing – as a result of the large quantity of cabbage. The smoked ham and mushrooms provide that traditional earthy, smoky flavour which is always so recognizable in authentic Chinese dishes.

Crispy and Aromatic Duck I

Serves 8–10, with other dishes

4–5 lb (1¾–2 kg) duck
2 teaspoons salt
¼ teaspoon freshly milled black pepper
¼ teaspoon five spice powder

3 slices root ginger
3 spring onion stalks
2 tablespoons soya sauce
1 tablespoon vinegar
1 tablespoon honey
oil for deep-frying

The process here is to steam first, and deep-fry afterwards. This is a party dish.

Preparation Clean the duck thoroughly, inside and out. Make a mixture of the salt, pepper, and five spice powder, and rub the duck inside and out with this mixture. Shred the ginger, and cut the onions into 1 inch (2½ cm) segments. Stuff half of them inside the duck, and place the other half on top of it. Leave to marinate in a covered container overnight. Mix the soya sauce, vinegar, and honey.

Cooking Place the duck in a heat-proof dish, covered with a lid or tinfoil (or wrap the bird in tinfoil). Place it in a steamer to steam for 1½ hours; then remove. When cool, truss it, and brush liberally with the soya/vinegar/honey mixture. Allow to dry. Place the duck in a wire basket and double deep-fry it for 3–4 minutes (that is, deep-fry it twice: deep-fry for 3–4 minutes, drain; then repeat the deep-frying, again for 3–4 minutes, after which it should be

The Complete Chinese Cookbook

golden-brown and crispy). The meat should be tender enough to be taken to pieces with a pair of chopsticks.

Serving Like Peking Duck, it should be eaten wrapped in pancakes, with strips of crunchy vegetables (spring onion and cucumber) and brushed with soya paste and plum sauce.

Crispy and Aromatic Duck II

Serves 8–10, with other dishes

4–5 lb (1¾–2 kg) duck

5–6 pints (3 litres) Herbal Stock
oil for deep-frying

The process here is to simmer first in Herbal Stock, and then to deep-fry. As Herbal Stock is a highly-spiced liquid it heightens the duck's aromatic qualities.

Preparation Clean the duck thoroughly, removing the oil sacs.

Cooking Place the duck in a pan of boiling water and simmer for 10 minutes. Drain; then discard the water. Heat the stock, and when it begins to boil, lower the duck into it and simmer for 55 minutes. Lift the duck out to drain and cool for 15 minutes. Joint the bird with a chopper, and quarter the body. Double deep-fry the pieces until golden and crispy; about 3–4 minutes for *each* frying.

Serving Serve on a well-heated, flat serving dish, banked with green vegetables. It is best eaten with pancakes.

Deep-Fried and Steamed Eight-Precious Duck

Serves 10–12 people as a party dish

5–6 lb (2–2½ kg) duck
1 clove garlic
1 slice root ginger
6 tablespoons glutinous rice
4 dried oysters
4 dried scallops (root muscles)
6 Chinese dried mushrooms
1 Chinese sausage
3 tablespoons water chestnuts
3 tablespoons green peas
2 teaspoons sugar
1 teaspoon salt
2 tablespoons soya sauce
oil for deep-frying
½ pint (250 ml) superior stock
2 heads of lettuce

Preparation Crush the garlic and shred the ginger. Soak the rice, oysters, and scallops separately for 1 hour, and soak the mushrooms for 30 minutes. Discard the mushroom stalks; then dice the caps, sausage, and water chestnuts into small cubes and mix them with the garlic, ginger, rice, oysters, scallops, peas, sugar, and salt. Blend well. Clean the duck thoroughly inside and out; remove the oil sacs. Hang up to dry for 3 hours. Rub with soya sauce, and then lower into boiling oil to deep-fry for 9–10 minutes, or until golden-brown. Rinse quickly under running water; then drain.

Cooking Stuff the duck with the rice mixture, and then sew up and skewer firmly. Transfer the bird to a heat-proof bowl or casserole. Pour the stock over the duck; cover with lid or tinfoil; and steam for 1¾ hours. Take the stuffing out of the duck, and spread in the centre of a large, well-heated serving dish. Disjoint the duck with a sharp cleaver, and flatten the body with the side of the chopper, before placing it on the stuffing. Arrange the legs and wings around the body; place dish in a steamer, and steam for a further 10 minutes.

Serving Arrange lettuce leaves around the duck and stuffing, and bring the dish steaming to the table.

Nanking Salt Duck

Serves 6–10, with other dishes

4–5 lb (1¾–2 kg) duck

6 tablespoons coarse salt
2 teaspoons freshly milled black pepper

Preparation Heat the salt in a dry frying pan over a low heat for 1½ minutes, spreading it thinly over the pan. Stir and toss several times; then add pepper to the salt, and continue to stir, heating for 1½ minutes. When this salt and pepper mixture is cool, put aside 1 tablespoon for use as a table dip. Use the remainder to rub thoroughly into the duck, both inside and out. Do this twice. Wrap the duck securely in tinfoil, and refrigerate for 5–6 days.

Cooking Cook the duck by dipping it in boiling water for 5–6 seconds; then drain, and steam vigorously for 35 minutes. Or simmer it very gently (with an asbestos sheet under the pan) for 40 minutes in 3½ pints (2 litres) water. Reserve this stock for other uses.

Serving Chop the duck through the bone into double-mahjong-size pieces (or fricassée pieces), and arrange on a serving dish.

The unique flavour of the duck comes from its cooking, most of which is achieved through seasoning and marinating in the salt and pepper mixture. The flavour of this mixture is increased by the heating. This method is unlike the usual hanging of birds, fowls, or meats which is found in European cuisine. Although the actual cooking time is comparatively short, the meat is usually very tender.

The Complete Chinese Cookbook

Chinese Peppered Duck

Serves 6–10, with other dishes

Chinese Peppered Duck is prepared by rubbing the duck *once*, inside and out, with the same heated salt and pepper mixture as in the recipe for Nanking Salt Duck. Wrap in tinfoil, and leave to season overnight in the refrigerator. Just before cooking, rub the duck over with 1½ tablespoons soya sauce.

Preheat the oven to 400°F (205°C or Gas Mark 6), and roast the duck for 1 hour. Chop through the bones into double-mahjong-size pieces, and arrange on a serving dish.

Peking Duck

Serves 6–10, with other dishes

4–5 lb (1¾–2 kg) Aylesbury duck
10 spring onion stalks
6 oz (150 g) cucumber
1 tablespoon sugar
1 teaspoon salt

pancakes
variety of sauces, including
   3 tablespoons plum sauce, and
   2 tablespoons hoisin sauce
3 tablespoons soya bean jam
1 tablespoon sesame oil
2 teaspoons sugar

Peking Duck is now a world famous dish. It owes its fascination and fame, I think, not only to the way it is cooked, but also to the way it is eaten, wrapped in a pancake or doiley with spring onion and strips of sliced cucumber, and heavily dabbed with the appropriate sauces. It is this heavenly combination of fresh and crunchy raw vegetables with the crackling of the duck's skin, the tender meatiness of the duck's meat, and the sweet piquancy of the sauces, all wrapped in one roll, that gives the dish its distinction and inimitable quality.

Preparation Cut the spring onions into 2 inch (5 cm) segments, and cut the cucumber into slightly thicker strips of the same length. Clean the duck inside and out, and lower it momentarily into a pan of boiling water for a quick scald – 2–3 seconds. Drain; wipe dry with paper towels, then hang it up to dry overnight in a cool, airy place. Prepare a bowl of sugar water by mixing the sugar with ½ pint (250 ml) water and 1 teaspoon salt, if desired; rub the duck with this sugar-salt solution several hours before roasting. Hang up to dry. When dry, the duck is ready for roasting.
Cooking Preheat the oven to 400°F (205°C or Gas Mark 6). Place the duck on top rack, and roast for exactly one hour, with a pan underneath to catch the drippings. After 60 minutes of roasting, the duck should be well-cooked

Duck, Pigeon, Turkey and Frogs

and the skin very crispy.

Serving and Eating Peking Duck is the one thing which is carved beside the dining table in China; or to be more precise, it is peeled, for the motion of slicing the duck is one of peeling – a one-handed action, where the thumb and blade of the knive held in the same hand act in unison in a peeling action. In the initial carving, the peeling or slicing is restricted only to the crackling skin. The skin is first peeled off, then placed in a well-heated dish and passed around. Each diner will then open a pancake or doiley on the small dish provided in front of him. The pancake is brushed with sauce, and the diner places 2 pieces of crackling skin on the pancake, along with several segments of spring onion, and some strips of cucumber. He wraps the pancake up like a bed roll, turning up the bottom end so that nothing will fall or drip out; then uses his fingers to hold the roll, which is eaten like a sausage roll. After the duck skin has been eaten, the carver peels off the meat: it is eaten in the same way as the skin – wrapped in a pancake with spring onions and cucumber, and heavily brushed with sauce. Plum sauce and hoisin sauce for use with the duck should be served in separate sauce dishes. Soya bean pastes or jams should be blended with sesame oil and sugar, and stirred over a low heat for 2–3 minutes before being placed in a sauce dish for use.

Normally, a medium-sized duck will peel to make 1 dish of crackling skin, and 2 dishes of sliced duck meat. When these are complemented by other dishes (there are usually at least 6–10 dishes at a party or banquet), a 4–5 lb (1¾–2 kg) duck will be sufficient for 6–10 people.

Pancakes for Peking Duck

Serves 6–10

12 oz (300 g) flour

½ pint (250 ml) boiling water
2 tablespoons sesame oil

Preparation Sift the flour into a large basin. Pour in the boiling water very slowly, and gradually work into a warm dough. Knead gently for 10–12 minutes, then leave to stand for 10–12 minutes. Form the dough into a roll 2 inches (5 cm) in diameter, then cut it into ½ inch (1 cm) thick slices. Brush one slice with sesame oil and lay another slice on top of it. Using a rolling pin, roll the double piece, until it spreads out to a diameter of about 5–6 inches (11½–15 cm), rolling from the centre out. Use up all the dough in this way. Heat a large heavy frying pan over low heat. When it is very hot, place the rolled pieces of dough evenly over the pan. Move the pan over the heat so that the heating is even and well spread. When any piece of dough starts to bubble, turn it over to heat the other side. When ready (i.e. both sides have patches of brown), pull each piece of dough apart into the two original slices. Fold each slice into a half circle on the side which has been greased. Pile the pancakes up on a plate, and steam them for 10 minutes, before they are used to wrap the duck.

In China, these pancakes are called 'thin pancake cakes' (bao pin) and they are indispensable for eating with Peking Duck. They can be kept in a refrigerator for several days, and re-steamed when required.

Lotus Leaf Rolls

Serves 6–10

12 oz (300 g) flour
3 teaspoons sugar
3 teaspoons baking powder
¼ pint (125 ml) water *or* milk
4 tablespoons vegetable oil

Peking Duck is eaten with pancakes, but most of the other duck dishes, or red-cooked dishes which are often served with ample gravy, are usually accompanied by Lotus Leaf Rolls, which are more absorbent.

Preparation Sift the flour and mix with sugar and baking powder. Add water or milk very slowly; stir with fork into a soft dough. Knead for 5–6 minutes. Cover dough with a dry cloth, and allow to stand for 20 minutes. After the dough has risen, knead again for 2–3 minutes. Form the dough into a roll 1½ inches (3½ cm) in diameter. Slice into 1 inch (2½ cm) thick slices. Brush the top with a little oil, and fold over on the greased side into half moon shapes. Use a fork to press down the edges, making indentations all around.

Cooking Place the pieces of dough on a large heat-proof plate and steam for 12 minutes. Because of their absorbent quality they are extremely useful for soaking up gravy.

These Lotus Rolls can be kept for a day or two, and re-steamed for 7–8 minutes when required.

Pigeons

Braised Pigeon in Fruit Juice

Serves 4

This is a highly savoury Cantonese 'semi-soup' dish which is served among the earlier courses of a southern dinner to facilitate drinking.

Duck, Pigeon, Turkey and Frogs

Repeat the recipe for Red-Cooked Lemon Pigeon, but after the initial frying and draining away of excess fat, add 2½ tablespoons of apple sauce, 2 tablespoons of orange juice, 3 tablespoons of peeled and chopped tomato, 1 tablespoon of sweet chutney, and 1 tablespoon of chopped chives or spring onion, to the lemon juice.

When braised pigeons are arranged in quarters on the serving dish, they can be surrounded not only by the slices of lemon, but also by slices of tomato, apple, orange; that is, all the constituents which make up the sauce.

Deep-Fried Pigeon

Serves 4

4 fat pigeons, total weight
 4–5 lb (2–2¼ kg)
1 teaspoon salt
2 tablespoons soya sauce
1 tablespoon sherry
pepper
1½ tablespoons cornflour
oil for deep-frying

Preparation Chop each bird into four pieces with a sharp cleaver. Rub each piece with a mixture of salt, soya sauce, and sherry, and sprinkle with pepper. Dust each piece with cornflour.

Cooking Heat oil in the deep-fryer. When it is very hot, place eight pieces of pigeon in a wire basket, and double deep-fry them for a total of 6–8 minutes; that is, deep-fry them for 2–3 minutes first, and keep hot for 3–4 minutes while the next eight are being fried, and finally deep-fry them all together for another 3 minutes.

Serving The pieces of pigeon can be placed on a bed of 3 inch (7½ cm) segments of spring onions, and lemon slices. The usual dips for this dish are Salt and Pepper Mix, and Lemon juice-Soya-Ginger Mix (see Index).

Casserole of Pigeon with Mushrooms

Serves 4

4 fat pigeons, total weight
 4–5 lb (2–2¼ kg)
6 large Chinese dried mushrooms
12 medium-sized fresh
 mushrooms
1 teaspoon salt
3 tablespoons soya sauce
4 oz (100 g) streaky pork
4 golden needles (lily bud stems)
1 large sweet pepper
½ tablespoon cornflour
4 tablespoons vegetable oil
2 slices root ginger
2 oz (50 g) ham
2 tablespoons sherry
½ tablespoon light-coloured soya
 sauce
½ teaspoon flavour powder

The Complete Chinese Cookbook

Preparation Slit each pigeon along the backbone with a sharp cleaver, and flatten with the side of a chopper. Rub with salt and 2 tablespoons of the soya sauce. Slice the pork into four thin slices, and rub with the remaining soya sauce. Soak the dried mushrooms for 20 minutes, and remove the stems. Soak the golden needles in warm water for 30 minutes; then drain, and discard the water. Clean and rinse the fresh mushrooms under running water and remove the stems. Slice the sweet pepper thinly, and blend the cornflour with 2 tablespoons water.

Cooking Preheat oven to 375°F (190°C or Gas Mark 5). Heat the oil in a large frying pan. Turn the pigeons in the hot oil for 3–4 minutes until slightly brown. Line a large heat-proof dish or casserole with slices of pork. Arrange the pigeons and ginger on top of the pork, and place the dried mushrooms, the golden needles, the sliced sweet pepper, and the ham on the pigeons. Pour in ¾ pint (375 ml) boiling water, and place the dish or casserole in the oven for 1 hour. Open the casserole and scatter the fresh mushrooms over the contents. Sprinkle with half of the sherry, and the light-coloured soya sauce; then return to the oven for a further 30 minutes. Remove the casserole from the oven and pour the liquid into a small saucepan. Add the cornflour mixture, the remaining sherry, and the flavour powder, and heat, stirring, until the sauce thickens.

Serving Arrange the pieces of pigeon and other ingredients decoratively on a large serving dish. Pour the sauce over, and serve.

Turkey

Turkey is neither a common nor a popular bird in China, although by Christmas time each year, we seem to encounter them; and every now and then there is a turkey dish on the table. As turkey is not a traditional food ingredient, the recipes for cooking it do not go back hundreds of years, but are improvisations of accepted well-tried methods, which, being traditional, usually have points to recommend them.

Steamed Roast Turkey

Serves 12–16 for a large party or for several meals

10–12 lb (4–5 kg) turkey
3 tablespoons black beans
12 spring onion stalks
6 slices root ginger
4 tablespoons sherry
6 tablespoons soya sauce
1 tablespoon sugar
2 teaspoons chilli oil
2 tablespoons sesame oil

Duck, Pigeon, Turkey and Frogs

Preparation Wipe the turkey inside and out with a warm, damp cloth, and leave in an airy place to dry for 3 hours. Soak the black beans for 30 minutes; then drain and mash them, and put them in a basin. Chop the spring onions and shred the ginger; then add them to the basin, with the sherry, soya sauce, sugar, and chilli oil. Mix them well, then rub the turkey over twice, inside and out, with the mixture. Pile all the loose spring onions on top of the bird, wrap securely in a large piece of tinfoil, and place in the refrigerator overnight.

Cooking Place the turkey, still wrapped in tinfoil, on a heat-proof dish, and steam in a steamer for 1½ hours. Preheat the oven to 400°F (205°C or Gas Mark 6). Unwrap the turkey, and place it in a roasting pan. Rub it all over with sesame oil, and roast for 1¼ hours.

Serving Chop the bird through the bone with a Chinese chopper or sharp cleaver into double-mahjong-size pieces. Serve in two large serving dishes, banked with fresh or quick-fried green vegetables (lettuce, or hearts of greens).

There are enough turkey pieces here for at least two banquet tables. Hoisin sauce and plum sauce are good dips to provide.

Cold White-Cut Salted Turkey

Serves 12-16

10-12 lb (4-5 kg) turkey
3 tablespoons salt

2 teaspoons pepper
2 tablespoons sesame oil
1 teaspoon chilli oil

Preparation Cut the wings and legs off the turkey, and chop the body into four pieces. Mix the salt and pepper, and heat the mixture in a dry frying pan for 2 minutes, stirring constantly. Rub the pieces of turkey with this mixture as soon as it is cool. Mix the sesame oil and chilli oil, and rub the turkey with this. Wrap the bird securely in a long sheet of tinfoil, and leave to season in a cool place for 2-3 days.

Cooking and Serving Bring a large pan of water to the boil. Unwrap the turkey, and place the pieces in the water. Bring back to a slow boil, reduce the heat to a rapid simmer, and cook for 20 minutes; then drain. Slice the meat into thin 2 × 3 inch (5 × 7½ cm) pieces, and serve.

Turkey cooked this way is very savoury and juicy, and does not fall to pieces like ordinary left-over turkey. Serve it cold as a Chinese *hors d'œuvre*, or as a main cold dish for a Western buffet.

Good dips for white-cut turkey are hoisin sauce, Plum Sauce, Chilli-Soya Dip, and Salt and Pepper Mix (see Index).

The Complete Chinese Cookbook

'Field Chickens' or Frogs

It is not without reason that frogs are called 'field chickens' in China. The meat is really very similar to chicken, but it is more tender and delicate. They are often served during banquets in south and east China where frogs thrive in the paddy fields. Definitely regarded as a delicacy.

Quick-Fried Frog Legs with Sweet Pepper

Serves 4 or 5, with other dishes

8–10 fat frogs
1 medium-sized sweet pepper
½ teaspoon salt
2½ tablespoons soya sauce
1 tablespoon hoisin sauce
2 tablespoons tomato purée
1 teaspoon chilli oil
2 tablespoons sherry
½ tablespoon cornflour
1 egg white
2 slices root ginger
3 tablespoons vegetable oil

Preparation Remove the drumsticks (hind legs) of the frogs – use the bodies to make stock. Rub the legs with salt. Blend the soya sauce, half of the hoisin sauce and tomato purée, and the sherry, and marinate the frog legs in this mixture for 30 minutes. Mix the cornflour with the egg white and 1 tablespoon water. Batter the frog legs with this paste. Cut the sweet pepper into strips approximately the same size as the frog legs. Remove the pips, and discard. Shred the ginger.

Cooking Heat 2 tablespoons of the oil in a large frying pan. Add the sweet pepper and ginger, and stir-fry over a medium heat for 2 minutes. Put aside. Add the remainder of the oil to the pan, with the rest of the hoisin sauce, tomato purée, and chilli oil. Stir and blend together. Turn the heat to high, and pour in the frog legs. Stir-fry quickly for 3 minutes, then add the sweet pepper; stir-fry together for a further minute, and serve.

Szechuan Home-Cooked Frog Legs

Serves 4 or 5, with other dishes

10 pairs frog legs
4 oz (100 g) bamboo shoots
4 oz (100 g) young leeks
1 tablespoon black beans
2 cloves garlic
2 slices root ginger
½ tablespoon cornflour
½ teaspoon flavour powder
6 tablespoons vegetable oil
2 tablespoons lard
2 tablespoons sherry
1½ tablespoons soya sauce
6 tablespoons superior stock
2 teaspoons sesame oil

Duck, Pigeon, Turkey and Frogs

Preparation Clean and dry the frog legs. Slice the bamboo shoots into thin slices, and cut the leeks into 1 inch (2½ cm) segments. Soak the black beans in water for 30 minutes; then drain. Crush the garlic and shred the ginger. Blend the cornflour with 2 tablespoons water and the flavour powder.

Cooking Heat the oil in frying pan, and when hot, add the frog legs. Stir-fry over high heat for 2 minutes, then set aside to keep warm. Add the leeks and bamboo shoots, and stir-fry in the remaining oil for 2 minutes. Drain away any excess oil. Add the lard and black beans to the pan. Stir-fry over a medium heat for 1½ minutes, then remove and discard the black beans. Add the crushed garlic, ginger, sherry, and soya sauce. After 10 seconds stirring and quick-frying together, pour in the frog legs, bamboo shoots, leeks, and stock. Cover and simmer for 5–6 minutes. Add the cornflour mixture, and stir-fry for a further ½ minute. Sprinkle with sesame oil, and serve.

Fried Steamed Frog Legs

Serves 4 or 5, with other dishes

- 10 pairs frog legs
- 1½ teaspoons salt
- 1 tablespoon cornflour
- 4 oz (100 g) thin stem bamboo shoots
- 2 spring onion stalks
- 4–5 oz (100–125 g) cucumber
- 3 oz (75 g) smoked ham
- 2 slices root ginger
- 2 tablespoons light-coloured soya sauce
- 2 tablespoons sherry
- 2 tablespoons chicken stock
- ½ teaspoon flavour powder
- 1½ teaspoons sugar
- 1 teaspoon sesame oil
- 6 tablespoons vegetable oil

Preparation Rub the frog legs with salt, and dredge with cornflour. Cut the bamboo shoots and spring onions into 1 inch (2½ cm) segments, and slice the cucumber thinly. Cut the ham into six slices, shred the ginger, and parboil the bamboo shoots for 5 minutes. Drain. Mix the soya sauce with the sherry, chicken stock, flavour powder, sugar, and sesame oil until well-blended.

Cooking Heat the oil in a frying pan. When hot, pour in the frog legs and stir-fry over a high heat for 2 minutes. Drain away the oil. Arrange the bamboo shoots and cucumber as a bed at the bottom of a heat-proof dish or casserole. Lay the frog legs on top, and sprinkle evenly with the spring onion and the ginger, soya/sherry/chicken broth mixture, and the ham. Place the heat-proof dish in a steamer and steam vigorously for 30 minutes.

Serving Serve on the table in the heat-proof dish or casserole.

Fish

魚

In China, in the past, fish had to be eaten fresh or not at all as there was no refrigeration; except, of course, when it was salted and dried – a very different kettle of fish altogether.

When dried salted fish is fried it gives off a strong inimitable smell, which can only be adequately described in English with words which are unmistakably rude. In China we always fry this fish to such a degree of crispiness that even the bones become crispy and edible. Salted fish fried in such a way is very similar to concentrated cheese, except that it is crispy. But there is a unique 'melting' quality about its crispiness. It is one of the best-loved side-dishes for eating with soft or semi-soft (porridgy) rice, and is considered a delicacy by the Japanese.

The only way to keep fish fresh in China was to keep them alive in jars, vats, or ponds. Fish kept in this way are naturally immeasurably fresher and sweeter than frozen fish. It is strangely ironical that in a country where there was no refrigeration we ate fresh fish all the time, but in the West, where you have every modern aid and convenience, the only times most people ever see fresh fish are in zoo aquariums, or else when they go fishing – and then even if they do catch any fish at all, they throw most of them back into the water! It seems that with the advance of civilization, and having got into the habit of only buying dead fish laid out on tiles or marble slabs, we forget the quality of live or fresh fish.

Although China has a coastline of over three thousand miles with an abundance of salt-water fish, fresh-water fish play a much bigger part in the Chinese diet than fish from the sea. This is not only due to the fact that there are several mighty rivers and tens of thousands of miles of streams, tributaries, canals, and other waterways in China, as well as many fresh-water lakes, but also because we Chinese make a practice of fish-farming. There is a pond in most villages in which

Fish

fish are reared, and grass and other natural fish foods are thrown in to keep the fish alive. Each year the ponds are drained, and the fish sifted; the smaller ones are returned to the re-flooded ponds for another season's growing, while the larger ones are taken out for food or sold to markets. These 'fish-farms' are undoubtedly a large source of fresh fish in China. To some extent, in supplying the necessary proteins, they must have partly compensated for the lack of dairies in China.

We Chinese eat all edible fish: the varieties are numerous, and some fish may not have any exact Western equivalent. Some of the favourites are bass, sea-bass, sea-bream, carp, flounder, halibut, mackerel, perch, pike, cod, salmon, sole, shad, trout, plaice, sardines, and herring.

The principal ways of cooking fish are to steam, clear-simmer, deep-fry, pan-fry, stir-fry, or braise them; or else they may be minced or ground for making into fish balls and fish cakes.

Unlike meat, which often has to be hung to be tasty, fish are best cooked and eaten completely fresh. To retain that sweet, fresh juiciness in fish, they are best when cooked only for a short time. All the additional, supplementary seasonings and flavours are impregnated into the fish by a period of marinating, and then they are given a short, sharp blast of steam for about 10–20 minutes, or a sizzle in oil. Alternatively, after being cut into smaller pieces or slices, they are turned over a few times in hot oil, often pre-impregnated with ginger, garlic, and onion; and then the various supplementary ingredients are added for a final stir-fry to give the flavour of the dish a balanced orchestration. Such cooking usually lasts no more than 2–3 minutes. Although fish cooked in this manner is very popular, it is suitable only for very fresh fish with firm flesh which does not break up too easily during the stir-frying.

Otherwise, we Chinese prefer to have fish cooked whole, especially a large fresh-water specimen. We seem to have the same conception of a fish as the English have of a joint: it is best served whole on a large serving dish, and brought in steaming, succulent, and garnished. Whole fish are steamed, clear-simmered, or deep-fried; draped with a few supplementary materials, and served covered with a rich sauce. In contrast to Western cooking, the Chinese sauce for fish is very seldom, if ever, a fish sauce. It is usually a meat sauce, or a hot sauce, incorporating pickles and dried mushrooms. The only times when any additional fish or seafood is introduced into a fish dish is when it is dried or pickled such as dried prawns, dried scallop-muscles, or oyster sauce, when all the fishiness has gone out of them or has changed. One of the things we always try to avoid is adding more fishiness to a fish dish.

Red-Cooked Fish with Vegetables

Serves 4–6, with other dishes

1 3 lb (1¼ kg) fish
3 golden needles
 (lily bud stems)
3 large Chinese dried mushrooms
1 oz (25 g) dried wood ears
2–3 oz (50–75 g) bamboo shoots
1 green sweet pepper
1 large onion
2–3 water chestnuts
3 spring onion stalks
3 oz (75 g) ham
2 teaspoons salt
2 tablespoons flour
oil for deep-frying
4 tablespoons soya sauce
3 tablespoons sherry
3 teaspoons sugar
6 tablespoons chicken stock
pepper to taste

This is really a slightly more elaborate version of the previous recipe, using ham instead of pork, and with the addition of many more vegetables.

Preparation Soak the golden needles, mushrooms, and wood ears separately for 30 minutes. Cut the needles into 2 inch (5 cm) segments. Remove the mushroom stalks and cut the caps into strips. Retain 4 tablespoons of the mushroom water. Slice the bamboo shoots and sweet pepper into strips. Cut the onion and water chestnuts into thin slices. Cut the spring onions into 2 inch (5 cm) segments. Cut the ham into strips. Make five or six slashes on each side of the fish, then rub it with salt, inside and out, and dredge with flour.

Cooking Fry the fish in oil in a deep-fryer for 5 minutes, or semi-deep-fry it in a large frying pan in 1 inch (2½ cm) of oil. If you use the latter method, cook the fish over a high heat for 1 minute on each side, then reduce the heat to medium and fry for 2½ minutes on each side. Drain the fish and keep it warm. Pour away most of the oil. Stir-fry the bamboo shoots, water chestnuts, green pepper, onion, mushrooms, wood ears, golden needles, and half of the spring onions in the remaining oil for 2 minutes. Add the mushroom water, soya sauce, sherry, sugar, chicken stock, and pepper. Cook this sauce, stirring, for 2 minutes; then lower the fish into the enriched sauce to baste and cook gently for 5–6 minutes.

Serving Place the fish on a large oval dish and pile all the solid ingredients from the pan on top. Garnish with the strips of ham and the remaining spring onions.

Fish

Red-Cooked Fish in Chunks

Serves 4–6, with other dishes

2 lb (1 kg) fish
1 teaspoon salt
2 tablespoons flour
2 slices root ginger
3 spring onion stalks

4 tablespoons oil
3 tablespoons soya sauce
4 tablespoons meat *or* chicken stock
pepper to taste
2 teaspoons sugar

Large fish such as halibut, cod, or haddock, which are normally available in big pieces or chunks, can be red-cooked in a similar fashion to the method described in the two previous recipes. The fish should be cut into cubes about 1 inch (2½ cm) square. As this is a home-cooked dish for domestic consumption, no mushrooms or bamboo shoots are used.

Preparation Cut the fish into cubes approximately 1–1½ inches (2½–3½ cm) in size. Rub them with salt and dredge with flour. Shred the ginger and cut the spring onions into 1 inch (2½ cm) segments.
Cooking Heat the oil in a frying pan. Fry the fish cubes for 2 minutes on each side. Remove them from the pan and keep warm. Add the ginger and half of the spring onions to the pan. Stir-fry for 1 minute. Add the soya sauce, stock, pepper, and sugar, and stir-fry for 1 minute. Return the pieces of fish to the pan and baste them with the sauce for 1 minute. Cover the pan and cook the fish and sauce over a medium heat for 4 minutes.
Serving Place the pieces of fish on a serving dish and pour the sauce from the pan over them. Sprinkle with soya sauce and the remaining spring onions; then serve.

This is a useful dish as it can be prepared and cooked in a very short time.

Sweet and Sour Red-Cooked Fish

In the majority of sweet and sour fish dishes, the fish is made crispy by frying before the sauce is added at the last minute, or towards the end of the cooking time. All red-cooked fish dishes can be converted into sweet and sour dishes by reducing the quantity of sauce in the original recipe and adding the sweet and sour sauce towards the end. The original sauce can be reduced simply by not including stock in the liquid ingredients and by reducing the quantities of sherry and mushroom water added. Through such elimination and reduction, the dish would become quite dry after a period of braising. The sweet and sour sauce is then poured over this comparatively dry dish. The ingredients for making the sauce are given in the following recipe.

Sweet and Sour Yellow River Carp

Serves 4–6, with other dishes

1 3 lb (1¼ to 1½ kg) carp
2 teaspoons salt
2 tablespoons flour
1 oz (25 g) wood ears
2 oz (50 g) bamboo shoots
3 cloves garlic
3 slices root ginger
4 spring onion stalks
1 oz (25 g) water chestnuts

1 small sweet pepper
1 tablespoon cornflour
2 tablespoons sugar
3 tablespoons vinegar
1 tablespoon tomato purée
3 tablespoons orange juice
2 tablespoons sherry
3 tablespoons stock *or* water
oil for deep-frying
2 tablespoons lard

The term 'Yellow River' is used here mainly to provide a certain geographical nostalgia – to give the feeling that the dish and ingredients are something special, when, in fact, Yellow River carp is no different from or better than many other Chinese varieties of carp, except that it lives in muddier water and should be kept in clear water for a few days before consumption.

Preparation Wash the fish thoroughly, then slash it on both sides at 2 inch (5 cm) intervals, to a depth of about ¼ inch (½ cm). Rub with salt and dredge lightly with flour. Soak and rinse the wood ears. Cut the bamboo shoots into strips. Crush the garlic and shred the ginger. Cut the spring onions into 1 inch (2½ cm) segments. Slice the water chestnuts thinly. Cut the sweet pepper into thin slices. Mix the remaining ingredients, except the oil and lard, and blend well into a smooth sauce.

Cooking Heat the oil in a deep-fryer and deep-fry the fish for 8–10 minutes until quite crispy. Remove it and place it in the oven to keep warm, on a well-heated dish. Heat the lard in a frying pan. Add the ginger, garlic, and half of the spring onions. Stir-fry for 2 minutes, then pour most of the impregnated lard over the fish. Put the bamboo shoots, water chestnuts, wood ears, sweet pepper, and remaining lard in the frying pan. Stir-fry together for 2 minutes. Pour in the sauce mixture. As soon as it thickens and becomes translucent, pour it and all the solid ingredients over the length of the fish, and serve.

This is a banquet dish, popular at most party dinners.

Fish

Deep-Fried Fresh Salted Fish Steaks

Serves 4-6, with other dishes

2 lb (1 kg) fish (cod, haddock, halibut)
2 slices root ginger

4 teaspoons salt
1¼ tablespoons plain flour
¼ tablespoon self-raising flour
1 egg
oil for deep-frying

Preparation Cut the fish into 2 × 1½ inch (5 × 3½ cm) pieces. Shred the ginger and chop finely. Mix 2 teaspoons salt with the ginger. Rub each piece of fish with this mixture and leave to season for 2 hours. Mix the remaining salt with the plain and self-raising flours. Beat the egg lightly. Wet the pieces of fish with the beaten egg and dredge with the seasoned flour.
Cooking Heat the oil in a deep-fryer. Lower three or four pieces of fish into the oil in a wire basket and fry for 3-4 minutes, or until lightly browned. Repeat until all the pieces of fish have been fried, then arrange them on a well-heated white serving dish in fish-scale fashion, and serve. A few leaves of lettuce or young cabbage can be used to garnish the fish, if desired.

The sharp saltiness on the surface of the fish contrasting with the freshness within makes this a very appealing dish for rice-eating fish-lovers, in spite of its apparent simplicity.

Squirrel Fish

Serves 4-6, with other dishes

1 3 lb (1¼ kg) carp *or* bream
3 teaspoons salt
2 tablespoons flour
6 Chinese dried mushrooms
2 slices root ginger
3 spring onion stalks
2 oz (50 g) bamboo shoots

1 tablespoon cornflour
3 tablespoons water
1½ tablespoons soya sauce
1½ tablespoons sugar
2½ tablespoons vinegar
6 tablespoons chicken stock
2 tablespoons sherry
oil for deep-frying
1½ tablespoons lard *or* butter

In contrast to Yellow River carp, this is a Yangtze River dish, well-known in the city of Nanking, which is situated on the great river.
Preparation Chop off the head of the fish. Clean the rest of the fish and slice it open lengthwise. Remove the vertebrae and bones. Clean again thoroughly. Rub with salt and dust lightly with flour. Make ten slashes on each side of the fish. Leave it to season for 2 hours. Soak the mushrooms for 30 minutes, remove the stalks and shred the caps. Shred the ginger and cut the

spring onions into 1 inch (2½ cm) segments. Slice the bamboo shoots into strips. Blend the remaining ingredients, except the oil and lard, into a smooth sauce.

Cooking Place the fish in a wire basket and lower it into the boiling oil to fry for 5–6 minutes. When the sizzling stops, which means most of the water has evaporated, turn off the heat or remove the pan from the heat. The fish will now curl up like a squirrel. Allow it to continue cooking in the oil for 2 minutes without returning the pan to the heat; then turn the heat up to maximum and fry the fish for 2 minutes, which should turn it golden-brown and cause the tail to turn up even more like that of a squirrel. Meanwhile, prepare the sauce by frying the bamboo shoots and mushrooms in the lard over a medium heat for 1½ minutes. Pour in the sauce mixture. When it thickens and boils, drain the fish quickly and put it on a well-heated serving dish; then bring the fish and sauce to the table. Pour the sauce over the fish in front of the diners and the fish should emit a noise like a squeaking squirrel (does a squirrel squeak?). Anyway, the thought and description seem to tickle the Chinese fancy.

Carp Braised in Chicken Fat Sauce

Serves 4–6, with other dishes

1 2½–3 lb (about 1¼ kg) carp
4–5 tablespoons chicken fat
2 teaspoons salt
1½ tablespoons flour
2 slices root ginger
2 cloves garlic

4 spring onion stalks
3 tablespoons soya sauce
1 tablespoon hoisin sauce
1 teaspoon chilli sauce
2 teaspoons sugar
2 tablespoons sherry
2 cakes fresh bean curd
⅓ pint (160 ml) chicken stock

Preparation Clean the carp thoroughly and rub with salt, inside and out. Leave to season for 1 hour. Dust and dredge the fish with the flour. Shred the ginger, crush and chop the garlic, and cut the spring onions into 1 inch (2½ cm) segments.

Cooking Heat the chicken fat in a large, oval, heat-proof casserole. Add the ginger, garlic, and half of the spring onions. Stir-fry for 1 minute. Add the soya sauce, hoisin sauce, chilli sauce, sugar, and sherry. Stir and mix well. When the mixture boils, lay the carp on the hot oil-sauce mixture to cook for 2 minutes. Turn the fish over and cook for another 2 minutes. Meanwhile, cut each bean curd cake into six pieces and place them against the sides of the casserole. Pour in the stock, sprinkle in the remaining spring onions and cover the casserole firmly. Simmer gently for 10 minutes and serve from the casserole.

Fish

Pan-Fried Sliced Fish in White Sauce

Serves 4-6, with other dishes

1½ lb (600 g) fillet of sole *or* flounder
1 oz (25 g) wood ears
1½ teaspoons salt
1 egg white
2 tablespoons cornflour
1 teaspoon self-raising flour
7 tablespoons chicken stock
3 tablespoons white wine
¼ teaspoon flavour powder
1½ teaspoons cornflour
1 tablespoon chicken fat
1 tablespoon lard
2 slices root ginger

Preparation Soak the wood ears for 30 minutes, rinse and drain. Cut fish with a sharp knife into 2 × 1 inch (5 × 2½ cm) strips. Rub them with salt. Beat the egg white with a fork for 10 seconds. Wet the fish slices with the egg white, then dust and dredge them with 2 tablespoons cornflour, blended with the self-raising flour. Blend together 4 tablespoons of the chicken stock, the wine, flavour powder, 1½ teaspoons cornflour, and 1 tablespoon chicken fat, until a smooth sauce is formed.

Cooking Heat the lard, ginger, and remaining chicken stock in a frying pan and stir over a medium heat. Put the slices of fish into the liquid to heat for just over 1 minute on each side. Remove the fish carefully with a fish-slice, place on a well-heated dish, and keep hot in the oven. Pour away the remaining liquid from the pan. Add the chicken fat and wood ears to the pan and stir-fry quickly over a medium heat for 30 seconds. Pour in the sauce mixture and stir gently until the liquid thickens and becomes translucent. Pour the sauce and wood ears over the fish in the serving dish.

This is a delicate dish which requires precise timing to succeed. It is a very well-known and well-liked dish from Peking. The term 'pan-fried' is used here to distinguish the cooking method from quick-frying or stir-frying, where stirring, turning, mixing, and scrambling are involved. Pan-frying is static and the ingredients are handled carefully and slowly so that they do not break up. Usually the ingredients employed are few and all are cooked individually. They are not meant to be mixed up in a scramble. The sauce is the constituent part of the dish that combines all the ingredients together.

Double-Fried Eel

Serves 4–6, with other dishes

1 3–4 lb (1¼–1¾ kg) eel
3 teaspoons salt
2 slices root ginger
2 cloves garlic
4 spring onion stalks
oil for deep-frying
2 tablespoons lard

2 tablespoons soya sauce
2 tablespoons sherry
4 tablespoons chicken stock
¼ teaspoon flavour powder
1 teaspoon sugar
¼ teaspoon five spice powder
pepper to taste
2 tablespoons chopped parsley

This is a rich, highly-spiced dish from Shanghai, and is an excellent accompaniment to rice.

Preparation Dip the eel in boiling water for 1 minute; then drain and dry it, and rub it with salt. Leave to season for 1 hour. Shred the ginger; crush and chop the garlic. Cut the spring onions into 1 inch (2½ cm) segments.
Cooking Heat the oil in a deep-fryer. Place the eel in a wire basket and deep-fry it for 4–5 minutes. Drain; then cut the meat neatly into 2 × 1 inch (5 × 2½ cm) strips. Discard the head and tail. Place the pieces of eel-meat in the wire basket, deep-fry for a second time over a high heat for 2–3 minutes until golden-brown; then drain thoroughly. Meanwhile, heat the lard in a frying pan. Add the ginger, garlic, spring onions, soya sauce, sherry, chicken stock, flavour powder, sugar, five spice powder, and pepper. Stir-fry together for 1 minute. Add the pieces of eel, spreading them over the pan. Turn and baste them with the sauce for 2½ minutes
Serving Place the pieces of eel on a well-heated dish, pour the sauce over, and sprinkle with chopped parsley.

This dish is best served immediately.

Smoked Fish

Serves 4–6, with other dishes

4 fish steaks
2 spring onion stalks
2 tablespoons soya sauce
1 tablespoon sherry

2 teaspoons sugar
½ teaspoon flavour powder
1½ teaspoons salt
4 tablespoons vegetable oil
3 tablespoons brown sugar
2 large sheets of tinfoil

Fish

Chinese smoked fish is usually made with fish or pieces of fish which have already been thoroughly marinated and seasoned, then fried in oil until they are quite dry, so that they appear as if they have already been smoked. When smoke is actually used, it is applied only to provide a slight touch of flavour. This recipe describes the best way to go through the whole process in a modern kitchen. It sounds fairly complicated, but the result is well worth it.

Preparation Chop the spring onions finely. Mix them with the soya sauce, sherry, sugar, and flavour powder. Rub the fish with the salt and leave the pieces to marinate in the mixed sauce for approximately 1 hour, turning a couple of times.

Cooking Heat the oil in a large, heavy frying pan. Spread the pieces of fish evenly over the pan and fry for 2 minutes on each side, over a medium heat. Reduce the heat to very low, pour the remainder of the marinade over the fish, and continue to fry very slowly and gently until nearly all the sauce has dried up, or is encrusted on the fish. The fish should now be dark brown in colour.

Smoking Place the pieces of fish in a tin dish or small roasting pan. Spread the brown sugar in the centre of a sheet of tinfoil and place the dish containing the fish on top. Wrap the foil loosely over the dish of fish and seal over the top by twisting or screwing the edges together (thus forming a tinfoil 'tent'). Repeat with another sheet of tinfoil, but this time without sealing the top, and puncture a small hole in the top of the inner layer. Place the foil-wrapped dish of fish in a heavy saucepan or large roasting pan. Place the pan over a medium heat for 3–4 minutes, or until smoke starts to come out of the hole in the inner sheet of the foil. The smoke is caused by the burning sugar. Now seal the outer layer of tinfoil, heat for a few more seconds; then turn the heat off and leave the fish to stand in the smoke-filled tent for 10 minutes.

Serving Unwrap the layers of tinfoil, arrange the pieces of fish on a dish, and serve.

This is a more elaborate type of Chinese smoked fish dish. The less elaborate method, as mentioned at the beginning of this recipe, does not require any smoking at all. All it requires is low-heat frying until all the marinade and fish have become dried enough for the fish to appear to have been smoked. The fish turns brown because of the soya sauce and other ingredients becoming encrusted on it during the slow process of gentle, low-heat frying.

The Complete Chinese Cookbook
Drunken Fish

Serves 4–6, with other dishes

- 2 lb (1 kg) very fresh cod or salmon
- 1 medium-sized onion
- 3 slices root ginger
- 1 teaspoon salt
- 2 tablespoons soya sauce
- 2 tablespoons dry sherry
- 2 teaspoons brandy *or* Mowtai liqueur *or* Kaoliang liqueur
- ⅛ teaspoon freshly-milled black pepper
- ½ teaspoon chilli oil
- 2 tablespoons chopped chives
- 3 teaspoons sesame oil

It is in the Japanese tradition to eat raw fish. We Chinese also have some raw fish dishes. These are generally very well seasoned.

Preparation Chop the onion. Boil the ginger and onion in 6 tablespoons of water for 2 minutes. Retain the water. Cut the fish into very thin slices about 2½ × 1½ inches (6 × 3½ cm) in size. Rub them with salt, then add the soya sauce, ginger/onion water, sherry, brandy or liqueur, pepper, chilli oil, and half of the chives. Mix thoroughly. Leave to season for 3 hours in a refrigerator.

Serving Spread the pieces of fish on a flat serving dish. Brush them with sesame oil, sprinkle with the remaining chopped chives; then serve.

Stir-Frying, Steaming, and Simmering Fish

Fish is never stir-fried in the vigorous way in which pieces of meat, vegetables, or pasta are stir-fried in Chinese cooking. This is for the simple reason that pieces of fish would break up into uneven pieces if treated with such violence. Hence, slices of fish are usually cooked by static frying (Chien) or by wet frying (Liu) in a thickened sauce. To cook sliced fish either way, the actual cooking time is generally not more than 4–5 minutes, and all the flavourings and supplementary ingredients are generally added after the cooking has started. Apart from having to cut or slice the fish neatly and carefully to the required size, cooking by these methods is very quick – they are equivalent to quick stir-frying (Chow) in meat cookery, which produces an inexhaustible number of dishes; and although there are far fewer fish dishes in these categories than meat dishes, some of the best-known and best-liked fish dishes are wet-fried (Liu) dishes.

On the other hand, when fish is available fresh and whole, perhaps 'clear-steaming' or 'clear-simmering' are two of the simplest ways of handling it. Perhaps by not doing too much to fish, more of its native qualities, such as its sweet-freshness, can be retained. Here, the Chinese habit of adding fresh

Fish

root ginger, with perhaps a few drops of wine and a sprinkle of sugar, can work miracles to reduce the fishiness in fish. Once again, the use of soya sauce or fermented salted beans, in conjunction with leeks, onions, and just a trace of garlic, seems to enhance the savoury quality of fish in a way which few other flavourers are able to surpass.

In contrast with wet-frying, when fish is steamed or simmered it is often well-marinated before cooking starts. In the cooking itself, the fish is simply subjected to a vigorous blast of steaming for 15–25 minutes, depending on the size or quantity of the fish to be cooked. It is cooked by 'open steaming', that is, without a lid. All the dressing and garnishing is usually arranged prior to the steaming, so once the cooking has been completed, the dish of fish can usually be brought direct from the steamer to the table, all spick and span and well-presented.

Clear-Steamed Fish

Serves 4–6, with other dishes

1 3 lb (1¼ kg) whole fish
1½ tablespoons dried shrimps
2 large Chinese dried mushrooms
3 slices root ginger
2 teaspoons salt
½ teaspoon flavour powder
6 spring onion stalks

2 cloves garlic
3 tablespoons soya sauce
2 tablespoons sherry
3 teaspoons sugar
3 tablespoons chicken stock
2 teaspoons cornflour
2 rashers of bacon
dash of pepper

Various types of fish can be cooked by clear-steaming, including carp, bream, sea-bream, mullet, bass, and sole. It is preferable to choose the thicker, chunkier varieties rather than the thin, flat type, such as plaice, which is more suitable for frying. The Chinese conception of a good fish dish is not unlike the Western conception of a good joint: something big, which can be carved on the table.

Preparation Soak the dried shrimps in a bowl of water for 1 hour. Soak the mushrooms, remove the stalks, and slice the caps into strips. Chop the ginger finely and mix with the salt and flavour powder. Rub the fish with this mixture, inside and out, and leave to season for 30 minutes. Chop half of the spring onions into fine pieces and the other half into 2 inch (5 cm) segments. Crush and chop the garlic and mix it with the spring onions, soya sauce, sherry, sugar, stock, and cornflour blended with 2 tablespoons water. Mix together well. Pour the mixture over the fish and turn it in the marinade a couple of times. Slice the bacon into strips. Sprinkle the shrimps evenly over the fish, drape it with bacon and mushroom strips; then sprinkle lightly with pepper.

The Complete Chinese Cookbook

Cooking Place the fish in a deep heat-proof dish and steam vigorously for 20–22 minutes.

Serving Bring the dish from the steamer and serve in a cloud of steam. This is particularly effective on a winter's day. Although the cooking of this dish is simple, the unbiased opinion of many people is that this is one of the great fish dishes of the world.

Seafood & Crustaceans

海味

Not all shellfish or crustaceans can be classified as seafoods in China. Most of the crabs and shrimps eaten are, in fact, fresh-water products from the lakes, rivers, canals, and ponds. Fresh-water shrimps and crabs are considered sweeter and more delicate than the coarser products of the sea, which are enjoyed by the coastal people.

Some of the shellfish or seafoods are used mainly dried, as flavourers, rather than as a dish or food in themselves. There are few abalone dishes because it is most frequently used in small quantities just to give flavour. As a food, abalone is of no importance; as a flavourer it is one of the essential supplementary materials in Chinese cooking.

Although great quantities of shrimps and squid are eaten and cooked fresh, equal quantities of them are used dried as flavourers. The same applies to oysters and the root-muscles of scallops, which are considered to possess a very delicate taste. As cross-cooking and inter-blending of flavours are an integral part of Chinese cooking, these ingredients have a double function in Chinese food and cooking. They are always available as dried foods in Chinese provision shops, and should be found in any well-stocked Chinese pantry. They must always be soaked before being used for flavouring.

On the other hand, when crustaceans and seafoods are used fresh, they have to be very fresh (because, as mentioned before, it is only recently that refrigeration came to China). Some are even cooked alive – one of the best ways of eating oysters is to cook them in their own shells. It was the tradition of the coastal people of south-east China to stick bamboo-sticks in oyster beds, and over a period of time the sticks became encrusted with oysters. To harvest the oysters they had only to pull up the sticks. I remember many enjoyable and exciting winter evenings spent in grilling sticks of oysters (usually there were six to twelve oysters on a stick) over blazing braziers, and listening to the popping noise of the oyster-shells opening when they were cooked.

Cooking fresh, live crabs, lobsters, clams, prawns, and scallops seems to be the practice wherever freshness is valued. As a rule they are only subjected to very brief cooking, usually by stir-frying, deep-frying, or steaming. In many parts of the world today, however, these crustaceans and seafoods are available only canned or frozen. The frozen varieties have to be completely thawed and strained before being used in Chinese cooking. There are some excellent canned varieties of crab-meat, but for prawns and shrimps to have any resemblance to the original fresh variety, it is best to buy them frozen.

As variety is the keynote to Chinese food, and since crustaceans and seafoods provide such a distinctive difference in taste and flavour from other types of materials, one almost invariably finds a dish or two made from crustaceans during a multi-course Chinese dinner. In their use as flavourers – usually in small quantities in made-up dishes – they are to be found in almost every Chinese meal, if it is one which is above subsistence level. For these reasons seafoods and crustaceans are perhaps better known and more universally appreciated by the Chinese than by any other continental people.

Abalone

Abalone has a rubbery texture, is brownish-yellow in colour, and has an extremely savoury flavour. It is usually available canned – only occasionally in dried form. When the can is opened the liquid or abalone water should always be reserved for later use, especially for adding a savoury flavour to soups, and stewed, or braised dishes.

In all normally available forms, abalone requires very little cooking – generally not more than a few minutes. Because of its rubbery texture, it becomes monotonous when chewed, and therefore is not a very interesting food to eat on its own. Although there are one or two pure abalone dishes, it is far more interesting when cooked with other ingredients.

Seafood and Crustaceans
Abalone Stir-Fried with Mushrooms and Bamboo Shoots

Serves 4-8, with other dishes

8-16 oz (200-400 g) can abalone
6 Chinese dried mushrooms
4 oz (100 g) bamboo shoots
2 teaspoons cornflour

2 spring onion stalks
3 tablespoons vegetable oil
1 tablespoon soya sauce
2 teaspoons hoisin sauce
1 tablespoon sherry

Preparation Soak the dried mushrooms for 20 minutes, then drain, reserving 4 tablespoons of the mushroom water. Remove the stalks and cut each mushroom cap into four. Cut the abalone and bamboo shoots into ⅛ inch (¼ cm) thick slices. Blend the cornflour with 2 tablespoons of the abalone water. Chop the spring onions into 1 inch (2½ cm) segments.
Cooking Heat the oil in a frying pan, add the mushrooms and bamboo shoots, and stir-fry over a medium heat for 2 minutes. Add the soya sauce, hoisin sauce, sherry, and mushroom water; stir-fry gently for another minute. Pour in the abalone water and cornflour mixture. As soon as the liquid thickens slightly, add the slices of abalone and spring onion. Stir-fry for 2 minutes, then serve on a light-coloured, well-heated dish, and eat immediately.

Simmered Chicken with Abalone

Serves 8-10, with other dishes

1 3-4 lb (1½-1¾ kg) chicken
4-6 oz (100-150 g) can abalone
1 lb (400 g) broccoli

2 slices root ginger
2 teaspoons salt
1 teaspoon flavour powder
4 tablespoons sherry

The flavour of chicken seems to combine well with most seafoods, particularly with abalone. There are many dishes in which these two ingredients are used together with excellent effect. The following is one in which they are in 'wet combination'.

Preparation Clean the chicken. Cut the abalone into ⅛ inch (nearly ½ cm) thick slices, reserving the abalone water. Clean the broccoli and cut it into individual leaves and branches, discarding the outer, coarser parts.
Cooking Place the chicken in boiling water for 3 minutes, then discard the water. Remove the chicken to a large heat-proof casserole and pour in 2 pints (generous litre) of water. Add the ginger and salt, cover the casserole, and simmer the chicken gently, either over a low heat or in the oven for 1 hour. Put the broccoli and abalone into the liquid surrounding the chicken.

The Complete Chinese Cookbook

Add the flavour powder, and pour in the abalone water and sherry; then simmer, covered, for a further 30 minutes. Serve in the casserole or in a large soup bowl or tureen.

This makes a very attractive dish, with the greenness of the broccoli balancing the whiteness of the chicken. (Chinese celery cabbage can be used instead of broccoli.) The tastiness of the chicken, accentuated by the presence of abalone, causes the dish to rise to a degree of flavour which can only be described as 'the ultimate in savouriness'. This is a large dish, often made for dinner parties, and it is usually served in a tureen or 'ocean bowl' – the largest dish used on a Chinese dining table.

Red-Cooked Abalone with Chicken, Mushrooms, and Bamboo Shoots

Serves 6–8, with other dishes

- 4 large Chinese dried mushrooms
- 1 chicken breast
- 3 oz (75 g) bamboo shoots
- 4 oz (100 g) abalone
- 2 tablespoons lard
- 1 slice root ginger
- 1¼ tablespoons soya sauce
- ½ tablespoon oyster sauce
- ½ tablespoon hoisin sauce
- 1 tablespoon sherry
- 1 teaspoon cornflour
- ½ teaspoon sesame oil

Preparation Soak the mushrooms for 20 minutes; then remove the stalks and cut the caps into quarters. Reserve 4 tablespoons of the mushroom water. Slice the chicken, bamboo shoots, and abalone into ⅛ inch (¼ cm) pieces.
Cooking Heat the lard in a frying pan. Add the chicken, ginger, and bamboo shoots; stir-fry over a medium heat for 2 minutes. Add the abalone, mushrooms, soya sauce, oyster sauce, hoisin sauce, and sherry. Continue to stir-fry for 2 minutes. Blend the cornflour with the mushroom water; then pour this mixture into the pan, add the sesame oil, and stir-fry gently for 5 minutes.
Serving Serve on a well-heated plate. This dish is considered a delicacy and is usually served only at party meals.

Bêche de Mer

Bêche de mer, also called sea cucumber, is considered a delicacy in China, and is served only during banquets and party dinners. It is quite tasteless in itself, but it is a great conveyor and orchestrator of other tastes and flavours. It has an interesting texture: jelly-like but firm. It is usually available dried, and requires long soaking before cooking.

Seafood and Crustaceans

Red-Cooked Bêche de Mer with Pork, Mushrooms, and Bamboo Shoots

Serves 6, with other dishes

6 pieces bêche de mer (about 1 lb *or* 400 g)
6 large Chinese dried mushrooms
3 oz (75 g) bamboo shoots
4 oz (100 g) lean pork
1 spring onion stalk
2 tablespoons lard
1 slice root ginger
3 tablespoons soya sauce
6 tablespoons sherry
1 tablespoon cornflour
¼ pint (125 ml) chicken stock
½ teaspoon flavour powder
1 teaspoon sesame oil

Preparation Soak the bêche de mer overnight. Next day, dip it in boiling water for 15 minutes; then drain. Repeat the dipping. Soak the mushrooms for 30 minutes; then remove the stalks and cut the caps in half. Reserve ¼ pint (125 ml) of the mushroom water. Cut the bamboo shoots into ¼ inch (nearly ½ cm) slices, shred the pork into matchstick strips, and cut the spring onion into ½ inch (1 cm) segments.

Cooking Heat the lard in a covered frying pan. Add the pork and ginger, and stir-fry over a medium heat for 3 minutes. Add the bamboo shoots and mushrooms, and continue to stir-fry for 2 minutes. Add the soya sauce, sherry, mushroom water, and bêche de mer. Leave to cook over a low heat for 40 minutes. Mix the cornflour, chicken stock, and flavour powder: pour the mixture into the pan, and simmer for a further 20 minutes.

Serving Pour the contents of the pan into a deep, heat-proof dish. Sprinkle with sesame oil and spring onion, then place the dish in a steamer and steam for 30 minutes.

At the end of the steaming the bêche de mer has a rich, glistening gloss, and is tender but firm – highly palatable to connoisseurs.

Butterfly Bêche de Mer

Serves 6, with other dishes

10 pieces bêche de mer (about 1 lb *or* 400 g)
2 eggs
1 oz (25 g) smoked ham
2 oz (50 g) cooked chicken breast meat
4 spring onion stalks
2 oz (50 g) bean sprouts
3 teaspoons cornflour
1 teaspoon flavour powder
half a small chicken
1 lb (400 g) knuckle of pork
2 slices root ginger
3 teaspoons salt
4 tablespoons sherry
2 tablespoons lard

The Complete Chinese Cookbook

Preparation Soak the bêche de mer overnight. Clean thoroughly, then cut the pieces into butterfly shapes. Dip them in boiling water and leave to soak. Hard-boil the eggs. Discard the yolks and cut the whites into thin slices. Slice the ham and chicken thinly into 1½ × 1 inch (3½ × 2½ cm) pieces. Cut the spring onions into 1 inch (2½ cm) segments. Mix the bean sprouts with the cornflour, flavour powder, and 3 tablespoons water.

Cooking Boil the half chicken and the knuckle of pork in water for 5 minutes. Discard the water. Place the chicken and pork in a heavy pan or heat-proof casserole with 2½ pints (nearly 1½ litres) water, half of the ginger, half of the salt, half of the sherry, and half of the spring onions. Bring to the boil and simmer over a very low heat for 3 hours, with an asbestos sheet under the pan. Strain the resulting 'soup', skim away the fat, and put the soup aside. Heat the lard in a deep-fryer and add the remaining ginger and spring onions. Stir-fry for 2 minutes, then remove the ginger and spring onions. Lower the bêche de mer into the impregnated oil to fry gently over a medium heat for 3 minutes, turning the pieces over a few times. Add the ham, sliced chicken, egg whites, pork/chicken soup, the remaining sherry, and the salt. Lower the heat and simmer gently for 35 minutes. Add the bean sprout mixture and cook for a further 2 minutes.

Serving Serve in a large soup dish or tureen.

Clams

In contrast to bêche de mer, which needs long soaking and cooking with ingredients which have been cooked for a long time, clams are usually cooked very quickly, by steaming, simmering, poaching, or simply by pouring boiling water over them. The keynote for preparing clams in Chinese cookery is purity. The refinement comes with serving a wide range of dips and mixes on the dining table to accompany the dishes. The following are some of the most suitable dips and mixes to serve with clams: Soya-Mustard Dip, Soya-Sherry Dip, Ginger-Soya-Vinegar Dip, Soya-Chilli Oil Dip, Dip for Clams, Plum Sauce, hoisin sauce, mustard, and tomato sauce (see chapter on Table Condiments).

Steamed Clams

Allow 4–6 clams per person, depending on size

Preparation Clean the clams thoroughly with a brush, under running water.
Cooking Place the clams on a flat, heat-proof dish. Put the dish in a steamer and steam for 7–8 minutes, until the shells open.

Serving Provide each diner with a bowl in which to mix his own dip from a selection of condiments arranged on the table. Let the diners cut the white meat from the shells and dip it into their dips and sauces.

Pork-Stuffed Steamed Clams

Serves 4

16 clams
8 oz (200 g) streaky pork
1 slice root ginger
2 spring onion stalks
½ teaspoon salt
1 tablespoon soya sauce
1 teaspoon sugar
1 tablespoon sherry

Preparation Steam the clams for 15 minutes. Mince the pork. Remove the clam-meat from the shells, reserving them for later use. Chop the clam-meat coarsely and mix with the minced pork. Chop the root ginger and spring onions and add them to the clam/pork mixture. Mix in the remaining ingredients, blend well, and stuff the mixture into the half-shells.
Cooking Arrange the shells on a heat-proof dish, place in a steamer and steam vigorously for 25 minutes. Alternatively, roast the stuffed clams in the oven for 20 minutes at 400°F (205°C or Gas Mark 6).
Serving Serve the clams with a variety of dips and mixes.

Pork-Stuffed Deep-Fried Clams

Serves 4

Preparation Repeat the instructions given in the recipe for Pork-Stuffed Steamed Clams, adding 1 egg and 1½ tablespoons cornflour to the pork/clam mixture.
Cooking Put the stuffed half-shells into a wire basket, six at a time. Lower into boiling oil and deep-fry for 4 minutes. Repeat until all the stuffed clams are cooked. Drain well; then serve, decorating each stuffed clam with a sprig of parsley, if desired.

An additional condiment which can be used with deep-fried clams is Salt-Cinnamon Mix (see page 50).

Crabs

In Chinese cooking, crabs play a very different role from abalone, bêche de mer, and clams. They are eaten in much greater quantity, and although crab-meat is sometimes used as a flavourer or cooked with other foods, it is most frequently eaten on its own. Indeed, there are a number of restaurants in Peking which serve nothing but crabs when they are in season. These are fresh-water river crabs which are served plain-steamed. On the rough table tops in the restaurant, each diner is issued with a wooden hammer with which to crack open the shells of the crabs. They are then eaten after dipping them in the dips and mixes which are amply provided in sauce dishes on the table. The meat is half-chewed, half-sucked out of the crabs while the diner holds on to the claws or feet. (We Chinese are past-masters at the art of extricating the shells and bones which get stuck between the teeth and in the mouth.) The claws are usually cracked last and eaten in the same manner. The favourite dip for crabs is Vinegar-Ginger Dip.

Stir-Fried Crabs in Egg Sauce

Serves 4–6, with other dishes

3–4 medium-sized crabs
¼ pint (125 ml) Egg Sauce
  (see page 40)
3 slices root ginger
3 cloves garlic
3 spring onion stalks
3 tablespoons lard
1½ teaspoons salt

Use the Egg Sauce recipe given on page 40.

Preparation Remove the top shell from each crab and chop the body into four pieces. Leave a leg attached to each piece as a 'handle'. Reserve the shell for other uses. Shred the ginger and crush the garlic. Chop the spring onions into ½ inch (1 cm) segments.

Cooking Heat the lard in a covered frying pan. Add the salt, ginger, garlic, and spring onions, and stir-fry for 30 seconds over a medium heat. Put the crab pieces (including the shell) into the pan, turn the heat up to maximum, and stir-fry for 3 minutes. Pour in the Egg Sauce slowly. This causes almost an explosion of steam: the onion/ginger/garlic impregnated steam shoots its way through the pieces of crab. Cover the pan and cook in this explosive situation for 1 minute. Serve immediately.

After the final explosive cooking with the crab, the Egg Sauce becomes extraordinarily tasty and makes a good accompaniment to rice. The dish should be eaten while very hot. It is a favourite dish with the southern Cantonese.

Plain Deep-Fried Crabs

Serves 4-6, with other dishes

4 medium-sized crabs
3 slices root ginger
3 spring onion stalks

2 eggs
6 tablespoons flour
2 teaspoons salt
oil for deep-frying

Preparation Steam the crabs for 10 minutes. Clean them, remove the top shell, and chop the body of each crab into six pieces, leaving each piece with a leg or claw attached as a 'handle'. Slightly crack the claws with the side or back of a chopper. Chop the ginger and spring onions finely. Beat the eggs lightly, blend with the flour, 2 tablespoons of water, ginger, spring onions, and salt, and mix to a smooth batter. Dip the meat-end of each section of crab into the batter to coat.
Cooking Heat the oil in a deep-fryer. Place six sections of crab in a wire basket and deep-fry for 3-3½ minutes over a high heat, then keep warm on a heated plate. Repeat until all the crab sections are cooked.
Serving Serve hot with a variety of dips and mixes.

Crab-Meat in Steamed Eggs

Serves 4-6, with other dishes

3 eggs
4-5 oz (100-125 g) can crab-meat
1 pint (500 ml) chicken stock *or*
superior stock (cold)
1 teaspoon salt
2 spring onion stalks
1 tablespoon vegetable oil
1 oz (25 g) ham

Preparation Beat the eggs lightly and mix them with the stock and salt in a heat-proof serving bowl. Cut the spring onions into 1 inch (2½ cm) segments. Divide the crab-meat into two piles. Add half of the crab-meat to the egg mixture, together with the crab water. Stir to mix. Reserve the other half of the crab-meat for later use.
Cooking Place the heat-proof bowl in a steamer and steam gently for 25 minutes. Meanwhile, heat the oil in a frying pan. Add the ham, spring onions, and remaining crab-meat. Stir-fry together for 1½ minutes.
Serving Remove the heat-proof bowl from the steamer. Garnish the top of the steamed egg and crab mixture with the stir-fried crab mixture. Serve from the heat-proof bowl.

The Complete Chinese Cookbook
Lobster

Although popular in Western cuisine, lobsters do not occupy nearly so important a place in Chinese food and cooking as crabs do. This is mainly due to their much higher cost and lack of availability. Lobsters are called Lung Hsia or Dragon Prawns in Chinese, and almost all crab dishes can be prepared with lobsters, except for those in which flaked crab-meat is scramble-fried with eggs, as lobster-meat does not flake in quite the same manner as crab-meat.

Plain Deep-Fried Lobster

Serves 4–6, with other dishes

1 1½–2 lb (¾ kg) lobster
1 slice root ginger
2 spring onion stalks
1 clove garlic
1 egg
4 tablespoons flour
1 teaspoon salt
oil for deep-frying

A rather extravagant dish with an excellent flavour.

Preparation Chop the ginger and spring onions, and crush the garlic. Beat the egg lightly and blend it with the flour, salt, 2 tablespoons water, ginger, garlic, and spring onions. Slice the lobster in half through the shell lengthwise, using a sharp cleaver; then chop it into 1½ inch (3½ cm) sections, including the claws. Dip each piece of lobster into the batter.
Cooking Heat the oil in a deep-fryer. Place half of the batter-coated pieces of lobster in a wire basket and deep-fry in the boiling oil for 3 minutes. Repeat this process with the remaining lobster pieces.
Serving When all the lobster pieces have been fried, serve them quickly on a well-heated dish. Eat with the usual array of table dips and mixes.

Lobster Stir-Fried with Minced Pork

Serves 4–6, with other dishes

1 1½–2 lb (¾ kg) lobster
4 oz (100 g) pork
2 slices root ginger
2 cloves garlic
2 spring onion stalks
4 tablespoons vegetable oil
1 teaspoon salt
¼ pint (125 ml) chicken stock
1 tablespoon soya sauce
2 eggs
2 tablespoons sherry
¾ tablespoon cornflour

Seafood and Crustaceans

Sections of unshelled lobster, fried with minced pork, are called 'Cantonese Lobster'.

Preparation Slice the lobster in half lengthwise through the shell, using a sharp cleaver; then chop it into 1½ inch (3½ cm) sections, including the claws. Mince the pork, ginger, and garlic finely; chop the spring onions into ¼ inch (½ cm) sections.
Cooking Heat the oil in a covered frying pan. Add the pork, garlic, ginger, and salt, and stir-fry over a high heat for 2 minutes. Add the lobster pieces and spring onions, and continue to stir-fry for 2½ minutes. Pour in the chicken stock and soya sauce, and cook, covered, for 3 minutes. Meanwhile, beat the eggs lightly with 1 tablespoon water and the sherry; mix the cornflour in another bowl with 5 tablespoons water. Add the cornflour mixture to the frying pan and stir until the liquid in the pan thickens. Stir in the egg/water/sherry mixture, streaming it evenly over the contents of the frying pan. Stir, and dish out on to a well-heated serving plate.

This is an excellent dish to eat when drinking wine or to accompany rice.

Steamed Marinated Lobster

Serves 4–6, with other dishes

1 1½–2 lb (¾ kg) lobster
2 slices root ginger
1 clove garlic
2 spring onion stalks

1½ tablespoons soya sauce
2 tablespoons sherry
1 tablespoon vegetable oil
1 teaspoon sugar
1 tablespoon chopped chives

Preparation Slice the lobster in half lengthwise through the shell, using a sharp cleaver; then chop it into 1½ inch (3½ cm) sections, including the claws. Arrange the pieces of lobster, meat side up, on a large heat-proof dish. Chop the ginger, garlic, and spring onions finely, and mix with the soya sauce, sherry, oil, and sugar. Beat them together lightly, then pour the mixture over the lobster sections. Leave to stand for 1 hour.
Cooking Place the dish in a steamer and steam vigorously for 20 minutes, until the lobster turns bright red.
Serving Sprinkle the meat side of the lobster pieces with chopped chives; then serve.

Stir-Fried Lobster with Red Wine-Sediment Paste

Serves 4–6, with other dishes

1 1½–2 lb (¾ kg) lobster
2 tablespoons red wine sediment paste
2 slices root ginger
2 cloves garlic
2 spring onion stalks
3 tablespoons lard
¼ teaspoon salt
1 tablespoon hoisin sauce

This is a dish from Fukien. In this south-east coastal province, red wine-sediment paste is a favourite cooking ingredient.

Preparation Slice the lobster in half lengthwise through the shell, using a sharp cleaver; then chop it into 1½ inch (3½ cm) sections, including the claws. Shred the ginger, crush and chop the garlic, and cut the spring onions into ½ inch (1 cm) segments.

Cooking Heat 2 tablespoons of the lard in a frying pan. Add the ginger, garlic, spring onions, and salt, and stir-fry over a medium heat for 30 seconds. Add the pieces of lobster and stir-fry over a high heat for 2 minutes. Remove the lobster pieces from the pan, put them aside, and keep them warm. Put the remaining lard in the pan together with the hoisin sauce and wine-sediment paste (or substitute). Stir-fry over a medium heat for 30 seconds until the oil and sauces are well blended. Return the pieces of lobster to the pan. Raise the heat to maximum and stir-fry the lobster pieces in the oil and sauce for 30 seconds. Serve immediately.

Wine-Sediment Paste Substitute

1 medium onion
2 cloves garlic
2 slices root ginger
2 tablespoons vegetable oil
1 tablespoon soya bean paste
1 teaspoon sugar
1 tablespoon tomato purée
1 teaspoon red soya bean cheese
1 tablespoon sherry
2 teaspoons brandy

If you are unable to obtain red wine-sediment paste, use the following recipe to prepare a substitute.

Preparation Chop the onion, garlic, and ginger finely.
Cooking Stir-fry the onion, garlic, and ginger in oil for 2 minutes. Add all the remaining ingredients. Stir and mix for 1 minute. Allow the mixture (or paste) to stand and cool before use.

Seafood and Crustaceans

Oyster Dishes

Fresh oysters are a little-known food item to the Chinese population, except to people who live along or near the east coast of China. After all, China is an enormous continental country and fresh oysters could not travel very far and remain fresh before the days of refrigeration. To the majority of Chinese people oysters come only in dried form, and in that state they are used primarily for flavouring other types of food. As such, oysters are merely one among a number of similar types of dried seafood flavourers, the most important being abalone and squid.

It is not surprising, therefore, that there are not many fresh oyster dishes. Two of the most delicious ways of eating oysters are oyster omelettes (or oyster cakes) and barbecued oysters. The following are several of the more widely-practised dishes.

Deep-Fried Oysters in Batter

Serves 4–8, with other dishes

24 oysters
3 spring onion stalks
salt to taste
pepper to taste
chilli pepper to taste
2 eggs
4 oz (100 g) flour
vegetable oil for deep-frying

Preparation Shell the oysters. Mince the spring onions finely, and season the oysters with salt, pepper, chilli pepper, and half of the minced onion. Mix the eggs, flour, and 6 tablespoons of water into a smooth batter. Dip the oysters into the batter.
Cooking Heat the oil in a deep-fryer (or Chinese semi-deep-frying pan), using ½–1 inch (1–2½ cm) oil. Place a few oysters at a time in the boiling oil to fry for 2½–3 minutes until golden-brown. Remove them with a perforated spoon, and drain.
Serving Place the oysters on a well-heated dish, garnish with the remaining spring onion, and serve.

Deep-Fried Oysters with Bacon

Serves 4–8, with other dishes

Preparation and Cooking Repeat the recipe for Deep-Fried Oysters in Batter, using an extra egg, and 1 oz (25 g) extra flour in the batter. You will also need 6 rashers of bacon. Cut each rasher crosswise into four pieces; dip oysters and bacon pieces into the batter. Heat the oil in a deep-fryer. Wrap each oyster in 1 piece of bacon, and with the help of a pair of bamboo chopsticks (not plastic, as they would melt in the hot oil), immerse the bacon-wrapped oyster in the boiling oil. Repeat until six wrapped oysters are frying at the same time. Fry for 3 minutes; then remove with a perforated spoon, and drain. Serve garnished with minced spring onion. The crispy bacon adds a new interest to the oyster.

Scallops

Although scallops are frequently used dried, the flesh has a texture similar to that of clams, and can easily be stir-fried or steamed to excellent effect. The dried scallop used for flavouring is usually not a whole scallop, but the root muscles. Hence the regular shape of dried scallop is an amber-coloured disc, with a diameter of ½–1 inch (1–2½ cm) and a thickness of about ⅓ inch (1 cm). It is considered to have a more delicate flavour than any other type of dried seafood, and is usually added to slow-cooking foods and dishes, such as soups, soft rice, and stewed dishes. Dried scallop must be soaked overnight, and when simmered and shredded, it can be used in various stir-fried combinations.

Steamed Scallops with Ham, Ginger, and Onion

Serves 4–8, with other dishes

12–16 oz (300–400 g) scallop meat
2 oz (50 g) smoked ham
1 slice root ginger
2 spring onion stalks
4 tablespoons sherry
1 teaspoon sugar
2 tablespoons soya sauce

Preparation Cut each scallop into four pieces. Marinate them in sherry, sugar, and soya sauce for 30 minutes; then drain, reserving the marinade. Shred the ginger, and chop the ham and spring onions coarsely.
Cooking Place the pieces of scallop neatly on a heat-proof dish. Sprinkle with ginger, onion, ham, and the remaining marinade. Steam vigorously for 15 minutes, and serve.

Seafood and Crustaceans

Stir-Fried Scallops with Diced Chicken, Mushrooms, and Cucumber

Serves 4–8, with other dishes

12 oz (300 g) scallop meat
4 large Chinese dried mushrooms
5 oz (125 g) chicken breast meat
quarter of a medium cucumber
3 tablespoons vegetable oil

2 tablespoons light-coloured soya sauce
4 tablespoons chicken stock
1 tablespoon sherry
½ tablespoon cornflour
½ teaspoon flavour powder
pepper to taste

Preparation Soak the mushrooms in warm water for 30 minutes. Drain, discard the stems, and cut the caps into quarters. Dice the scallop meat, chicken, and cucumber (unpeeled) into ⅓ inch (½ cm) cubes.
Cooking Heat the oil in a large frying pan. Add the cucumber, chicken, and scallops, and stir-fry over a high heat for 2 minutes. Pour in the mushrooms and soya sauce, lower the heat to medium, and stir-fry for another minute. Add the chicken stock and sherry, and stir-fry for a further minute. Mix the cornflour, flavour powder, and pepper with 3 tablespoons water, and stream evenly into the frying pan. When the contents of the pan thicken, pour on to a well-heated dish, and serve immediately.

Squid

Although the squid is not considered the most refined seafood in China, it has many points to recommend it. Firstly, it is plentiful and cheap – it is eaten in quantity by poorer people. Secondly, it is quick to cook. Thirdly, although it has less flavour than many other types of seafood, it can be made tasty very easily by seasoning or cross-cooking with other types of food; and fourthly, although its texture is like neither meat nor fish, it has a certain firmness which enables it to be chewed with great satisfaction, especially when eaten with rice.

Fresh Squid Stir-Fried with Vegetables

Serves 4–8, with other dishes

1 lb (400 g) fresh squid
2 spring onion stalks
4 oz (100 g) celery
2 oz (50 g) bamboo shoots
2 oz (50 g) lettuce
3 tablespoons vegetable oil
2 slices root ginger
½ teaspoon salt
1 tablespoon lard
1 tablespoon soya sauce
½ tablespoon hoisin sauce
½ tablespoon oyster sauce
1 tablespoon sherry
½ teaspoon red bean curd cheese
1 tablespoon cornflour
½ teaspoon flavour powder
6 tablespoons chicken stock

Preparation Cut the squid into 1½ × ½ inch (3½ × 1 cm) strips. Chop the spring onions into 1 inch (2½ cm) segments, and shred the celery, bamboo shoots, and lettuce.

Cooking Heat 2 tablespoons of the oil in a frying pan. Add the squid, spring onions, ginger, and salt, and stir-fry for 3 minutes over a high heat. Remove the pieces of squid and put aside. Discard the ginger. Add the remaining oil, celery, bamboo shoots, and lettuce and stir-fry gently for 4 minutes over medium heat. Remove from the pan and put aside. Place the lard in the pan, add the sauces, sherry, and bean curd cheese, and stir until the fat and the sauces are well blended. Return the squid to the pan, stir-fry for 1 minute, then remove and keep hot. Return all the vegetables to the pan, toss and mix well with the gravy for 30 seconds; then blend the cornflour and flavour powder with the chicken stock and stir the mixture into the pan, mixing well with the contents. Heat for 2 minutes, and serve in a deep dish, using the vegetables as a base and piling the squid on top.

Fresh Squid Stir-Fried with Red-Cooked Pork and Mushrooms

Serves 5 or 6, with other dishes

1 lb (400 g) squid
4 oz (400 g) Red-Cooked Pork (see page 106)
6 Chinese dried mushrooms
2 spring onion stalks
2 tablespoons vegetable oil
4 tablespoons Red-Cooked Pork gravy
1 tablespoon sherry
½ tablespoon soya sauce
½ tablespoon cornflour

Preparation Cut the squid into 1½ × ½ inch (3½ × 1 cm) pieces. Soak the mushrooms for 30 minutes in warm water; drain and discard stalks, but

reserve 4-5 tablespoons mushroom water. Cut each mushroom cap into four. Slice the pork thinly and cut the spring onions into 1 inch (2½ cm) segments.
Cooking Heat the oil in a frying pan and fry the squid and spring onions quickly over high heat for 1 minute. Add the pork, pork gravy, mushrooms, mushroom water, sherry, and soya sauce, and continue to stir-fry for 3 minutes. Blend the cornflour with 3 tablespoons water and stir into the pan. Serve as soon as the liquid thickens.

This is a quickly cooked dish which can be prepared in a short time if the Red-Cooked Pork is available; this is why it often appears on a Chinese dinner table.

Shark's Fin

Shark's fin, like bêche de mer, is a delicacy which belongs to the sphere of Chinese haute cuisine. It is only served at party dinners and banquets. The two materials have a curiously similar texture, jelly-like but firm. Shark's fin is somewhat stickier in the body and crunchier in the fin bones, which makes it more interesting than bêche de mer. As both come in dried form, they need prolonged soaking and many changes of water before they are ready for cooking. In China, a shark's fin dish can almost be considered a culinary joke, for it takes 3 days to prepare, and only 3 minutes to eat. The reason why preparation of shark's fin takes such a long time is because in its original state it is as tough as rhinoceros' horn. If it is to be softened into a jellified state without destroying or changing its essential texture, it requires very careful handling. Since this ingredient seems to intrigue Western fancy, we will go into it in some detail.

Braised Red-Cooked Shark's Fins

Serves 6-10, with other dishes

1 lb (400 g) dried shark's fins
1 tablespoon dried prawns
4 oz (100 g) Chinese cabbage (*or* celery)
4 large Chinese dried mushrooms
2 oz (50 g) bamboo shoots
1 spring onion
½ pint (250 ml) chicken stock
1 slice root ginger
2 tablespoons lard
⅓ teaspoon salt
2 tablespoons soya sauce
4 tablespoons white wine
6 tablespoons red-cooked meat gravy
¾ tablespoon cornflour
⅓ teaspoon flavour powder
1 teaspoon sesame oil

The Complete Chinese Cookbook

Preparation Soak the shark's fins overnight. Soak the dried prawns for 30 minutes in warm water, then drain, discarding the water. Blanch the cabbage or celery, and drain. Soak the mushrooms for 30 minutes, remove the stalks, and shred the caps (discard the water). Shred the bamboo shoots and cut the spring onion into 1 inch (2½ cm) segments. Scrub, clean, and simmer the shark's fins gently in 2 pints (generous litre) of water for 1 hour; change the water and simmer for another 1½ hours; then drain.

Cooking Heat the chicken stock in a pan. Add the ginger and prawns, simmer gently for 30 minutes; then drain and discard the prawns and ginger. Add the cabbage to the stock, and simmer for 15 minutes. Heat the lard in another pan, and stir-fry the spring onion, bamboo shoots, mushrooms, and salt for 1 minute; add the soya sauce, wine, shark's fins, and meat gravy. Simmer for 3 minutes; then pour in the chicken stock and cabbage, and simmer for a further 20 minutes. Blend the cornflour and flavour powder with 3 tablespoons water, add to the pan, and stir until the contents thicken. Sprinkle with sesame oil.

Serving Serve in a large soup bowl or tureen, arranging the fins on top of the cabbage.

Crab-Egg (Spawn) Shark's Fins

Serves 6–10, with other dishes

4 oz (100 g) crab-eggs (*or* spawn)
3 lb (1¼ kg) dried raw shark's fins
4 slices root ginger
6 tablespoons lard
6 tablespoons white wine
4 pints (generous 2 litres)
secondary stock
2 tablespoons sherry
2 pints (generous litre) superior stock
4 oz (100 g) crab-meat
1½ tablespoons cornflour
2 tablespoons finely minced ham

This is the recipe for the dish as prepared by the famous Lee Ho Foo Restaurant, Canton.

Preparation Trim and pare the shark's fins with a sharp knife. Soak them in water for 6 hours; drain and discard water. Transfer the fins to an earthen pot or casserole, add 2 pints (generous litre) water and simmer for 1 hour. Change the water and simmer gently for another hour. Remove the fins, clean and scrub away any impurities; then place them in fresh water and simmer gently for another 2 hours. Take out the fins for a final trimming, paring, and cleaning. Change the water again and simmer very gently for 8 hours. The fins are at last partially ready for cooking. Simmer the slices of root ginger in 8 tablespoons water for 6 minutes. Leave to stand for 1 hour, then discard the ginger. Heat 2 tablespoons of the lard in a heavy pot; add half of the white wine, 3 tablespoons of the ginger water, and 2 pints (generous litre) of the secondary stock. Place the fins in the pot and simmer for 30 minutes, then repeat, using equal amounts of the same ingredients, and simmering the shark's fins for another 30 minutes. Drain the fins, and keep warm.

Cooking Heat 1 tablespoon of the lard in an earthen or heat-proof china pot over a medium heat. Add the sherry and superior stock, the fins, and the fresh crab-meat. Bring to a gentle boil, add the cornflour, blended with 6 tablespoons water, stir for 30 seconds and remove from the heat. Add the crab-eggs, and replace on the heat, and when the contents start to simmer again, add the remaining lard. (Lard is used in Chinese cooking to give smoothness.)

Serving Pour the contents of the pot into a large well-decorated soup bowl or tureen. Garnish with finely minced ham and serve.

Shark's fins are appreciated for their texture and their savouriness.

Shrimps and Prawns

We make no distinction in China between shrimps and prawns. They are both called 'Hsia'. However, Hsia from the muddy coasts of Chihli, usually known as Pacific Prawns in Britain, and very popular with restaurants both abroad and in Peking and Tientsin, are about ten times the size of the smaller fresh-water specimens from the lakes and rivers of the south.

Shrimps and prawns are very important items of the Chinese diet. This is partly because of their wide availability, and partly because of the quality of their flesh, which enables them to combine so well with numerous other items of food, both meat and vegetables. After pork and chicken, they are probably one of the most widely-used animal products for human consumption in China.

Although the demand for shrimps and prawns has shot up both in the West and in the world as a whole in recent years (indeed, there now appears to be a general shortage), they have been popular in China for centuries. Unlike other seafoods which are time-consuming to prepare, and still others which are in themselves tasteless and require a host of other materials to be cooked with them in order to make them palatable and appealing, shrimps and prawns are highly tasty, and can generally be prepared within a very short time. Because of their shape and size, they are particularly suitable for the Chinese practice of cross-cooking, requiring no further cutting, shaping, or reduction. Hence the number of recipes using these two items is inexhaustible. The following are a few of the more popular ones. Except for dishes in which very large prawns are needed, prawns and shrimps are usually interchangeable.

The Complete Chinese Cookbook
Stir-Fried Shrimps with Green Peas

Serves 4–8, with other dishes

10 oz (250 g) unshelled shrimps
8 oz (200 g) green peas
1 slice root ginger
½ tablespoon cornflour

4 tablespoons chicken stock
1 oz (25 g) bamboo shoots
2½ tablespoons vegetable oil
¼ teaspoon salt
1 tablespoon sherry
pepper to taste

Preparation Shred the ginger, blend the cornflour with the chicken stock, shell the shrimps, and cut the bamboo shoots into ¼ inch (½ cm) cubes.
Cooking Heat 1½ tablespoons of the oil in a frying pan over medium heat. Add the shrimps, ginger, and salt; stir-fry for 1 minute, and set aside. Add the remaining oil to the pan together with the bamboo shoots and peas, and stir-fry gently over a high heat for 2 minutes. Return the shrimps to the pan and stir a few times. Add the cornflour mixture, the sherry, and pepper, and stir-fry gently for 1 minute. Serve immediately, and eat while hot.

Stir-Fried Shrimps with Bean Curd, Mushrooms, and Minced Pork

Serves 4–8, with other dishes

8 oz (200 g) shelled shrimps
2 cakes bean curd
1 small can button mushrooms
2 oz (50 g) streaky pork, minced
1 spring onion stalk
½ tablespoon cornflour
¼ teaspoon flavour powder

6 tablespoons chicken stock
3 tablespoons vegetable oil
1 slice root ginger
¼ teaspoon salt
1 tablespoon soya sauce
1 tablespoon sherry
½ tablespoon oyster sauce
½ tablespoon hoisin sauce
1 teaspoon sesame oil

Preparation Cut each cake of bean curd into eight pieces. Drain the button mushrooms and discard the water. Cut the spring onion into 1 inch (2½ cm) segments. Blend the cornflour and flavour powder with the chicken stock.
Cooking and Serving Heat 1½ tablespoons of the oil in a frying pan. Add the pork, ginger, and salt, and stir-fry for 2 minutes over a high heat. Add the shrimps, and continue to stir-fry for 1½ minutes. Remove the pork and shrimps, and put them aside to keep warm. Pour the remainder of the oil into the pan. Add the onion and stir-fry for 15 seconds. Add the bean curd and stir-fry for 2 minutes, then add the soya sauce, sherry, oyster sauce, hoisin sauce, and mushrooms. Stir-fry for another minute. Pour in the stock

mixture. Return the pork and shrimps to the pan. Cook, stirring gently, for 3 minutes; then sprinkle with sesame oil, and serve in a deep dish.

Plain Stir-Fried Shrimps in Shells

Serves 4–8, with other dishes

1½ lb (600 g) large unshelled shrimps
2 teaspoons fermented black beans
2 cloves garlic
2 slices root ginger

2 spring onion stalks
3 tablespoons vegetable oil
½ teaspoon salt
½ tablespoon soya sauce
1½ tablespoons sherry
2 tablespoons chicken stock
¼ teaspoon sugar
dash of pepper

Preparation Soak the black beans for 1 hour; then drain. Wash the shrimps thoroughly, and remove the legs but leave the tails intact. Chop the garlic, ginger, and spring onions finely.

Cooking Heat the oil in a frying pan. Add the salt, fermented beans, garlic, ginger, and onions. Stir-fry vigorously over medium heat for 1 minute, mixing the ingredients together. Add the shrimps, raise the heat to maximum, and stir-fry for another 2 minutes. Add the soya sauce, sherry, stock, sugar, and pepper, and continue to stir-fry for a further minute. Serve and eat immediately.

This is a famous Metropolitan Chinese dish, seen and served throughout China. Prawns 3–5 inches (7½–12½ cm) long can be, and often are, cooked in precisely the same manner with the same ingredients, but with an increase in the cooking time of 1 minute.

Deep-Fried Phœnix-Tail Prawns

Serves 4–8, with other dishes

1½ lb (600 g) unshelled fresh giant prawns
1 slice root ginger

2 eggs
3 oz (75 g) plain flour
½ oz (15 g) self-raising flour
1½ teaspoons salt
vegetable oil for deep-frying

This way of cooking prawns came to be so-called because the tail shell is left on and is unbattered. When the prawns are fried, the tails turn bright red, and can be conveniently used by the diners as 'handles'. This is a very popular way of presenting prawns in Chinese restaurants abroad today; so prepared, the prawns can be more easily managed by Westerners – yet it is an authentically Chinese custom.

The Complete Chinese Cookbook

Preparation Chop the ginger finely. Beat the eggs for 15 seconds, then fold in both types of flour, the salt, ginger, and 4 tablespoons water. Beat for another minute into a light batter. Shell the prawns, leaving the tail shells on. Clean them thoroughly, and scrape away any dark and gritty bits.

Cooking Heat the oil in a pan. Hold each prawn by its tail and dip it into the batter, then lower it into the boiling oil. Fry six prawns simultaneously for 3 minutes, then remove them with a perforated spoon, draining off the excess oil. When the first batch has been fried, it can be kept hot and crispy in the oven while the remaining prawns are being cooked. Repeat until all the prawns have been cooked.

Serving Serve on a well-heated platter, garnished with parsley if desired.

The dips recommended for this dish are Salt and Pepper Mix and the dip recommended for Prawns (see pages 50 and 54).

Deep-Fried Butterfly Prawns

Serves 4–8, with other dishes

1¼ lb (600 g) unshelled fresh giant prawns
1 slice root ginger
1 clove garlic
1 spring onion stalk
2 eggs
3 tablespoons cornflour
½ tablespoon self-raising flour
8 oz (200 g) breadcrumbs
oil for deep-frying
1 lemon
parsley sprigs

The term 'butterfly' simply means that after shelling, the prawn's body is sliced open along two thirds of the inner curve, and spread-eagled into two butterfly wings. The tail shell is left intact. When prawns are stuffed they are usually butterflied first. In Chinese cooking there are numerous items which could be stuffed into prawns. Unstuffed butterfly prawns are usually coated with batter.

Preparation Chop the ginger, garlic, and spring onion finely. Beat the eggs for 15 seconds. Add the chopped ingredients and both types of flour to the eggs, and beat together for a further 30 seconds, making a light batter. Shell the prawns, leaving the tail shells on, as in the previous recipe. Hold the prawns by their tails, and dip the bodies into the batter; then sprinkle with breadcrumbs to coat.

Cooking Heat the oil in a deep-fryer. Lower six prawns at a time into the oil to fry for 3 minutes. Remove, and drain. When all the prawns are ready, serve decorated with lemon wedges and parsley. The dips and mixes recommended for Deep-Fried Phœnix-Tail Prawns can be served.

Cantonese Crystal Shrimps

Serves 4–8, with other dishes

1 lb (400 g) fresh shelled shrimps
1½ tablespoons salt
½ tablespoon cornflour *or* water chestnut flour
2 tablespoons chicken stock
3 tablespoons white wine
¼ teaspoon flavour powder
2 cloves garlic
2 slices root ginger
2 spring onion stalks
2½ tablespoons vegetable oil
1 tablespoon lard

Preparation Mix the salt in 1 pint (500 ml) water. Soak the shrimps in this salted water, and place in the refrigerator for 2 hours. Drain, rinse quickly, and dry thoroughly. Mix the cornflour or water chestnut flour with the chicken stock, white wine, and flavour powder, blending until smooth. Chop the garlic and ginger finely, and cut the spring onions into ¼ inch (½ cm) segments.

Cooking Heat the oil in a pan over a high heat. Add the ginger, garlic, and onions and stir-fry for 30 seconds. Pour the shrimps into the pan and stir-fry vigorously for a further 30–40 seconds. Drain, and put aside. Return the pan to the heat. Add the lard, and when it has all melted, pour the cornflour mixture into the pan. Stir and mix gently until smooth and translucent. Return the shrimps to the pan, and stir and turn them for 30 seconds until they have taken on a glossy finish. Serve and eat immediately.

Toasted Shrimps

Serves 6–8, with other dishes

This is a suitable dish for party dinners as well as for a family meal.

Preparation Using the ingredients given in the recipe for Shrimp Balls, make the shrimp paste by mixing the minced pork, water chestnuts, shrimps, etc. together. In addition, you will need 4–5 thin slices of bread. Cut each slice into four, and trim off the crusts. Three beaten eggs and 8 oz (200 g) breadcrumbs or sesame seeds are also required. Spread shrimp paste mixture very thickly and firmly on one side of the bread, then wet with the beaten egg. Sprinkle and dredge with breadcrumbs. If you are using sesame seeds, sprinkle them on the spread, as they help greatly in providing a pleasant aroma.

Cooking Place four pieces of shrimp-spread-bread at a time in a wire basket. Lower them to fry in hot oil for 2½–3 minutes; then drain. When all the pieces have been fried, arrange them on a well-heated dish, either decorated with parsley, or built up in the form of a pyramid. Serve and eat immediately.

The crispness of the fried bread contrasting with the meatiness of the shrimps makes this a very appealing and interesting dish – yet one which is very easy to make.

Drunken Shrimps

Serves 6–8, with other dishes

1¼ lb (500 g) fresh shrimps
3 slices root ginger
3 spring onion stalks
3 tablespoons sherry
1½ tablespoons brandy
1½ teaspoons salt
⅛ teaspoon black pepper
juice of half a lemon
2 teaspoons sesame oil
1 tablespoon chopped parsley

Preparation Rinse and clean the shrimps thoroughly, removing the heads, tails, and legs. Rinse again to remove any impurities; then rinse a third time. Chop the ginger and onion coarsely. Prepare a marinade by adding the onion and ginger to the sherry and brandy. Stir, and leave to mature for 1 hour. Place the shrimps in a flat-bottomed bowl or basin. Sprinkle and rub with salt and pepper. Strain the impregnated sherry and brandy on to the shrimps, and mix well. Place the basin in the refrigerator, and leave the shrimps to marinate for 3 hours; then drain, and discard the marinade. Sprinkle the shrimps with lemon juice and sesame oil. Arrange them nicely on a plain white dish, sprinkle with chopped parsley, and serve.

This is an excellent dish to accompany wine. Favourite dips include Chilli Sauce, mustard, hoisin sauce, Ginger-in-Vinegar, and Garlic-in-Vinegar (see the section on Table Condiments).

Eggs

蛋

Because there is an abundance of poultry in China, eggs are a universal dish. Egg dishes – usually the scrambled, stir-fried type – are those most likely to be brought to the table to add to the existing dishes if unexpected guests arrive. Since we live much more communally in China, unexpected guests are always arriving, and it is the custom to share your meal – if you can afford to eat at all. As stir-fried egg dishes are the quickest to cook, and as almost any other ingredient can be blended in, they are the most convenient to prepare at a moment's notice. Hence they are a favourite with housewives and restaurants with limited resources.

Another form in which eggs are frequently served is 'gravied eggs' – hard-boiled eggs which have been simmered in soya-meat stock. These are usually cut into slices with a thread (by sawing) and laid out neatly in wedges on a dish, their rich yellow yolk contrasting with the brownness of the skin. As hard-boiled eggs impregnated with soya sauce keep well, they are also the most common type of egg for taking on journeys, or buying from street-vendors, or from the sampans which crowd around ships and liners anchored in port.

For breakfast, the type of eggs most frequently eaten is salted eggs, usually hard-boiled duck eggs which have been soaked in their shells in brine for varying lengths of time.

As many Chinese dishes are created to go with rice, two types of egg dish are very popular in China: savoury steamed egg-custards, and Yellow Flowing Oil-Scrambled Eggs (Liu Huang T'sai). This latter form of egg dish differs from ordinary stir-fried egg dishes (which are not very different from scrambled eggs), in that much more oil or lard is blended into the eggs during the final cooking stages, and they are usually very savoury.

Steamed savoury egg-custards are popular because they can be

The Complete Chinese Cookbook

very light. Often, no more than a couple of eggs are used, combined with stock, for a large bowl of custard. In fact, egg-custards are part-egg and part-soup in composition (90% soup). Although they are solid dishes, they are very suitable for invalids and the aged.

In Chinese restaurants in the West, all Fu-Yung dishes are egg dishes, either stir-fried or in the form of omelettes or soufflés. But in China, Fu-Yung only refers to dishes prepared from egg whites beaten up with minced chicken or pork. They are usually very light and delicate dishes.

Finally, we have Tea Eggs and 1000 Years Old Eggs. Tea Eggs are very much an acquired taste. They are hard-boiled eggs, which are again boiled in tea, with salt added. The shell is somewhat cracked, but not detached, during the second boiling.

1000 Years Old Eggs are not exactly antiques. They are duck eggs preserved in lime, pine ash, and salt for about 50 days. They are normally obtainable from Chinese provision stores, coated with dried mud and husks, which give them the appearance of dating from the Tang or Han dynasty. When the mud has been washed off and the shell removed, the egg is greenish-black in colour, with a yellowish-green yolk. It has a pungent cheesy taste. Once you have acquired the taste, there can be no substitute!

Huang-Pu Scrambled Stir-Fried Eggs

Serves 4–6, with other dishes

9 eggs
1 teaspoon salt
1 tablespoon finely chopped chives *or* the green tops of spring onions
¾ teaspoon flavour powder
5 tablespoons vegetable oil

This is probably the best-known plain, scrambled stir-fried egg dish. It originates from the boat-dwellers of Huang-Pu, which is a section of the Pearl River flowing past the city of Canton. Although originally what one might term a 'coolie dish' – a true product of the proletariat – it has come to be so well-liked that it is now on the menus of many famous restaurants in Kwangtung, for the delight of connoisseurs.

Preparation Beat the eggs up in a basin for about 10 seconds with a pair of chopsticks or a fork. Mix in the salt, chopped chives or spring onions, and flavour powder. Beat for a further 5 seconds.
Cooking Heat 3 tablespoons of the oil in a smooth, medium-sized frying pan over a low heat. Wait until the oil is very hot, then pour in one third of the

Eggs

egg mixture. Take the handle of the pan and manœuvre it so that the egg flows and spreads evenly over the surface. Remove the pan from the heat as soon as most of the egg is solid. Stir once or twice; then lift the egg with a spatula or fish-slice on to a well-heated serving dish, and keep it warm. Add 1 tablespoon of the oil to the pan and repeat the process. Repeat again until all the beaten egg has been used up, piling the scrambled omelettes one on top of the other. In this way, you will have several layers of soft and runny egg sandwiched between firmer, well-fried eggs.

Because of the conjunction of firm and soft layers, the highly savoury flavour, the delicate egg-quality, and the appealing scent of freshly-fried chives, eggs cooked in this way are indeed a delicacy; yet they can be cooked quickly in any kitchen.

Scrambled Stir-Fried Eggs with Shredded Ham

Serves 4–6, with other dishes

4 oz (100 g) cooked ham
8 eggs
¼ teaspoon flavour powder
4 tablespoons vegetable oil
1 tablespoon chopped chives *or* spring onion tops
1 tablespoon sherry

As Chinese cooking tends to go into cross-cooking, eggs are bound to be cooked with many other foods, resulting in a wide range of dishes. This is one of the favourites.

Preparation Slice the ham into strips about half the length of matchsticks. Beat the eggs in a bowl for 10 seconds with the flavour powder.
Cooking Put the oil into a frying pan over a medium heat. When it is quite hot, pour in the beaten eggs and sprinkle with the chives or spring onions, and ham. Lift the handle of the pan and manœuvre the pan so that the eggs spread over the surface. When practically all of the egg is solid, sprinkle with sherry and remove the pan from the heat. Scramble the eggs a few times.
Serving Lift the 'omelette' on to a well-heated dish, and serve immediately.

The Complete Chinese Cookbook

Chinese Omelettes

As often as not, Chinese omelettes come in miniature size (miniature by Western standards), and it takes eight to ten omelettes to make a complete dish. Each omelette probably consists of no more than half an egg, with fillings. The fillings can consist of any of the wide variety of ingredients used in stir-fried eggs, together with such ingredients as lobster, oysters, large prawns, and shrimps. These fillings have to be cooked or fried separately, and then added to the beaten eggs after the egg mixture has had a moment's frying. They should be added when the top of the omelette is still a little runny. This facilitates the sealing, when both sides, or just one side, of the omelette are turned over and the omelette is pressed lightly against the side of the pan. Some boiling oil is then poured over the omelette to seal it well and the whole omelette is turned over for 20–30 seconds of frying on the opposite side. Because of their size, these small omelettes are intriguing to Westerners. They usually have some sauce (such as Sweet and Sour Sauce, a meat sauce, or Hot Sauce) poured over them when served.

Oyster Omelette

Serves 4–6, with other dishes

10 oysters
6 eggs
4 oz (100 g) lean pork
2 spring onion stalks
1 slice root ginger
2 oz (50 g) bamboo shoots
1 teaspoon salt
6 tablespoons milk
dash of pepper
6½ tablespoons vegetable oil
2 teaspoons soya sauce
1 teaspoon vinegar
2 teaspoons sherry
½ teaspoon sugar
2 teaspoons cornflour

Oyster is used for cooking with other ingredients much more extensively in China than is customary in the West. In seaboard provinces such as Fukien, where I lived for over a decade, oysters were used for cooking with noodles, pancakes, and soups. Here is a recipe where they are cooked in an omelette. Albeit expensive, it is well worth a trial.

Preparation Shell the oysters, reserving 2 tablespoons oyster water. Mince the pork and spring onions; then shred the ginger and bamboo shoots. Beat the eggs and ½ teaspoon of the salt together for 10 seconds; then add the milk and pepper and beat for a further 5 seconds.

Eggs

Cooking Heat 3 tablespoons of the oil in a frying pan, add 3 oz (75 g) of the pork, ½ teaspoon of the salt, and the ginger and onion. Stir-fry for 3 minutes. Add the bamboo shoots and oysters, stir-fry for 2 minutes more, then remove the mixture from the pan and set aside. Wipe the pan and pour in the remainder of the oil. When it is quite hot, pour in a ladleful of beaten egg and spread it over the pan. When the bottom of the omelette has become firm, place a spoonful of the oyster/pork mixture in the centre. Fold the omelette down the middle and push it with a spatula to one side of the pan. Push it lightly against the side of the pan and pour some hot oil over it to seal. Turn the omelette over and fry the other side for 20 seconds. Lift it from the pan with a perforated spoon, then drain, and place it on a well-heated dish. Repeat this procedure until all the beaten eggs and filling are used up.

Serving Whilst the omelettes are keeping warm, drain away all the oil from the pan. Add the remaining 1 oz (25 g) of pork and fry it for 1 minute. Then add the soya sauce, vinegar, sherry, oyster water, sugar, and cornflour blended with 1½ tablespoons water. As soon as the sauce thickens, pour it over the omelettes, and serve.

Crab-Meat, Prawns, and Lobster Omelettes

Serves 4–6, with other dishes

True to the liberal tradition and high flexibility of Chinese cooking, any of the above seafoods can be substituted for oysters when making omelettes.

Preparation Follow the instructions given in the previous recipe, but substitute either crab-meat, prawns, or lobster for the oysters. It is a matter of choice whether or not to prepare a sauce to pour over the omelettes before serving.

Yellow Flowing Eggs

Serves 4–6, with other dishes

4 egg yolks
2 eggs
1 teaspoon flavour powder
1½ tablespoons cornflour
1 teaspoon salt
2 tablespoons oil
3 tablespoons lard
2 tablespoons minced smoked ham

This is a favourite dish in Peking and the north, possibly created primarily to accompany rice. Its high savouriness and well-oiled lubricating qualities perform this function to perfection.

Preparation Beat the egg yolks, eggs, and flavour powder together for 10 seconds. Add the cornflour, blended with 4 tablespoons water, and the salt. Mix well together.

Cooking Heat the oil and 1½ tablespoons of the lard in a pan. When very hot, pour in the beaten eggs. Stir quickly in one direction, and reduce the heat to low. Add the remaining lard and continue to stir in the same direction until the mixture is glistening, smooth, and thick. Pour the mixture into a serving bowl or deep dish. Sprinkle with minced ham; then serve.

Basic Steamed Eggs

Serves 4–6, with other dishes

3 eggs
1 teaspoon salt
1 teaspoon vegetable oil
½ teaspoon flavour powder
½ pint (250 ml) water
½ tablespoon chopped chives *or* spring onion tops
½ tablespoon soya sauce

Preparation Beat the eggs with the salt, oil, and flavour powder for 10 seconds in a heat-proof bowl. Mix in the water and beat for 5 seconds.

Cooking Place the bowl in a steamer or in a large saucepan with about 1 inch (2½ cm) of boiling water. Boil gently and steam for 20 minutes. Remove the bowl from the pan and sprinkle the surface of the eggs, which should now have hardened into a shimmering custard, with the chives or spring onions and soya sauce. Serve from the bowl.

Fancy Steamed Eggs

Serves 4–6, with other dishes

3 eggs
1 teaspoon salt
1 teaspoon flavour powder
1½ tablespoons chopped smoked ham
1 teaspoon vegetable oil
½ pint (250 ml) chicken stock
¼ pint (125 ml) water
2 tablespoons crab-meat *or* shrimps
1 tablespoon chopped chives *or* spring onion tops
1 tablespoon soya sauce

Preparation Beat the eggs with the salt, flavour powder, ham, and oil for 10 seconds in a heat-proof bowl. Add the stock and water, and mix well.

Cooking Place the bowl in a steamer or in a large saucepan with 1 inch (2½ cm) of boiling water. Steam for 18 minutes, by which time the surface of the egg mixture should have hardened. Arrange the crab-meat or shrimps on top of the eggs and sprinkle with chives or spring onions, and soya sauce. Steam for a further 4–5 minutes and serve from the bowl.

Eggs

To vary Mix flaked cooked or smoked fish, such as haddock or kipper, with the eggs before steaming them. Garnish with chopped ham and chives.

Yellow Flower Pork

Serves 4–6, with other dishes

- 12 oz (300 g) streaky pork
- 5 eggs
- 2 tablespoons wood ears
- 1 slice root ginger
- 2 oz (50 g) bamboo shoots
- 2 spring onion stalks
- 1 teaspoon salt
- 3 tablespoons vegetable oil
- 1 tablespoon light-coloured soya sauce
- 6 tablespoons superior stock
- ½ teaspoon flavour powder
- 1 tablespoon sherry
- 2 teaspoons sesame oil

Preparation Soak the wood ears for 30 minutes and rinse them in two changes of water. Slice the pork into shreds. Shred the ginger and bamboo shoots. Cut the spring onions into 1 inch (2½ cm) segments. Beat the eggs with half of the salt for 10 seconds.

Cooking Heat 2 tablespoons of the vegetable oil in a pan. Pour in the beaten eggs. As soon as the mixture hardens and sets, scramble lightly, and set aside. Pour the remaining vegetable oil into the pan. Add the ginger, pork, and remaining salt. Fry for 2 minutes over a high heat. Add the bamboo shoots, soya sauce, wood ears, and spring onions, and continue to stir-fry for another minute. Pour in the stock and add the flavour powder. Cook, stirring gently, for 1 minute. Return the egg mixture to the pan and break it up into small pieces. Stir the ingredients together for 30 seconds. Sprinkle with sherry and sesame oil, and serve in a well-heated dish.

Yellow Flower Pork is a well-known favourite dish in the north, but it is not so popular in the south.

Steamed Eggs

Steamed eggs are designed primarily for the accompaniment of rice. In contrast to Yellow Flowing Eggs, steamed eggs are very light dishes, made with only two or three eggs, and with a very small amount of oil, if any. The beaten eggs are usually mixed with stock or water before being steamed. Although stock is more savoury, many people prefer the lightness of water. It is an ideal dish for invalids and the aged.

Steamed Three Variety Eggs

Serves 4–6, with other dishes

2 salt eggs
2 preserved '1000 Years Old Eggs'
3 fresh eggs
2 spring onion stalks
⅓ pint (160 ml) superior stock, heated
½ teaspoon salt
dash of pepper
1 teaspoon vegetable oil
1 tablespoon chopped smoked ham

This is one of those domestic dishes which are sometimes served up as a change from the normal stir-fried egg dishes.

Preparation Dice the salt eggs and preserved eggs separately into small cubes or neat pieces. Cut the spring onions into 1 inch (2½ cm) segments. Beat the fresh eggs in a bowl.
Cooking Place the cubes of preserved egg at the bottom of a heat-proof dish. Mix the diced salt eggs with the beaten eggs. Stir in the heated stock, together with the salt, pepper, and oil. Pour the mixture into the heat-proof dish containing the preserved eggs. Place the dish in a steamer or a large saucepan with 1 inch (2½ cm) of water, and steam for 20 minutes. Sprinkle with the chopped onions and ham, and serve from the heat-proof dish.

Tea Eggs or Marbled Eggs

Serves 6

6 eggs
2 tablespoons Indian tea leaves

Preparation and Cooking Hard-boil the eggs for 10 minutes, then slightly crack the shells, but do not remove them. Boil tea leaves in ¾ pint (scant ½ litre) water for 5 minutes or until it becomes very strong and dark. Immerse the cracked-shell eggs in the tea for 45 minutes or until cool. When you remove the shells from the eggs you will notice that some of the tea has seeped through the cracks and formed a marbled pattern on the whites of the eggs. The tea also gives the eggs a very distinctive flavour.

Soya Eggs

Soya Eggs are made by simmering hard-boiled eggs in soya sauce for 15–20 minutes. Drain, cool, and slice them lengthwise into four to six wedges. Hard-boiled eggs can also be simmered in the gravy of red-cooked dishes, such as Red-Cooked Pork or Beef (see index), during the last 30–40 minutes of cooking time.

Thousand Years Old Eggs

Serves 4–6, with other dishes

2 dozen duck eggs
6 tablespoons salt

1 pint (500 ml) water
30 tablespoons pine ash
6 tablespoons lime

We cannot allow a chapter on eggs to end without dealing with and giving a picture of Thousand Years Old Eggs. These eggs are, in fact, seldom made at home in China. They are almost always bought from food stores or provision shops. They are nowadays frequently obtainable from Chinese food stores in the West. In China, for some reason, they are called 'Pine Flower Eggs' (Sung Hwa Dan). Is it because pine ash is used in the making of them?

Preparation First of all, dissolve the salt in the water in a large basin. Gradually add the pine ash and then the lime. Stir into a thick, consistent, muddy mixture with a spoon or stick. Wash the eggs in hot water. Coat them completely in a ¼ inch (½ cm) layer of 'mud-pack' from the basin (as they do with ladies' faces in beauty-parlours). See that they are completely coated. Roll the mud-covered eggs in a tray of husks (rice or any other dry husk) so as to take on a coating, thus preventing the eggs from sticking to each other or anything else. Place the eggs in a pile at the bottom of a large earthenware jar and cover with a lid. After 3 days, take the eggs out and rearrange them, placing those on the top at the bottom of the pile and vice versa. Repeat the procedure five times in 15 days. After 15 days of chopping and changing, seal the jar by placing the lid on firmly, and leave the eggs to stand for 1 month. At the end of the total 45 day period, the Thousand Years Old Eggs should be ready. The mixture of salt, lime, and ash provides a process of 'slow cooking' which acts as a time-machine to shorten the time from 1000 years to 50 days. The eggs, covered in husks and grey dried mud, appear remarkably like antique eggs.

Serving To eat the eggs, wash off the mud under a tap and crack the shells gently. Remove the shells and slice the eggs lengthwise into quarters. The eggs should be greenish-yellow in colour and they taste pungent and cheesy. There is nothing quite like them in the Western culinary world.

Sweets & Snacks

點心甜菜

Sweets or desserts do not really have the same function in China as in the West where the dessert ends the meal. At an ordinary Chinese dinner, the dessert does not occur at all: in fact there is no sweet after any Chinese meal.

Sweets are eaten in China on two occasions. Firstly, during a multi-course party dinner or banquet, where they have the same function as soups, that is to punctuate the long, endless procession of savoury dishes. In many cases, Chinese sweets not only have the function of soups, they *are* soups – sweet soups! (Some are such thick soups that they are really creams or custards!) Sweets are also eaten between meals, as snacks. Then they are often simply dumplings or steamed buns stuffed with sweet fillings. Sometimes they are sprinkled or studded with sesame seeds to give them an aromatic flavour. They are either steamed or deep-fried; if deep-fried they are called 'crispies'.

Compared with the enormous range and sophistication of Western desserts, Chinese sweet dishes are almost primitive. They can only be of purely academic interest to the Western connoisseur. Nonetheless, some of the Chinese practices could contribute to Western concepts and experiments with desserts.

On the other hand, we Chinese have a vast tradition of savoury snacks. The majority are steamed, poached, simmered, fried, dry-fried, or dry-heated.

Savoury snacks are eaten in China not only between meals, but also at the numerous tea-houses which serve them all day long. The tea-houses are, in a way, Chinese pubs or coffee-houses, where people – the lazy bourgeoisie who can afford the time and money – can sit and nibble all day long!

Sweets and Snacks

Almond 'Tea'

Serves 4–6

6 oz (150 g) almonds

4 oz (100 g) rice
3½–4 tablespoons sugar

Preparation Soak the almonds in boiling water, then remove the skins. Grind the rice and almonds together with 1 pint (500 ml) water, which should be added gradually. Filter the resulting smooth, thin paste through a fine sieve or gauze. Put the paste and the filtered rice and almonds through the grinder a second time. Add the sugar and ½ pint (250 ml) water to the strained mixture. Stir until smoothly blended.
Cooking Put the mixture into a heavy saucepan. Bring to the boil slowly (it burns very easily), and insert an asbestos sheet under the pan. Stir continually. As the liquid thickens, add 2 tablespoons water (or use milk or cream if you prefer) at a time to prevent it getting too thick. Continue to stir for 30 minutes.
Serving Pour the Almond Tea into individual bowls, one for each diner.

Walnut Soup

Serves 4–6

12 oz (300 g) walnuts

4 tablespoons sugar
4 oz (100 g) powdered rice *or* rice flour

Preparation Blanch the walnuts and remove the skins. Grind them to a powder, then add 1½ pints (¾ litre) water.
Cooking Bring the mixture to the boil and simmer gently for 40 minutes. Filter and strain through fine gauze. Add the sugar, powdered rice, and ½ pint (250 ml) water to the strained walnut 'milk'. Put the mixture into a heavy saucepan and bring to the boil, stirring constantly. Insert an asbestos sheet under the pan and continue to stir for 25 minutes. Serve in soup bowls.

Lotus Seed Soup

Serves 4–6

8 oz (200 g) dry lotus seeds

8 oz (200 g) crystallized candied lotus seeds
4 tablespoons sugar

Preparation Blanch the dry lotus seeds, then remove the skins. Grind them into a powder, then add 1½ pints (¾ litre) water.

The Complete Chinese Cookbook

Cooking Bring the mixture to the boil very gently in a heavy pan. Insert an asbestos sheet under the pan. Simmer very gently for 30 minutes, then strain. Place the candied lotus seeds in another heavy pan. Add ½ pint (250 ml) water. Bring to the boil and simmer for 20 minutes. Pour in the strained lotus seed 'milk' and insert an asbestos sheet under the pan. Bring the mixture slowly to the boil, add the sugar, and reduce the heat to low. Stir continually for 15 minutes. Serve in soup bowls.

To vary this recipe, add canned chopped pineapple instead of, or as well as, the candied lotus seeds.

Almond Junket

Serves 4–6

6 oz (150 g) almonds
4 oz (100 g) rice

3½–4 tablespoons sugar
1 envelope plain gelatine powder
¼ pint (125 ml) evaporated milk

Preparation Repeat the recipe for Almond Tea (see page 257).
Cooking In the final boiling, instead of adding water, stir in 1 envelope of plain gelatine powder, blended with 4 tablespoons water, and ¼ pint (125 ml) evaporated milk. Stir slowly for 3 minutes, then pour the liquid into a square heat-proof dish. Let it cool for 30 minutes; then place in refrigerator for 3 hours.
Serving After 3 hours, the liquid will have set into a jelly. Cut it up into neat pieces. Dissolve 1½ tablespoons sugar in 6 tablespoons water, then pour over the junket and serve on an attractive platter.

Peanut Cream

Serves 6–8

12 oz (300 g) shelled peanuts

4 oz (100 g) powdered rice
6 tablespoons sugar

Preparation Roast the peanuts and grind them to a powder as fine as castor sugar.
Cooking Mix the powdered rice and peanuts in a heavy pan. Pour in 2¼ pints (almost 1½ litres) water. Stir, and bring to the boil slowly; then insert an asbestos sheet under the pan. Simmer gently, stirring continually, until the mixture thickens. Add the sugar, bring to a slow boil once more, and stir for a further 5 minutes.
Serving Serve in bowls, like custard. In the West, a small amount of cream could be poured over the custard to make it even more interesting and acceptable.

Sweets and Snacks

Steamed Pears in Honey

Serves 6

6 pears
3 tablespoons honey

6 tablespoons sugar
2 tablespoons liqueur (Chinese Rose Dew, Kirsch, Cherry Brandy *or* Crème de Menthe)

This is an attractive sweet and can well be served as a Western dessert.

Preparation Peel the pears, leaving the stalks as 'handles'.
Cooking Stand the pears in a pan and barely cover with water. Simmer for 30 minutes, sprinkle the pears with sugar, and simmer for a further 5 minutes. Reserve half of the water in the pan for later use and pour away the remainder. Refrigerate the pears for 2 hours; then add the honey and liqueur to the reserved water and stir until well-blended. Put the mixture in the refrigerator.
Serving Place each pear in a dessert bowl and pour over the chilled liqueur/honey mixture. Serve with whipped cream if desired.

This is a very refreshing dessert to have after the 'long hot summer' of a multi-course Chinese dinner.

Chilled Melon Bowl

Serves 4–10

1 large melon

3 oz (75 g) Almond Junket (see page 258)
variety of fresh and canned fruit

This is simply serving a chilled fruit salad in a scooped-out melon, which is a very attractive way of serving a dessert. The full Chinese title for the dish is 'Ten Variety Chilled Melon Bowl', but it is not absolutely necessary to have ten different types of fruit in the salad.

Preparation Slice an inch off the top of a large melon and scoop out the inside of the fruit carefully in large pieces with a spoon. Cut the scooped-out pieces into regular triangular shapes. Cut the Almond Junket into similar pieces. Mix the pieces of melon and Almond Junket with six or more types of canned and fresh fruit, such as strawberries, honeydew melon, cherries, peaches, pears, apples, pineapple, lychees, grapes, plums, etc. Pack the cavity of the melon with this mixture. Chill the melon in the refrigerator for at least 2 hours.
Serving If desired, the pile of fruits in the melon can be topped with a piece of ice.

This dish can be a magnificent dessert if well-presented and decorated, especially if you can find an enormous melon or watermelon to use. A similar type of dessert could be concocted using a fresh pineapple instead of a melon.

Eight Precious Rice

Serves 10-12

1½ lb (600 g) glutinous rice
4 tablespoons lard
6 tablespoons candied fruit (raisins, cherries, ginger, dates, prunes, dragon eye meat, dried lychee meat *or* mixed glacé fruit)
4 tablespoons nuts (almonds, chestnuts, walnuts, melon seeds, gingko nuts)
6 tablespoons sugar
8 tablespoons sweetened red bean paste *or* date purée

This is the traditional Chinese steamed pudding, studded with a variety of candied fruits and nuts. It is often served during a banquet.

Preparation Cook the rice by boiling or steaming. Grease a large heat-proof bowl, about 8 inches (20 cm) in diameter, generously with half the lard. (The lard should be cold.) Stick the candied fruits and nuts on to the walls of the bowl as decoratively as possible, and arrange the remainder at the bottom of the bowl. Add the sugar and remaining lard to the cooked rice and mix well. Spoon half of the rice into the bowl, covering the fruits and nuts on the bottom, but without dislodging those studded on the walls. Spoon in the sweetened red bean paste on top of the rice. Cover the paste completely with the remaining rice, leaving nearly 1 inch (2 cm) space at the top of the bowl for expansion.

Cooking Place a cloth or piece of tinfoil over the bowl and put it in a steamer to steam vigorously for 60-70 minutes, or until cooked through.

Serving Invert the pudding on to a dish and serve. The fruits and nuts showing on the top and sides should make an interesting pattern. Eight Precious Rice is almost a kind of Chinese Christmas Pudding!

Drawn Thread Toffee Apples

Serves 4-6

4 crisp apples
1 egg
4 oz (100 g) flour
oil for deep-frying
6 tablespoons sugar
3 tablespoons vegetable oil
3 tablespoons syrup

Sweets and Snacks

This is a popular **Peking** sweet. It came to be so called because when the pieces of apple immersed in hot, sticky syrup are pulled apart, they draw with them long threads of thick syrup, which rapidly begin to harden into brittle caramelized sugar. The process begins immediately the pieces of apple are dipped into ice-cold water, giving each piece of apple a very sweet, but thin, encrustation.

Preparation Peel and core the apples, slice each into six wedges, then cut each wedge in half. Blend the egg, flour, and ¼ pint (125 ml) water to make a smooth batter. Dip each piece of apple in the batter.

Cooking Deep-fry the pieces of apple in the oil for 2½–3 minutes, then drain. Heat the sugar, vegetable oil, and 2 tablespoons water in a heavy saucepan over a gentle heat for 5 minutes, stirring constantly. Add the syrup and stir for a further 2 minutes. Add the fried apple-fritters and stir slowly, covering each piece of apple completely with the syrup.

Serving Bring the pan to the dining table and quickly spoon the hot, syrup-covered apple slices into a large bowl of ice-water. Remove them quickly and distribute the apple slices among the dessert bowls of the diners. Alternatively, if the diners are adept with chopsticks, put the syrup-covered apple slices in a well-heated bowl in the centre of the table, and let the guests use their chopsticks to pick up slices and dip them in the ice-water.

In pulling an apple slice away from the other pieces, the diner will find long, thin threads of syrup trailing from the piece of fruit. Before eating, he must remember to plunge the piece of apple into the ice-water, which transforms the syrup instantly into a brittle coating with dangling threads (a kind of sugar stalactite!). The coating and threads are extremely fragile. They crackle when bitten into, which, together with the sensation of instant sweetness, creates an interesting experience which most Westerners enjoy.

Drawn Thread Toffee Apples are frequently served as a dessert in Chinese restaurants abroad.

Snacks

Chinese snacks or 'small eats' (T'ien Hsin) consist principally of noodles (which have already been dealt with in a separate section, dumplings (which are very thin-skinned small raviolis, usually cooked by boiling, poaching, or steaming), the larger steamed buns (which are a meal in themselves), and pancakes. The majority of these are stuffed with savoury foods, but a few have sweet stuffings. In preparing 'small eats' of this type, there are usually four steps to be considered: making the dough, rolling or shaping the pastry, making the filling, and the final heating or cooking.

Recipes for Chinese Dumplings and fillings are on the next page.

The Complete Chinese Cookbook

Chiao Tzu (*Stuffed Boiled or Steamed Dumplings*)

Makes approximately 30 dumplings

½ pint (250 ml) water
6 oz (150 g) plain flour

6 oz (150 g) self-raising flour
filling for the dumplings (see page 264)
soya sauce *or* vinegar *or* both

These dumplings are normally made 50–100 at a time. Wrapping dumplings is a kind of pastime in China. At festival seasons, Chinese women are often to be seen wrapping them on trays without looking at them – just like Western women knitting! Children are asked to join in.

Preparation Mix ½ pint (250 ml) of water with 12 oz (300 g) of sifted flour and knead until smooth. Cover with a wet cloth and let it stand for 30 minutes. Form the dough into a 14 inch (35 cm) roll about 1 inch (2½ cm) in diameter. Cut the dough into ½ inch (1 cm) thick slices. Roll the slices on a board lightly dusted with flour, until each piece is about 3 inches (7½ cm) in diameter. Place a heaped teaspoon of the filling in the centre of each dough circle. Fold over and seal the edges by pressing them together.

Cooking Bring a gallon of water to the boil and tip in all the dumplings. When the water comes to the boil again, let it boil for 10 seconds, then pour in ¾ pint (375 ml) of water. Repeat this process three times in the course of about 10 minutes, by which time the dumplings should be ready. Remove them with a perforated spoon, drain and arrange them on a well-heated serving dish.

Serving These dumplings are usually eaten dipped in soya sauce or vinegar, or both. In north China, savoury dumplings are frequently served as a full meal, in which case each person will need at least 18–24 of them. The 'dough-soup', which is the water in which the dumplings are boiled, is served in small bowls to accompany the dumplings. Because of its total neutrality (there being no seasonings added), it has the refreshing 'washing' effect which we Chinese love, especially when the dumplings are eaten with pickles and other salted dishes. For the more 'degenerate', chicken broth could be served instead of the dough-soup.

These dumplings can also be steamed. To do this, a piece of cheese cloth is spread out on the bottom of a steamer and the dumplings are arranged on top of the cloth. In China we usually use a round basket-like steamer. The dumplings should be steamed for 20–25 minutes (depending on the strength of the steam).

Some suggested fillings for Chiao Tzu are Pork and Chinese Celery Cabbage Filling, Shrimp, or Crab-meat Filling (recipes on page 264).

Sweets and Snacks

Kuo T'ieh (Steam-Fried Dumplings)

Makes approximately 30 dumplings

¼ pint (125 ml) water

1 teaspoon sugar
1 tablespoon soya sauce
1 tablespoon vinegar
2 tablespoons vegetable oil

When dumplings are steam-fried in the special way peculiar to north China they are called 'Kuo T'ieh'.

Preparation Make the dumplings according to the instructions in the previous recipe. Blend together the water, sugar, soya sauce, and vinegar.
Cooking Grease a flat frying pan, griddle, or roasting pan with the vegetable oil. Place pan over a medium heat and arrange the dumplings on it in one layer. Allow the dumplings to 'Tsien' (fry steadily) for 4–5 minutes until they are beginning to get brown at the bottom, moving the pan over the hot-plate now and then to ensure even heat. Sprinkle the dumplings with the soya sauce mixture, cover the pan with a lid, and heat the dumplings for a further 2–3 minutes.

This method of multi-process heating produces the desired effect of softness at the top, juiciness inside, and crispiness at the bottom, which makes these 'Kuo T'ieh' certainly one of the most interesting and appealing raviolis in the world. They are usually eaten with soya-vinegar dips, which are arranged in small saucer-style sauce dishes on the dining table.

Shao Mai (Steamed Open Dumplings)

Makes approximately 36 dumplings

Whilst 'Chiao Tzu' and 'Kuo T'ieh' are the favourites of the north, the dumpling which is very popular in the south, especially in Canton, is the 'Shao Mai'. Since this is an open dumpling, 'Shao Mai' must be steamed rather than boiled. As the Cantonese are fond of seafoods, more often than not shrimps, prawns, and crab-meat are incorporated into the fillings.

Preparation Make the dough-skins according to the instructions in the recipe for Chiao Tzu, adding 1 egg and 4 oz (100 g) cornflour for every 8 oz (200 g) flour. After kneading, form the dough into a 12 inch (30 cm) roll, 1 inch (2½ cm) in diameter. Cut off slices about ⅓ inch (¾ cm) thick from this dough roll and roll them out to circles about 2½ inches (7½ cm) in diameter. Form a ring by joining your index finger with the thumb on your left hand. Place dough circle on top of this ring, and make a hollow by gently pressing down the centre of the ring with the fingers of your right hand. The tucked-down part of the dough-sheet can then be supported by the remaining fingers and the rest of the hand. A small dough-bag is thus formed, with the index finger and thumb acting as a support to the mouth of the bag. When the bag is stuffed with the filling, the mouth is somewhat tightened. Push the filling into the dough-bag with a pair of chopsticks or the handle of a wooden spoon.

Cooking When the dumplings have been prepared, arrange them in a steamer covered with cheese cloth and steam vigorously for 15–20 minutes.

Serving Often these Shao Mais are decorated with a single shrimp placed on top of the filling so as to protrude slightly from the top of the casing. This indicates the abundance of fillings inside.

Pork and Chinese Celery Cabbage Filling for Dumplings

For 40–50 dumplings

8 oz (200 g) pork
8 oz (200 g) Chinese celery cabbage
2 spring onion stalks

1 slice root ginger
½ teaspoon salt
½ teaspoon flavour powder
1 tablespoon soya sauce
2 teaspoons sesame oil

Fillings for dumplings can be cooked or uncooked, but fresh ones are preferred. In the north, the favourite fillings are made of pork or lamb with Chinese Celery Cabbage. In the south, seafoods such as shrimps, prawns, and crab-meat are frequently used.

Preparation Chop the pork, cabbage, spring onions, and root ginger. Place all the ingredients in a basin, then stir and mix well. Allow the mixture to stand for 30 minutes before using as a filling for dumplings.

Shrimp or Crab-Meat Filling

8 oz (200 g) fresh shrimps *or* crab-meat
3 Chinese dried mushrooms
2 oz (50 g) pork
2 spring onion stalks

2 slices root ginger
½ teaspoon salt
1½ tablespoons soya sauce
1 tablespoon sherry
2 teaspoons sesame oil

Preparation Soak the dried mushrooms for 30 minutes, remove the stalks and chop the caps. Chop the shrimps or crab-meat, pork, spring onions, and root ginger. Place all the ingredients in a basin, stir and mix well. Allow the mixture to stand for 30 minutes before using as a filling. This should be sufficient for 40–50 dumplings.

Hun Tuns

Makes about 30 dumplings per 8 oz (200 g) flour

These miniature dumplings are called 'Wontons'. They are made more or less in the same manner as ordinary dumplings, except that the dough-skin used is much larger in relation to the stuffing inserted. The large dough-skin trails a 'skirt' which the Chinese think resembles a cloud. 'Hun Tun' means in Chinese 'swallow a cloud'! Hun Tuns are either used in soups, or deep-fried and eaten as snacks. When deep-fried, they are frequently served with Sweet and Sour Sauce (see page 42).

Preparation Hun Tun skins are usually made with one portion of water to three portions of flour, with ½ egg added for every 8 oz (200 g) flour. The dough is then kneaded until smooth and left for 30 minutes. Form the dough into a roll about 14 inches (35 cm) in length and about 1 inch (2½ cm) in diameter. Cut ½ inch (1 cm) thick slices from the roll on a flour-dusted board. Roll them out into thin pancakes about 3½ inches (9 cm) in diameter. Try to roll out the dough until it is paper-thin. Cut these round dough-skins into quarters, and wrap some of the filling in each quarter. After the filling has been wrapped and sealed into the skin, the two extremities of the skin should be brought together and pressed against each other. Thus the skin is double-folded.

Chicken Filling for Hun Tuns

4 oz (100 g) chicken breast meat
4 large Chinese dried mushrooms
2 spring onion stalks
1 slice root ginger

1 tablespoon soya sauce
¼ teaspoon salt
2 teaspoons sesame oil

Hun Tun fillings can be of the same ingredients as the fillings for other types of dumpling. But, being smaller in size, often daintier things such as chicken or bêche de mer are used.

Preparation Soak the mushrooms for 30 minutes, remove the stalks and chop the caps. Chop the chicken, spring onions, and root ginger. Place all the ingredients in a basin. Stir and mix well. Allow the mixture to stand for 30 minutes before using as a filling. Sufficient for 30–40 Hun Tuns.

The Complete Chinese Cookbook
Steamed Buns

Chinese steamed buns are principally of two types, those with fillings and those without. Those without fillings are eaten with meat, fish, vegetable, and savoury dishes. Among unfilled buns, the best known are the Man Tou and the Hua Chuan. Man Tou buns are made from wheat flour and are second in importance only to rice as the bulk food of China. Indeed, in the wheat-producing regions of north China, the consumption of Man Tou undoubtedly exceeds that of rice per head of population. If you walked into any dining hall north of the Yellow River, you would see Man Tou piled up in small, steaming mountains for the diners to fetch and bring to their own tables. Hua Chuan is a more refined form of Man Tou. It is, in fact, a steamed roll made in layers of raised dough, used more often during dinner parties and in restaurants than at ordinary meals.

Man Tou (Plain Steamed Buns)

Serves 10–12

¼ pint (160 ml) water

1½ tablespoons dried yeast
1 lb (400 g) flour

Preparation Heat 6 tablespoons of the water until warm, add the yeast, and stir until dissolved; then blend into the flour, and mix well. Add the remaining water gradually. Knead well for 7–8 minutes. Allow the dough to stand in the basin in a warm place for 2 hours, until it has expanded to twice its original size. Knead for a couple of minutes and repeat. Shape the dough into a roll 24 inches (60 cm) long and 2 inches (5 cm) in diameter. Cut off slices about 2 inches (5 cm) thick and form them into flat-bottomed buns.
Cooking Place the buns on a damp cheese cloth in a steam basket or steamer. Steam vigorously for 15–20 minutes.
Serving Hot Man Tou buns are served for breakfast, lunch, and dinner.

Hua Chuan (Flower Rolls)

Serves 10–12

Preparation Make the dough according to the instructions for Man Tou (Plain Steamed Buns). Divide dough into two portions and roll out each portion to a sheet ⅛ inch (⅓ cm) thick. Sprinkle each sheet with about ¼ teaspoon salt, and brush the surface of each with 1 tablespoon of sesame or vegetable oil. Place one sheet on top of the other, oiled surface against the non-oiled surface. Roll the two sheets into a scroll about 1½–2 inches (3½–5 cm) in diameter. Trim the ends and cut the scroll into 2½ inch (6 cm) segments. Press down the middle of each segment with a pair of chopsticks so that the opened ends will open out further.

Cooking Place these open-ended rolls in a steamer on top of a damp cheese cloth and steam vigorously for 15 minutes.

Serving Hua Chuan are essential and excellent for accompanying red-cooked meats and, indeed, all rich dishes.

Pao Tzu (Stuffed Steamed Buns)

Serves 6–10

There are two types of Pao Tzu or stuffed, steamed buns – those with savoury fillings and those with sweet fillings. Stuffed steamed buns are never served during meals; they are always eaten as snacks.

The dough used for stuffed buns is the same as Man Tou dough, except that 1 tablespoon of sugar is added. The presence of the sugar seems to have a very salutary effect. Since stuffed buns are eaten on their own, and not used just for soaking up the savouriness from the other dishes on the table, they have to be in themselves more appealing than unstuffed buns. Westerners take to these stuffed buns much more readily than to the plain Man Tou.

As in the making of Man Tou buns, the dough is first of all formed into a roll 2 inches (5 cm) in diameter, then sliced into thick discs. These discs are then rolled out again into 3 inch (7½ cm) diameter rounds. Between ½ and ¾ tablespoon of the filling is placed at the centre of each piece of dough, then the sides should be drawn up to a point and sealed. In this way, the filling is completely enveloped in the centre of a flat-bottomed ball. These flat-bottomed balls of dough are placed in a steamer on top of a damp cheese cloth and steamed vigorously for 25 minutes.

The stuffings for these buns can be made from any combination of meat and vegetables, either fresh or cooked.

Savoury Stuffing for Pao Tzu (1)

1 lb (400 g) pork
2 spring onion stalks
1½ lb (600 g) Chinese cabbage
2 tablespoons soya sauce
1 teaspoon salt
2 teaspoons sugar
2 teaspoons sesame oil

Preparation Mince the pork coarsely. Chop the spring onions and cabbage. Place all the ingredients in a basin and mix well. Leave the mixture to stand for 30 minutes before using. Sufficient for 30–40 buns.

The Complete Chinese Cookbook

Savoury Stuffing for Pao Tzu (2)

1½ lb (600 g) Cha Shao roast pork
3 spring onion stalks
2 tablespoons soya sauce
1 teaspoon salt
2 teaspoons sugar
2 teaspoons sesame oil

Preparation Mince the roast pork and chop the spring onions. Place all the ingredients in a basin and mix well. Allow the mixture to stand for 30 minutes before using. Sufficient for 30–40 buns.

Sweet Stuffing for Pao Tzu

2 oz (50 g) sesame seeds
6 oz (150 g) walnuts
4 oz (100 g) almonds
2 oz (50 g) pork fat
8 oz (200 g) sugar
1 tablespoon lard

Preparation Roast the sesame seeds in a dry frying pan for 1 minute, then crush them. Grind the walnuts and almonds. Chop the pork fat into tiny cubes. Mix all the ingredients together in a basin and use the mixture as a filling. Sufficient for 30–40 buns.

Sugar and Black Bean Filling for Pao Tzu

For approximately 40 buns

8 oz (200 g) sugar
12 oz (300 g) black *or* red bean purée
4 tablespoons lard

Cooking Stir-fry the ingredients together in a frying pan for 5 minutes over a gentle heat. Allow to stand and cool, then use as a filling.

Ping or Pancakes

The Chinese word 'Ping' refers to pancakes as well as to cakes of a much greater thickness, which have been cooked by frying with a little oil or on a dry pan or griddle. Although there are numerous types of cakes and pancakes, the majority of them are extremely mundane, usually incorporating a small amount of onion, grated radishes, or sesame seeds to provide flavour, pungency, or aroma. They are really only a poor man's way of making wheat flour edible. Through tradition or habit, many Chinese people have come to regard them with respect or even nostalgia, but they

Sweets and Snacks

really enjoy them only if they are accompanied by quantities of wholesome, rich, savoury foods. To Westerners, only the following types of Chinese pancakes are likely to be of much interest. Suggested fillings are given on page 270.

Spring Rolls, Pancake Rolls, and Egg Rolls

The above three are in fact the same thing. Spring rolls *are* pancake rolls, but in China they are called spring rolls because they are served and eaten on and after the Old New Year Day, usually falling sometime in February, which is getting fairly near to spring in many parts of the country. Egg rolls are pancake rolls with a little extra egg in the dough. The pancake rolls or egg rolls made and served by Chinese restaurants abroad are usually about 5 or 6 inches (12½–15 cm) in length and about ¾ inch (1½ cm) in diameter, which is larger than those usually served in China. In America, the egg rolls are usually cut into three pieces or into 1½ inch (3½ cm) sections when served. As probably more pancake rolls are eaten abroad than spring rolls are in China, the overseas version deserves a mention. I shall call the original Chinese version the spring roll and the overseas version the egg or pancake roll.

Egg or Spring Roll Skins

Makes 12–15

8 oz (200 g) flour

½ teaspoon salt
2 eggs
oil

Egg or spring roll skins are made in a way very similar to the method for making ordinary pancakes. The intention is simply to make a batter and produce extremely thin pancakes, which are then filled.

Preparation Combine the flour and salt. Beat the eggs lightly and add to the flour. Beat steadily in one direction, gradually adding ⅔ pint (320 ml) water. Continue beating until a thin, smooth batter is obtained.

Cooking Pour a small quantity of oil into a frying pan, swirl it around, and pour away the excess. Stir the batter, then place 2 tablespoons of it in the middle of the pan. Lift the handle of the pan and move it around until the batter has spread evenly over the whole surface of the pan. Pour away any excess batter. Place the pan over a low heat, and as soon as the dough-skin starts to peel and shrink from the sides, lift it from the pan and put it aside, covered with a damp cloth. Repeat this process until all the batter has been used, re-oiling the pan lightly by rubbing it with an oil-soaked cloth after each pancake has been made.

The Complete Chinese Cookbook

Wrapping the Rolls

Place about 2 tablespoons of filling just below the centre of the dough-skin or pancake, spreading it lengthwise. Fold the edge nearest to you over the filling, then roll up fairly tightly. When the pancake is rolled up, turn in the edges of the two ends. Continue to roll away from the body. Finally, fold the farthest side or corner inwards and seal it down with beaten egg.

Deep-Frying the Rolls

Fry the filled egg or spring rolls four or five at a time by placing them in a wire basket and lowering them into boiling oil, at a temperature of about 375°F (190°C or Gas Mark 5). After frying for 2 minutes, remove the pan from the heat for 1 minute, then replace it for a further 2 minutes. Alternatively, egg rolls and spring rolls can be pan-fried in shallow oil, just like sausages, by turning them in the oil and frying on all sides.

When the filling is composed of fresh, raw ingredients, it is sometimes advisable to steam the egg or spring rolls for 10 minutes before deep-frying. In such cases, the rolls are sometimes dipped in beaten egg or batter before deep-frying.

Meat and Other Fillings for Egg or Spring Rolls

As a rule, egg roll and spring roll fillings have to be cooked first before they are packed into the rolls. This is because the rolls are too thick for the meat ingredients to be thoroughly cooked during the 4–5 minutes the rolls are deep-fried. The majority of Chinese stir-fried dishes can, in fact, be packed into the rolls as fillings.

Chicken and Vegetable Filling

For 12–15 rolls

8 oz (200 g) chicken meat, cooked *or* uncooked
3 Chinese dried mushrooms
2 oz (50 g) bamboo shoots
4 oz (100 g) bean sprouts
2 spring onion stalks
1½ tablespoons vegetable oil
½ teaspoon salt
3 teaspoons soya sauce
1 teaspoon sugar
1 teaspoon cornflour

Preparation Soak the dried mushrooms for 30 minutes, then shred them. Shred the bamboo shoots, blanch the bean sprouts, and chop the spring onions. Shred the chicken meat.
Cooking Heat the oil in a frying pan. Add the chicken, bamboo shoots, and

spring onions. Stir-fry over a high heat for 1 minute; then add the bean sprouts and mushrooms. Stir-fry for a further minute. Add all the other ingredients and continue to stir-fry for 1 minute. Remove the mixture from the pan and put in a colander to cool and drain. Use as a filling for egg or spring rolls when it is thoroughly cooled and drained.

Stir-Fried Pork and Vegetable Filling

For 12–15 rolls

Cooking Repeat the previous recipe, substituting 10 oz (250 g) shredded pork for the chicken. Stir-fry the pork and salt together over a high heat for 1 minute before adding any other ingredients. Otherwise, the procedure is the same as in the previous recipe. The mixture must be thoroughly cooled and drained before use.

Roast Pork and Cooked Shrimp Filling

For 12–15 rolls

Cooking Use the same vegetables and seasonings as in the recipe for Chicken and Vegetable Filling (see above). Stir-fry the vegetables over a medium heat for 2 minutes, then add 3 oz (75 g) shrimps and 8 oz (200 g) shredded roast pork. Stir-fry for 1 minute, then add the seasonings for a final general stir-fry.

Glossary

ABALONE A rubbery-textured, limpet-like shellfish, which is used extensively for flavouring soups, mixed-fried foods, and red-cooked dishes. Occasionally cooked and presented as principal material of a banquet dish. It is ivory yellow in colour.

BAMBOO SHOOTS The young shoots of the bamboo plant which are harvested in the spring. They sometimes reach 2–3 inches (5–7½ cm) in diameter, are crunchy in texture, and have a mild and subtle flavour. Used extensively in Chinese cooking.

BEAN CURD Ground soya beans which have been lightly cooked with water and then left to set into a semi-solid 'custard'. This is cut into cakes approximately 2 inches (5 cm) square, and about 1 inch (2½ cm) deep. With its high protein content, it is a mainstay of Chinese vegetable and vegetarian cooking.

BEAN CURD CHEESE A type of fermented bean curd which has a very strong, savoury, cheesy taste. It is used extensively for flavouring, and is often eaten in small quantities with congee (plain, boiled rice-porridge) for breakfast in China.

BIRD'S NEST The regurgitated fish and seafoods that sea swallows in south-east Asia deposit in their nests for their young. An expensive delicacy, used in Bird's Nest Soup.

BLACK BEANS (Fermented) Small, black, salted soya beans, which must be soaked for about 15 minutes in water before use.

CHILLI SAUCE (and Chilli Oil) Chilli sauce is a hot sauce made from small chilli peppers. It is very similar in flavour to Tabasco. Chilli oil, which is even hotter, is made from small red peppers which are slowly fried in oil. The oil becomes coloured by the peppers in the process of the heating, and the chilli oil, when ready for use, is reddish in colour.

CHINESE CABBAGE A firm and flavoursome lettuce-like plant with long, crisp leaves. It can be braised, stir-fried or made into a salad.

CHINESE DRIED MUSHROOMS These are dark brownish-black in colour, and must be soaked for about 30 minutes before use. The stem should

Glossary

be removed as it is so tough that even one hour's cooking will not tenderize it. Dried mushrooms have a much more pronounced flavour than fresh mushrooms; they also have a much meatier texture. Fresh mushrooms are seldom used in Chinese cooking.

CHINESE PARSLEY Fresh coriander leaves that look like parsley but have a different, much stronger taste.

CHINESE SAUSAGES Smoked salami pork sausages, 4–8 inches (10–20 cm) long, often steamed or lightly fried, or cross-cooked with vegetables or other ingredients.

CLOUD EARS A form of fungus, usually available dried, that has to be soaked for at least 30 minutes before use. These fungi are cloud-shaped – hence their name. Cloud ears are used mainly for their textural effect – a sort of slippery crunchiness.

CONGEE RICE Congee is a word used in the Far East to describe rice-porridge, or watery rice, or rice which has been cooked for a long time in at least four to eight times its own weight of water. It is usually served for breakfast, or cooked by people who must augment their meagre rice ration with a very large content of water.

CRACKLING RICE The scrapings of rice from the bottom of the rice cooker, which have been further dried, then finally deep-fried until really hot and crackling. Often served with soup or sauce.

DOUBLE-MAHJONG-SIZE An average mahjong-size piece measures about $1 \times \frac{2}{3} \times \frac{1}{4}$ inch ($2\frac{1}{2} \times 1\frac{1}{2} \times \frac{1}{2}$ cm), so a double-mahjong-size piece is double that. It would probably have to be cut or bitten in half before being eaten.

EGG NOODLES Spaghetti-type noodles made from eggs and wheat flour.

FIVE SPICE POWDER A mixed, ground, herbal powder used in Chinese cooking. It consists of five types of ground, dried spices: star anise, anise pepper, fennel, cloves, and cinnamon.

GLUTINOUS RICE This is much the same type of thing as the round, glutinous rice used in the West. It is usually used in sweet dishes, but it is also used for Lotus Leaf Wrapped Rice.

GOLDEN NEEDLES Described under Lily Bud Stems.

HOISIN SAUCE Literally translated it means 'Sea-Fresh Sauce'. It is made from soya sauce, soya paste, ground yellow beans, garlic pulp, sugar, and vinegar. Sweet and spicy, it is frequently combined with other sauces for use as a dip. Used in the cooking of seafoods, meats, and vegetables.

KUMQUATS Like very small oranges or tangerines. Available in cans, or occasionally fresh.

LIGHT-COLOURED SOYA SAUCE Soya sauce in China is like wine in the West, in that it comes in numerous grades, strengths, colours, and flavours. The light-coloured variety is mostly used for preparing light-coloured dishes.

LILY BUD STEMS (DRIED LILY BUDS or GOLDEN NEEDLES) These are long, yellow strips of stem-like vegetables. Small quantities are often used in vegetable and semi-vegetable dishes, as they have a very distinctive (mouldy) flavour.

LOTUS LEAVES Often used to wrap up food materials before cooking – much the same as tinfoil is used in the West these days, except that Lotus Leaves impart a special flavour and aroma to the food. Poultry is frequently wrapped in a Lotus Leaf then steamed or roasted.

LOTUS ROOTS When fresh, these are usually used to prepare a sweet dish. Dried Lotus Roots require soaking, then may be used along with other vegetables in a mixed-fried or mixed-assembled dish.

LYCHEES Fleshy, white fruit with reddish-brown skin and a large stone. Has a sweet and very subtle flavour.

MANGE-TOUT The French term for pea pods. These are often quickly stir-fried into an extremely attractive, glistening, green vegetable dish.

OYSTER SAUCE A rich sauce made from oysters, oyster water, and soya sauce. Used to flavour seafood, meat, poultry, and vegetable dishes.

PEA-STARCH TRANSPARENT NOODLES These are white-coloured noodles which, when soaked, become transparent. Usually cooked with meat or vegetables. Because they tend to absorb a lot of liquid, the noodles

Glossary

become very meaty and flavoursome – ideal for consuming with plain rice.

PLUM SAUCE A spicy, fruity sauce made from plums, pepper, vinegar, and sugar. Frequently used as a dip.

RED BEAN CURD CHEESE A variety of Bean Curd Cheese.

RED-IN-SNOW PICKLED GREENS A variety of salted, pickled greens which are most often used coarsely chopped, and sprinkled over meaty or cross-cooked dishes, giving them a more piquant flavour.

RICE NOODLES Long, thin noodles made from rice flour. Can be boiled, stir-fried, or used in soups.

ROOT GINGER This is ginger in its raw state. It is either thinly sliced, or chopped, or minced. Root ginger is invariably used in the preparation of seafoods, fish, and all the stronger tasting meats, such as mutton, lamb, beef, or chicken.

SESAME OIL This is the oil produced from sesame seeds. It has a very strong nutty flavour, more often used in small quantities for flavouring than for cooking.

SHARK'S FIN The dried cartilage of a shark's fin. Very delicate flavour. Requires overnight or longer soaking.

SILVER EARS A type of fungus similar to Cloud Ears, except that they are usually white in colour. Most often used in sweet dishes.

SOYA BEAN PASTE This can almost be described as a solid version of soya sauce, but is somewhat less salty, often tastier, and should be applied in small quantities when cooking. It can often be used in conjunction with soya sauce.

STAR ANISE A dark brown eight-pointed seed called the 'eight point' in China. Used as a flavouring ingredient as it has a very distinctive flavour.

STOCKS: SUPERIOR; SECONDARY; MASTER; HERBAL Superior Stock is a meat broth produced by simmering pork, chicken, bacon, and bones together. Secondary Stock is usually produced by simmering just bones. Master Stock is made from good quality meat simmered with soya sauce, wine, sugar, and a variety of spices. Herbal Stock is a Master Stock where a much greater proportion of herbs is used in the preparation for cooking.

SZECHUAN PICKLED GREENS A hot pickle, to which a quantity of ground red chilli pepper has been added. Very hot. Often used in small quantities to flavour meats, vegetables, and soups.

TANGERINE PEEL The dried skin of tangerines. Used for flavouring duck and red-simmered dishes.

WATER CHESTNUTS An aquatic plant with white meat grown in East Asia. Usually available canned. They have a crunchy texture, and are often used in stir-fried, braised or steamed dishes. Often chopped coarsely and mixed with minced meat or prawns into meat balls or prawn balls.

WOOD EARS The more usual type of fungus which grows on trees, of which Cloud Ears and Silver Ears are different varieties. Wood Ears are usually black in colour and have to be soaked before use. They have very little taste or flavour, and are usually used in cooking for their colour and textural effect.

YELLOW WINE The most common type of wine used in Chinese cooking. It is made from rice, and tastes like medium dry sherry.

Index

Abalone
  Simmered Chicken with 225
  Stir-Fried with Mushrooms and Bamboo Shoots 225
  with Chicken, Mushrooms, and Bamboo Shoots, Red-Cooked 226
Almond
  Junket 258
  Tea 257
Apples, Drawn Thread Toffee 260
Aromatic
  Crispy Chicken (1) 164
  Crispy Chicken (2) 165
Asparagus
  Slivered Chicken with 185
  Tips, Shredded Pork with 128

Bacon, Deep-Fried Oysters with 235
Bamboo Shoots
  Double-Fried Vegetarian 100
  Red-Cooked Pork with 110
  Sliced Chicken with 180
  Sliced Pork Stir-Fried with 124
Barbecue
  Beef 148
  Pork 111
  Sliced Lamb, Peking Mongolian 157
Basic
  Dip for Seafoods 53
  Fried Rice 75
  Marinade for Roast Pork, Barbecued Pork, Spare Ribs, or Fish 44
  Noodles 85
  Pork Gravy Sauce for Noodles 37
  Soft Rice 78
  Soya-Vinegar Dressing 45
  Spare Ribs 120
  Steamed Eggs 252
  Sweet and Sour Sauce 42
  Vegetarian Stock 96
Bean
  Shoots, Splash-Fried 99
  Sprouts, Chicken Threads with 185
  Sprouts, Shredded Pork Stir-Fried with 127
Beaten Chicken 170
Bêche de Mer
  Butterfly 227
  Red-Cooked with Pork, Mushrooms and Bamboo Shoots 227
Beef
  and Cucumber Soup, Sliced 63
  and Tomato Sauce for Noodles 37
  and Watercress Soup, Sliced 64
  Balls
    with Oyster Sauce, Steamed 143
    with Szechuan Cabbage, Steamed 144
  Barbecue 148
  Broth
    and Marrow Soup 63
    and Spring Green Soup 62
    Basic 62
  Hot Spiced 148
  Moslem Long-Simmered 142
  Quick-Fried
    with Onion 146
    with Spring Onions and Shredded Carrots 147
    with Young Leeks 146
  with Star-Anise, Braised Marinated 142
  with Tomato, Red-Cooked 141
  with Yellow Turnip, Red-Cooked 141
Beggar's Chicken 168
Bird's Nest Soup 66
Black Beans
  Spare Ribs with (Chinese style) 121
  Spare Ribs with (Overseas style) 121
Braised
  Chicken with Chestnuts 177
  Marinated Beef with Star Anise 142
  Pigeon in Fruit Juice 204
  Red-Cooked Shark's Fins 239
  Spare Ribs with Pimento 120
Brazier-Grilled Sliced Lamb, Peking Mongolian 157
Broccoli, Shredded Pork with Bean Curd Skin and 129
Broth, Basic Beef 62
Butterfly Bêche de Mer 227

Cabbage
  Red-Cooked Chinese Celery 101
  Sliced Pork Stir-Fried with 123
  Soup
    Casserole of Chinese 59
    Meat Balls and Chinese Celery 60
    Spare Rib and Chinese Celery 59
  Sweet and Sour Chinese Celery 101
Cantonese
  Crystal
    Chicken 177
    Shrimps 245
  Roast
    Duck 195

277

Index

Cantonese
  Roast
    Pork 111
  Sliced Chicken in Fruit Sauce 182
Carp
  Braised in Chicken Fat Sauce 216
  Sweet and Sour Yellow River 214
Carrot Salad, Chinese 97
Carrots, Red-Cooked Pork with 110
Casserole
  of Chinese Cabbage Soup 59
  of Pigeon with Mushrooms 205
Cauliflower
  Fu-Yung 103
  Steamed Minced Pork with 129
Celery
  Salad, Chinese Chicken 186
  Shredded Pork Stir-Fried with 128
  Sliced Ham Stir-Fried with 137
Chestnuts
  Braised Chicken with 177
  Red-Cooked Pork with 109
Chiao Tzu (Stuffed Boiled or Steamed Dumplings) 262
Chicken
  Aromatic Crispy (1) 164
  Aromatic Crispy (2) 165
  Beaten 170
  Beggar's 168
  Cantonese Crystal 177
  Celery Salad, Chinese 186
  Chinese Roast 161
  Cold Crystal 165
  Crispy-Skin Pepper 161
  Cubes
    Kung-Po 173
    Vinegar-Tossed 172
    Deep-Fried Eight-Piece 174
  Distilled 167
  Drunken 168
  Eight-Precious Steamed 171
  Fried Rice 75
  Fu-Yung, Tri-Colour Scrambled 187
  Gold Coin 183
  Hot Pepper 175
  in Fruit Sauce, Cantonese Sliced 182
  in Ground Rice, Steamed 176
  in Soya Jam, Diced 173
  Legs, Crackling Aromatic 175
  Melon 169
  Paper-Wrapped 190
  Red-Cooked 160
  Royal Concubine 166
  Salt-Buried 163
  Sauce for Noodles, Plain 37
  Slices, Fu-Yung 188
  Soft Rice 79
  Soup, Whole 69
  Stock 58
  Sweet Corn and Velveteen of 189
  Tangerine Peel 180
  Threads
    with Bean Sprouts 185
    with Sliced Pepper 186
  Tramp's 164
  Velveteen Red, White, and Black with 190
  White-Cut 162
  Wine-Sediment Paste 170
  Wind-Cured 162
  with Asparagus, Slivered 185
  with Bamboo Shoots, Sliced 180
  with Chestnuts, Braised 177
  with Cucumber, Sliced 179
  with Cucumber, Slivered 185
  with French Beans, Slivered 184
  with Mushrooms, Sliced 178
  with Pea Pods or Mange-Tout, Sliced 183
  with Smoked and Salted Fish, Sliced 181
Chilled Melon Bowl 259
Chilli Oil, Hot 49
Chinese
  Carrot Salad 97
  Celery Cabbage
    Red-Cooked 101
    Soup, Spare Rib and 59
    Sweet and Sour 101
  Chicken
    and Ham Soup Noodles 86
    -Celery Salad 186
    Curried Chicken 231
    Peppered Duck 202
    Pork Escalope 116
    Roast Chicken 161
    Sausages 138
  Chops, Red-Braised Pork 118
Chow Mein 89
Clams
  Pork-Stuffed Deep-Fried 229
  Pork-Stuffed Steamed 229
  Steamed 228
Clear-Steamed Fish 221
Clear Stock 58
Cold
  Crystal Chicken 165
  White-Cut Salted Turkey 207
Congee 78
Cooked Rice with Toppings 77
Crab-Egg
  Soup, Shark's Fin and 67
  (Spawn) Shark's Fins 240
Crab-Meat
  in Steamed Eggs 231
  Prawns, and Lobster Omelettes 251
Crabs
  in Egg Sauce, Stir-Fried 230
  Plain Deep-Fried 231
Crackling
  Aromatic Chicken Legs 175
  Cream of Fish Soup 65
Cream of Pork Tripe Soup 64
Crispy
  and Aromatic Duck (1) 199
  and Aromatic Duck (2) 200

Index

Crispy
-Skin Pepper Chicken 161
Skin Roast Pork 118
Cucumber
Pan-Fried Stuffed 104
Sliced Chicken with 179
Slivered Chicken with 185
Soup
Sliced Beef and 63
Spare Rib and Sliced 60

Deep-Fried
and Steamed Eight-Precious Duck 200
Butterfly Prawns 244
Clams, Pork-Stuffed 229
Crabs, Plain 231
Eight-Piece Chicken 174
Fresh Salted Fish Steaks 215
Lobster, Plain 232
Meat Balls 130
Oysters
in Batter 235
with Bacon 235
Phœnix-Tail Prawns 243
Pigeon 205
Spare Ribs, Salt and Pepper 122
Diced
Chicken in Soya Jam 173
Pork Cubes Quick-Fried with Soya Paste 113
Dips and Mixes
Basic Dip for
Seafoods 53
Clams 54
Crab 59
Prawns 54
Hoisin or Plum Sauce for Pork 52
Hot
Chilli Oil 49
Mustard Sauce 50
Soya-Oil Dip 52
Pork, Soya-Sesame 53
Plum
Dip for Duck 53
Sauce 49
Salt
and Pepper Mix 50
-Cinnamon Mix 50
Seafood, Basic 53
Soya
-Ginger-Garlic Dip 52
-Mustard Dip 52
-Oil
Dip for Chicken 51
-Garlic Dip 51
-Ginger Dip 51
-Onion Dip 52
-Sesame Dip for Pork 53
Distilled Chicken 167
Double Fried
Eel 218
Vegetarian Bamboo Shoots 100
Drawn Thread Toffee Apples 260

Dressings
Basic Soya-Vinegar Dressing 45
Egg Dressing 46
Hot Soya Dressing 46
Mustard Dressing 46
Soya-Sesame Dressing 45
Drunken
Chicken 168
Duck 198
Fish 220
Shrimps 246
Dry-Fried
Beef Ribbons, Quick 144
Red-Cooked Duck 194
Duck
Cantonese Roast 195
Chinese Peppered 202
Crispy and Aromatic (1) 199
Crispy and Aromatic (2) 200
Deep-Fried and Steamed Eight-Precious 200
Eight-Precious 194
Hangchow Soya 196
Nanking Salt 201
Peking 202
Red-Cooked 193
Soup, Whole 69
Wine-Simmered 197
with Ham and Chinese Cabbage, White-Simmered 198
with Shredded Ginger, Quick-Fried Ribbon of 197

Eel, Double-Fried 218
Egg
Dressing 46
or Spring Roll Skins 269
Sauce
for Boiled White-Cut or Sliced Chicken 42
for Lobster, Crabs, or Giant Prawns 40
Soup, Sliced Pork and 61
Eggs
Basic Steamed 252
Crab-Meat in Steamed 231
Fancy Steamed 252
Huang-Pu Scrambled Stir-Fried 248
Omelettes see 'Omelettes'
Pork Trotters with Gravied 132
Soya 254
Steamed Three Variety 254
Tea or Marbled 254
Thousand Years Old 255
with Pork and Shrimps, Stir-Fried 249
with Shredded Ham, Scrambled Stir-Fried 249
Yellow Flowing 251
Eight-Precious
Duck 194
Hot Salad 98
Rice 260
Steamed Chicken 171

279

Index

Escalope, Chinese Pork 116

Fancy Steamed Eggs 252
Fillings
    for Egg or Spring Rolls 270
    for Hun Tuns 265
    for Savoury Dumplings 262-3
First Rank Hot-Pot 65
Fish
    Clear-Steamed 221
    Drunken 220
    in Chunks, Red-Cooked 213
    in White Sauce, Pan-Fried 217
    Sliced Chicken with Smoked and Salted 181
    Smoked 218
    Soup, Crackling Cream of 65
    Squirrel 215
    Sweet and Sour Red-Cooked 213
    with Vegetables, Red-Cooked 212
Five Willow Sauce for Fish 40
French Beans, Slivered Chicken with 184
Fresh Squid Stir-Fried with Red-Cooked Pork and Mushrooms 238
Fried
    Noodles
        with Beef Ribbons and Vegetable Topping 91
        with Chicken and Vegetable Topping 91
        with Crab-Meat and Vegetables 91
        with Fresh Shrimps and Vegetables 91
        with Pork and Vegetable Topping 90
        with Prawns and Vegetables 91
    Rice
        Basic 75
        Chicken 75
        Lobster 75
        Prawn 75
        Shrimp 75
Frog Legs
    Fried Steamed 209
    Quick-Fried with Sweet Pepper 208
    Szechuan Home-Cooked 208
Fu Yung
    Cauliflower 103
    Chicken Slices 188
    Tri Colour Scrambled Chicken 187

Ginger-Garlic Marinade 44
Gold Coin Chicken 183
Gravied Eggs, Pork Trotters with 132
Ground Rice, Steamed Chicken in 176

Ham
    Honey Pear 137
    Steamed 136
    Stir-Fried with Celery, Sliced 137
    Toasted Gold Coin 136
Hangchow Soya Duck 196
Hoisin or Plum Sauce for Pork 52
Honey Pear Ham 137

Hot
    and Sour Soup 68
    Five Willow Sauce for Fish 40
    Mustard Sauce 50
    Pepper Chicken 175
    -Pot
        First Rank 65
        Peking Mongolian Sliced Lamb 155
    Soya
        Dressing 46
        -Oil Dip 52
    Spiced
        Beef Ribbons Quick-Fried with Shredded Sweet Peppers and Chilli Pepper 148
        Chinese Peppered Steak 150
    Sweet and Sour Sauce 43
Hua Chuan (Flower Rolls) 266
Huang-Pu Scrambled Stir-Fried Eggs 248
Hun Tuns (Miniature Dumplings) 265

Junket, Almond 258

Kung-Po Chicken Cubes 173
Kuo T'ieh (Steam-Fried Dumplings) 263
Kweichow 'Salt and Sour' Tip Out Pork 113

Lamb
    Hot-Pot, Peking Mongolian Sliced 155
    of Lung Fu Ssi Long-Simmered 154
    Peking Mongolian
        Barbecued Sliced 157
        Brazier-Grilled Sliced 157
    Quick-Fried
        Triple 154
        with Ginger and Young Leeks, Shredded 153
        with Spring Onion, Sliced 153
    Red-Cooked 151
    Tung-Po Red-Cooked 152
Leeks
    Quick-Fried Beef Ribbons with Young 147
    Sliced Pork Stir-Fried with Young 125
Lions' Heads 131
Liver, Quick-Fried Pig's 134
Lobster
    Fried Rice 75
    Plain Deep-Fried 232
    Steamed Marinated 233
    with Minted Pork, Stir-Fried 232
    with Red Wine-Sediment Paste, Stir-Fried 234
Long
    Life Noodles in Egg Sauce 88
    -Simmered Lamb of Lung Fu Ssi 154
Lotus
    Leaf Rolls 204
    Seed Soup 257
Lu Mein 87

Index

Mange-Tout, Sliced Chicken with Pea-Pods or 183
Man Tou 266
Marbled Eggs 254
Marinades
Basic Marinade for Roast Pork, Barbecued Pork, Spare Ribs, or Fish 44
Ginger-Garlic Marinade 44
Marinade for Pork or Spare Ribs with Hoisin Sauce and Five Spice Powder 44
Soya-Red Bean Cheese Marinade for Pork or Spare Ribs 45
Marinated
Beef with Star Anise, Braised 142
Lobster, Steamed 233
Marrow Soup, Beef Broth and 63
Master Sauce 38
Meat
and Vegetable Sauce for Fish, Fancy 39
Balls
and Chinese Celery Cabbage Soup 60
Deep-Fried 130
Melon
Bowl, Chilled 259
Chicken 169
Minced
Pork Cakes, Steamed 130
Pork with Cauliflower, Steamed 129
Moslem Long-Simmered Beef 142
Mushroom Soup, Sliced Pork and 61
Mushrooms
Sliced
Chicken with 178
Pork Stir-Fried with 123
Mustard Dressing 46

Nanking Salt Duck 201
Noodles
and French Beans 194
Basic 85
Chinese Chicken and Ham Soup 86
in Egg Sauce, Long Life 88
in Lobster Sauce 93
in Meat Sauce 87
in Prawn Sauce 89
in Shrimp Sauce 89
with Beef Ribbons and Vegetable Topping, Fried 91
with Cha Shao Roast Pork and Spinach Topping, Soup 85
with Chicken and Vegetable Topping, Soup 85
with Crab-Meat and Vegetables, Fried 91
with Fresh Shrimps and Vegetables, Fried 91
with Pork and Vegetable Topping, Fried 90
with Prawns and Vegetables, Fried 91
with Red-Cooked Beef, Soup 86
with Red-Cooked Pork, Soup 86
with Stewed Meat and Vegetables, Pea-Starch Transparent 92
Wo Mein (Pot-cooked) 93

Omelette, Oyster 250
Omelettes, Crab-Meat, Prawns, and Lobster 251
Onion
and Spring Onion, Shredded Pork Stir-Fried with 128
Quick-Fried Beef Ribbons with 146
Oxtail, Red-Cooked 149
Oyster
Omelette 250
Sauce, Quick-Fried Spiced Steak in 145
Sauce, Steamed Beef Balls with 143
Oysters
in Batter, Deep-Fried 235
with Bacon, Deep Fried 235

Painted Soup 70
Pancakes
for Peking Duck 203
or Ping 268
Pan-Fried
Sliced Fish in White Sauce 217
Stuffed Cucumber 104
Pao T'sai (White Hot Pickle) 96
Pao Tzu (Stuffed Steamed Buns) 267
Paper-Wrapped Chicken 190
Peanut Cream 258
Pea Pods
or Mange-Tout, Sliced Chicken with 183
Sliced Pork Stir-Fried with 125
Pea Soup, Tripe and Green 61
Pea-Starch Transparent Noodles with Stewed Meat and Vegetables 92
Pear Ham, Honey 137
Pears in Honey, Steamed 259
Peking
Duck 202
Duck, Pancakes for 203
Mongolian Barbecued Sliced Lamb 157
Mongolian Brazier-Grilled Sliced Lamb 157
Mongolian Sliced Hot-Pot 155
Soya-Meat Sauce for Noodles 38
Peppered Steak, Hot Spiced Chinese 150
Pickle, Pao T'sai (White Hot Pickle) 96
Pigeon
Deep-Fried 205
in Fruit Juice, Braised 204
with Mushrooms, Casserole of 205
Pig's Liver, Quick-Fried 134
Ping or Pancakes 268
Plain
Chicken Sauce for Noodles 37
Deep-Fried
Crab 231
Lobster 232
-Fried Spinach with Vegetarian Stock 99
Stir-Fried Shrimps in Shells 243

281

Index

Plum
  Dip for Duck 53
  Sauce 49
Pork
  and Chinese Celery Cabbage Filling for Dumplings 264
  and Egg-Flower Soup, Sliced 61
  and Mushroom Soup, Sliced 61
  Barbecued 111
  Cakes, Steamed Minced 130
  Chops, Red-Braised 118
  Crispy Skin Roast 118
  Cubes Quick-Fried with Soya Paste, Diced 113
  Escalope, Chinese 116
  Gravy Sauce for Noodles, Basic 37
  in Pieces, Red-Cooked 107
  Kidney with Celery and Wood Ears, Quick-Fried 133
  Kweichow 'Salt and Sour' Tip Out 113
  Lobster Stir-Fried with Minced 232
  of Original Preciousness 108
  Quick-Fried with Leeks and Szechuan Pickle, Shredded 127
  Red-
    Cooked Leg of 106
    Cooked Round Knuckle with Spinach 109
  Spare Rib Soft Rice 80
  Stir-Fried
    with Bamboo Shoots, Sliced 124
    with Bean Sprouts, Shredded 127
    with Cabbage, Sliced 123
    with Celery, Shredded 128
    with Golden Needles and Transparent Noodles, Sliced 125
    with Mushrooms, Sliced 123
    with Onion and Spring Onion, Shredded 128
    with Pea Pods, Sliced 125
    with Szechuan Pickle, Sliced 126
    with Young Leeks, Sliced 125
  -Stuffed
    Deep-Fried Clams 229
    Steamed Clams 229
  Sweet and Sour 114
  Tip Out Steamed 112
  Tripe
    Red-Cooked 135
    Soup, Cream of 64
  Trotters with Gravied Eggs 132
  Tung-Po 116
  Twice-Cooked 115
  White-Cooked Sliced 111
  with Asparagus Tips, Shredded 128
  with Bamboo Shoots, Red-Cooked 110
  with Bean Curd Cheese, Red-Simmered 117
  with Bean Curd Skin and Broccoli, Shredded 129
  with Carrots, Red-Cooked 110
  with Cauliflower, Steamed Minced 129
  with Chestnuts, Red-Cooked 109
  with Dried Squid and Golden Needles, Red-Cooked 110
  Yellow Flower 253
Prawn
  Fried Rice 75
  Sauce, Noodles in 89
Prawns
  Deep-Fried Butterfly 244
  Deep-Fried Phœnix-Tail 243

Quick Dry-Fried Beef Ribbons 144
Quick-Fried
  Beef Ribbons
    with Onion 146
    with Spring Onions and Shredded Carrots 147
    with Young Leeks 147
  Frog Legs with Sweet Pepper 208
  Pig's Liver 134
  Pork Kidney with Celery and Wood Ears 133
  Ribbons of Duck with Shredded Ginger 197
  Sliced Steak with Tomatoes 146
  Spiced Steak in Oyster Sauce 145
  Triple Lamb 154

Red-Braised Pork Chops 118
Red-Cooked
  Abalone with Chicken, Mushrooms, and Bamboo Shoots 226
  Bêche de Mer with Pork, Mushrooms and Bamboo Shoots 227
  Beef 140
    with Tomato 141
    with Yellow Turnip 141
  Chicken 160
  Chinese Celery Cabbage 101
  Duck 193
  Duck, Dry-Fried 194
  Fish
    in Chunks 213
    Sweet and Sour 213
    with Vegetables 212
  Lamb 151
  Lamb, Tung-Po 152
  Leg of Pork 106
  Oxtail 149
  Pork
    in Pieces 107
    Tripe 135
    with Bamboo Shoots 110
    with Carrots 110
    with Chestnuts 109
    with Dried Squid and Golden Needles 110
  Round Knuckle of Pork with Spinach 109
  Shark's Fins, Braised 239
Red-Simmered Pork with Bean Curd Cheese 117
Red, White, and Black with Chicken Velveteen 190

282

Index

Rice
  Congee 78
  Cooked with Chinese Sausages 77
  Cooked with Toppings 77
  Eight Precious 260
  Fried
    Basic 75
    Chicken 75
    Lobster 75
    Prawn 75
    Shrimp 75
  Soft
    Basic 78
    Beef 80
    Chicken 79
    Congee 78
    Pork Spare Rib 80
    Roast Duck or Pork 80
    Sampan 81
  Topped 77
  Vegetable 76
Roast
  Chicken, Chinese 161
  Duck or Pork Soft Rice 80
  Pork, Crispy Skin 118
Rolls, Lotus Leaf 204
Royal Concubine Chicken 166

Salad
  Chinese
    Carrot 97
    Chicken-Celery 186
  Eight Precious Hot 98
  Three Fairies 97
  Vegetarian Cold 98
Salt
  and Pepper Deep-Fried Spare Ribs 122
  and Pepper Mix 50
  and Sour Tip Out Pork, Kweichow 113
  Beef with Heart of Spring Greens or Cabbage 103
  -Buried Chicken 163
  -Cinnamon Mix 50
Sampan Soft Rice 81
Sauce for Fish, Five Willow 40
Sauces
  Basic
    Pork Gravy Sauce for Noodles 37
    Sweet and Sour Sauce 42
  Beef and Tomato Sauce for Noodles 37
  Egg Sauce
    for Boiled White-Cut Chicken 42
    for Lobster, Crab or Giant Prawns 40
  Five Willow Sauce for Fish 40
  for Chicken 41
  Hot Five Willow Sauce for Fish 40
  Hot Sweet and Sour Sauce 43
  Master Sauce 38
  Meat and Vegetable Sauce for Fish 39
  Plum Sauce 49
Savoury Dumplings
  Chiao Tzu (Stuffed Boiled or Steamed) 262
  Kuo T'ieh (Steam-Fried) 263
  Shao Mai (Steamed-Open) 263
Scallops
  with Diced Chicken, Mushrooms and Cucumber, Stir-Fried 237
  with Ham, Ginger, and Onion, Steamed 236
Scrambled
  Chicken Fu-Yung, Tri-Colour 187
  Stir-Fried Eggs with Shredded Ham 249
Seafood & Crustaceans
  Abalone, Stir-Fried with Mushrooms and Bamboo Shoots 225
  Braised Red-Cooked Shark's Fins 239
  Butterfly Bêche de Mer 227
  Cantonese Crystal Shrimps 245
  Crab-Meat in Steamed Eggs 231
  Deep-Fried
    Butterfly Prawns 244
    Oysters
      in Batter 235
      with Bacon 235
    Phoenix-Tail Prawns 243
  Drunken Shrimps 246
  Fresh
    Squid
      Stir-Fried with Red-Cooked Pork and Mushrooms 238
      Stir-Fried with Vegetables 238
  Plain
    Deep-Fried
      Crabs 231
      Lobster 232
    Stir-Fried Shrimps in Shells 243
  Pork Stuffed
    Deep-Fried Clams 229
    Steamed Clams 229
  Red-Cooked
    Abalone with Chicken, Mushrooms, and Bamboo Shoots 226
    Bêche de Mer with Pork, Mushrooms, and Bamboo Shoots 227
  Steamed
    Clams 228
    Marinated Lobster 233
    Scallops with Ham, Ginger, and Onion 236
  Stir-Fried
    Crabs in Egg Sauce 230
    Lobster with Red Wine-Sediment Paste 234
    Scallops with Diced Chicken, Mushrooms, and Cucumber 237
    Shrimps
      with Bean Curd, Mushrooms, and Minced Pork 242
      with Green Peas 242
    Toasted Shrimps 245
Shao Mai (Steamed Open Dumplings) 263
Shark's Fin
  and Crab-Egg Soup 67
  Braised Red-Cooked 239

Index

Shark's Fin
  Crab-Eggs (Spawn) 240
Shredded
  Lamb Quick-Fried with Ginger and Young Leeks 153
  Pork
    Quick-Fried with Leeks and Szechuan Pickle 127
    Stir-Fried
      with Bean Sprouts 127
      with Celery 128
      with Onion and Spring Onion 128
      with Asparagus Tips 128
      with Bean Curd Skin and Broccoli 129
Shrimp
  Fried Rice 75
  or Crab Meat Filling for Dumplings 264
  Prawn, or Lobster Fried Rice 75
  Sauce, Noodles in 89
Shrimps
  Cantonese Crystal 245
  Drunken 246
  in Shells, Plain Stir-Fried 243
  Toasted 245
  with Bean Curd, Mushrooms, and Minced Pork, Stir-Fried 242
  with Green Peas, Stir-Fried 242
Silk-Thread Bamboo Shoots in Cream of Chicken 102
Sliced Beef
  and Cucumber Soup 63
  and Watercress Soup 64
Sliced Chicken
  in Fruit Sauce, Cantonese 182
  with Bamboo Shoots 180
  with Cucumber 179
  with Mushrooms 178
  with Pea Pods or Mange-Tout 183
  with Smoked and Salted Fish 181
Sliced Ham
  Stir-Fried with Celery 137
Sliced Lamb Quick-Fried with Spring Onion 153
Sliced Pork
  and Egg-Flower Soup 61
  and Mushroom Soup 61
  Stir-Fried 163
    with Bamboo Shoots 124
    with Cabbage 123
    with Golden Needles and Transparent Noodles 125
    with Mushrooms 123
    with Pea Pods 125
    with Szechuan Pickle 126
    with Young Leeks 125
  White-Cooked 111
Slivered
  Chicken with Asparagus 185
  Chicken with Cucumber 185
  Chicken with French Beans 184
Smoked
  and Salted Fish, Sliced Chicken with 181
  Fish 218
Snacks
  Chiao Tzu (Stuffed Boiled or Steamed) 262
  Egg or Spring Roll Skins 269
  Fillings for
    Egg or Spring Rolls 270
    Hun Tuns 265
    Savoury Dumplings 264
  Hua Chuan (Flower Rolls) 266
  Hun Tuns (Miniature Dumplings) 265
  Kuo T'ieh 263
  Man Tou 266
  Pancakes (Ping) 268
  Pao Tzu (Stuffed Steamed Buns) 267
  Shao Mai 263
  Stuffings for Steamed Buns 267-8
Soft Rice
  Basic 78
  Chicken 79
  or Congee 78
  Pork Spare Rib 80
Soup
  Basic Beef Broth 62
  Beef Broth
  and Marrow Soup 63
  and Spring Green Soup 62
  Bird's Nest Soup 66
  Casserole of Chinese Cabbage Soup 59
  Crackling Cream of Fish Soup 65
  Cream of Pork Tripe Soup 64
  First Rank Hot-Pot 65
  Hot and Sour Soup 68
  Lotus Seed 257
  Meat Balls and Chinese Celery Cabbage Soup 60
  Noodles 85-6
  Painted Soup 70
  Shark's Fin and Crab-Egg Soup 67
  Sliced Beef
    and Cucumber Soup 63
    and Watercress Soup 64
  Sliced Pork
    and Egg-Flower Soup 61
    and Mushroom Soup 61
  Spare Rib
    and Chinese Celery Cabbage Soup 59
    and Sliced Cucumber Soup 60
  Stock 55-9
  Tripe and Green Pea Soup 61
  Walnut 257
  Whole
    Chicken Soup 69
    Duck Soup 69
Soya
  Dressing, Hot 46
  Eggs 254
  -Ginger-Garlic Dip 52
  Jam, Diced Chicken in 173
  -Meat Sauce for Noodles, Peking 38
  -Mustard Dip 52
  -Oil
    -Dip for Chicken 51

Index

Soya-Oil
   -Dip, Hot 52
   -Garlic Dip 51
   -Ginger Dip 51
   -Onion Dip 52
   -Red Bean Cheese Marinade for Pork or Spare Ribs 45
   -Sesame
      Dip for Pork 53
      Dressing 45
   -Stock Sauce for Boiled, White-Cut or Sliced Chicken 41
   -Vinegar Dressing, Basic 45
   -Vinegar Sauce for Deep-Fried Chicken 41
Spare Rib
   and Chinese Celery Cabbage Soup 59
   and Sliced Cucumber Soup 60
   Soft Rice, Pork 80
Spare Ribs
   Basic 120
   Salt and Pepper Deep-Fried 122
   with Black Beans (Chinese Style) 121
   with Black Beans (Overseas Chinese Style) 121
   with Pimento, Braised 120
Spiced
   Steak in Oyster Sauce, Quick-Fried 145
Spinach
   Red-Cooked Round Knuckle of Pork with 109
   with Vegetarian Stock, Plain-Fried 99
Splash-Fried Bean Shoots 99
Spring
   Greens or Cabbage, Salt Beef with Heart of 103
   Green Soup, Beef Broth and 62
Spring Onion, Shredded Pork Stir-Fried with Onion and 128
Spring Rolls, Vegetarian 104
Squid
   and Golden Needles, Red-Cooked Pork with Dried 110
   Stir-Fried with Red-Cooked Pork and Mushrooms, Fresh 238
   Stir-Fried with Vegetables, Fresh 238
Squirrel Fish 215
Star Anise, Braised Marinated Beef with 142
Steak
   Hot Spiced Chinese Peppered 150
   in Oyster Sauce, Quick-Fried Spiced 145
   with Tomatoes, Quick-Fried Sliced 146
Steamed Beef Balls
   with Oyster Sauce 143
   with Szechuan Cabbage 144
Steamed
   Buns 266
      Man Tou (Plain) 266
      Hua Chuan (Flower Rolls) 266
      Pao Tzu (Stuffed) 267
   Chicken
      Eight-Precious 171
      in Ground Rice 176
   Clams 228
      Pork-Stuffed 229
   Eggs
      Basic 252
      Fancy 252
   Ham 136
   Marinated Lobster 233
   Minced Pork
      Cake 130
      with Cauliflower 129
   Pears in Honey 259
   Roast Turkey 206
   Three Variety Eggs 254
   Scallops with Ham, Ginger, and Onion 236
Stir-Fried
   Crabs in Egg Sauce 230
      Eggs with Pork and Shrimps 249
   Lobster with Red Wine-Sediment Paste 234
   Scallops with Diced Chicken, Mushrooms and Cucumber 237
   Shrimps
      in Shells, Plain 243
      with Bean Curd, Mushroom, and Minced Pork 242
      with Green Peas 242
Stock
   Basic Vegetarian 96
   Chicken 58
   Clear 58
   Secondary 58
   Superior 56
   White Soup or Milky Stock 58
Strengthened Sweet and Sour Sauce 42
Stuffings for Steamed Buns 267-8
Sweet and Sour
   Chinese Celery Cabbage 101
   Pork 114
   Red-Cooked Fish 213
   Sauce
      Basic 42
      Hot 43
      Strengthened 42
   Yellow River Carp 214
Sweet Corn and Velveteen of Chicken 189
Sweets
   Almond
      Junket 258
      Tea 257
   Chilled Melon Bowl 259
   Drawn Thread Toffee Apples 260
   Eight Precious Rice 260
   Lotus Seed Soup 257
   Peanut Cream 258
   Steamed Pears in Honey 259
   Walnut Soup 257
Szechuan
   Cabbage, Steamed Beef Balls with 144
   Home-Cooked Frog Legs 208
   Pickle, Sliced Pork Stir-Fried with 126

Index

Tangerine Peel Sweet and Sour Chicken 180
Tea
  Almond 257
  Eggs 254
Thousand Years Old Eggs 255
Three Fairies Salad 97
Tip Out Pork, Kweichow 'Salt and Sour' 113
Tip Out Steamed Pork 112
Toasted Gold Coin Ham 136
Toffee Apples, Drawn Thread 260
Tomato, Red-Cooked Beef with 141
Tomatoes, Quick-Fried Sliced Steak with 146
Topped Rice 77
Tramp's Chicken 164
Tri-Colour Scrambled Chicken Fu-Yung 187
Tripe
  and Green Pea Soup 61
  Red-Cooked Pork 135
  Soup, Cream of Pork 64
Tung-Po
  Pork 116
  Red-Cooked Lamb 152
Turkey
  Cold White-Cut Salted 207
  Steamed Roast 206
Turnip, Red-Cooked Beef with Yellow 141
Twice-Cooked Pork 115

Vegetable and Vegetarian Dishes
  Basic Vegetarian Stock 96
  Chinese Carrot Salad 97
  Double-Fried Vegetarian Bamboo Shoots 100
  Eight Precious Hot Salad 98
  Fu-Yung Cauliflower 103
  Pao T'sai (White Hot Pickle) 96

Pan-Fried Stuffed Cucumber 105
Plain-Fried Spinach with Vegetarian Stock 99
Red-Cooked Chinese Celery Cabbage 101
Salt Beef with Heart of Spring Greens or Cabbage 103
Silk-Thread Bamboo Shoots in Cream of Chicken 102
Splash-Fried Bean Shoots 99
Sweet and Sour Chinese Celery Cabbage 101
Three Fairies Salad 97
Vegetable Rice 76
Vegetarian
  Cold Salad 98
  Stock, Basic 96
Vinegar-Tossed Chicken Cubes 172

Walnut Soup 257
Watercress Soup, Sliced Beef and 64
White-Cooked Sliced Pork 111
White Cut Chicken 162
White-Simmered Duck with Ham and Chinese Cabbage 198
Whole
  Chicken Soup 69
  Duck Soup 69
  Happy Family 134
Wind-Cured Chicken 162
Wine-Sediment Paste
  Chicken 170
  Substitute 234
Wine-Simmered Duck 197
Wo Mein 93

Yellow
  Flower Pork 253
  Flowing Eggs 251